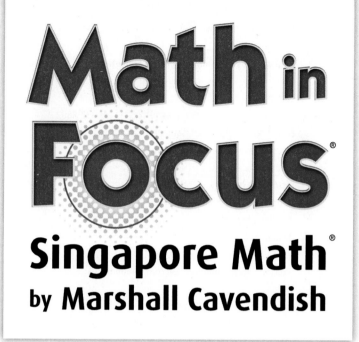

COURSE 1A

Student Book

Consultant and Author
Dr. Fong Ho Kheong

Authors
Gan Kee Soon and Dr. Ng Wee Leng

U.S. Consultants
Dr. Richard Bisk
Andy Clark

Marshall Cavendish
Education

U.S. Distributor

**Houghton
Mifflin
Harcourt**

© 2018 Marshall Cavendish Education Pte Ltd

Published by Marshall Cavendish Education
Times Centre, 1 New Industrial Road, Singapore 536196
Customer Service Hotline: (65) 6213 9444
US Office Tel: (1-914) 332 8888 | Fax: (1-914) 332 8882
E-mail: tmesales@mceducation.com
Website: www.mceducation.com

Distributed by
Houghton Mifflin Harcourt
222 Berkeley Street
Boston, MA 02116
Tel: 617-351-5000
Website: www.hmheducation.com/mathinfocus

Cover: © Henri Faure/Dreamstime.com

First published 2018

ISBN 978-1-328-87993-6

Printed in the United States of America

2 3 4 5 6 7 8   1401   23 22 21 20 19 18
4500709868   A B C D E

Course 1A Contents

In Student Book A and Student Book B, look for

Practice and Problem Solving	Assessment Opportunities
• **Practice** in every lesson • Real-world and mathematical problems in every chapter • Brain @ Work in every chapter • *Math Journal* exercises	• **Quick Check** at the beginning of every chapter to assess chapter readiness • **Guided Practice** after every Learn to assess readiness to continue lesson • **Chapter Review/Test** in every chapter to review or test chapter material • **Cumulative Reviews** four times during the year

Negative Numbers and the Number Line

4 Ratio

5 Rates

6 Percent

Algebraic Expressions

Welcome to

Math in FOCUS®

Singapore Math®
by Marshall Cavendish

What makes *Math in Focus®* different?

This world-class math program comes to you from the country of Singapore. We are sure that you will enjoy learning math with the interesting lessons you will find in these books.

▶ **Two books** The textbook is divided into 2 semesters. Chapters 1–7 are in Book A. Chapters 8–14 are in Book B.

▶ **Longer lessons** More concepts are presented in a lesson. Some lessons may last more than a day to give you time to understand the math.

▶ **Bar models and visual models** will help you make sense of new concepts and solve real-world and mathematical problems with ease.

About the book Here are the main features in this book.

Chapter Opener

Introduces chapter concepts and big ideas through a story or example. There is also a chapter table of contents.

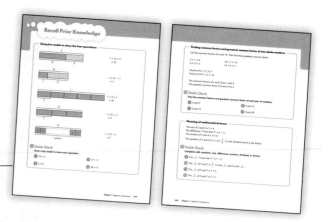

Recall Prior Knowledge

Assesses previously learned concepts, definitions, vocabulary, and models relevant to the chapter.

Quick Check assesses readiness for the chapter.

Look for these features in each lesson.

Learn shows steps that are easy to follow and understand. It often contains bar models or other visual models.

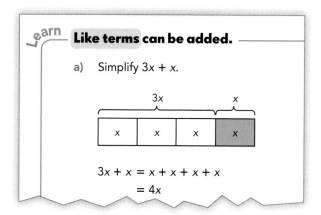

Like terms can be added.

a) Simplify $3x + x$.

$3x + x = x + x + x + x$
$= 4x$

Guided Practice exercises provide step-by-step guidance through solutions.

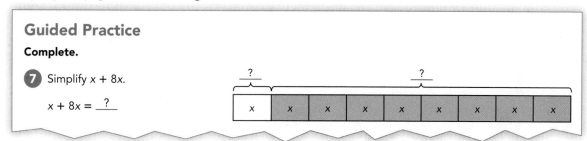

Guided Practice

Complete.

7 Simplify $x + 8x$.

$x + 8x = \underline{}$

Cautions alert you to common mistakes and misconceptions related to the topics.

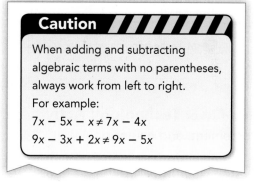

Caution

When adding and subtracting algebraic terms with no parentheses, always work from left to right.
For example:
$7x - 5x - x \neq 7x - 4x$
$9x - 3x + 2x \neq 9x - 5x$

Math Note

Commutative Property of Addition: Two numbers can be added in any order.

So, $4 + a = a + 4$.

Math Notes are helpful hints and reminders.

Practice 7.3

Simplify each expression. Then state the coefficient of the variable in each expression.

1 $u + u + u + u$

2 $v + v + 5 - 2$

Practice and **Math Journal** are included in practice sets.

c) *Math Journal* Explain how you can use your answers in **a)** and **b)** to show that the following expressions are equivalent.

$$3x + 6 \text{ and } 3(x + 2)$$

Hands-On Activities and Brain@Work combine logical thinking with math skills and concepts to help you meet new problem-solving challenges.

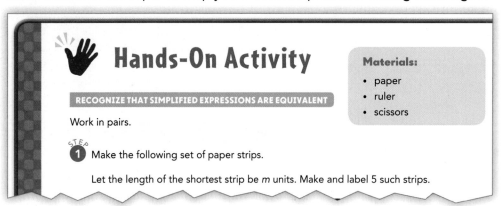

Hands-On Activity

RECOGNIZE THAT SIMPLIFIED EXPRESSIONS ARE EQUIVALENT

Work in pairs.

Materials:
- paper
- ruler
- scissors

STEP **1** Make the following set of paper strips.

Let the length of the shortest strip be *m* units. Make and label 5 such strips.

Hands-On or **Technology Activities** provide opportunities for investigation, reinforcement, and extension.

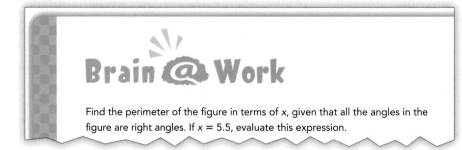

Brain @ Work

Find the perimeter of the figure in terms of *x*, given that all the angles in the figure are right angles. If *x* = 5.5, evaluate this expression.

Brain@Work problems, found at the end of each chapter, are challenging and promote critical thinking.

Chapter Wrap Up

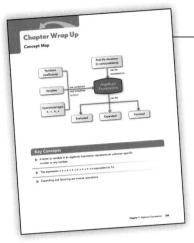

Key concepts, definitions, and formulas are summarized for easy review.

The Chapter Wrap Up summaries contain concept maps like the one shown below.

There may be more than one way to draw a concept map. With practice, you should be able to draw your own.

The center box contains the big idea for the chapter.

Other boxes represent key concepts of the chapter.

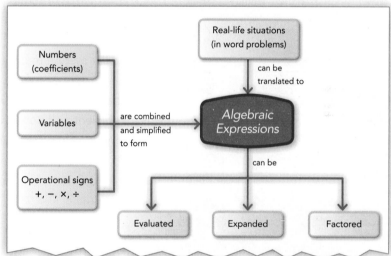

The lines and arrows show how all the concepts in the chapter are related to one another and to the big idea.

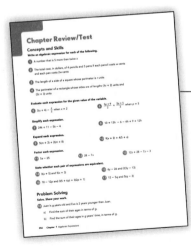

Chapter Review/Test

A practice test is found at the end of each chapter.

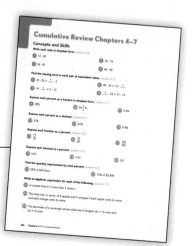

Cumulative Review

Cumulative review exercises can be found after Chapters 3, 7, 11, and 14.

Positive Numbers and the Number Line

How has the number system changed?

The first known use of numbers dates to about 35,000 B.C.E. At that time, people used tally marks to count things like animals, properties, and time. Unlike the number system used today, the tally system did not make use of place value, nor did it use symbols for numbers.

About 5,000 years ago, the Babylonians and the Egyptians began using number symbols.

The number system that we use today is called the decimal number system. It makes use of the ten numerals 0, 1, 2, 3, 4, 5, 6, 7, 8, and 9. Using these ten numerals, you can write a number of any magnitude. It is an efficient and powerful number system that became possible with the invention of the number 0 and the concept of place value.

BIG IDEA

▶ Whole numbers, fractions, and decimals are numbers that can be represented in several ways.

Recall Prior Knowledge

Finding factors of a whole number

Find the factors of 24.

$24 = 1 \times 24$

$24 = 3 \times 8$

$24 = 2 \times 12$

$24 = 4 \times 6$

The factors of 24 are 1, 2, 3, 4, 6, 8, 12, and 24.

✔ Quick Check

Find the factors of each number.

1 30

2 63

3 56

4 84

Finding multiples of a whole number

Find the first six multiples of 7.

$1 \times 7 = 7$
$2 \times 7 = 14$
$3 \times 7 = 21$
$4 \times 7 = 28$
$5 \times 7 = 35$
$6 \times 7 = 42 \ldots$

It is a good idea to write the multiples in order from least to greatest.

7, 14, 21, 28, 35, and 42 are the first six multiples of 7.

✔ Quick Check

Find the first five multiples of each number.

5 4

6 6

7 9

8 13

Identifying prime numbers

A prime number has only two different factors, 1 and the number itself.

Decide whether 11 and 14 are prime numbers.

Find the factors of 11.

$11 = 1 \times 11$

The factors of 11 are 1 and 11.
11 is a prime number.

Find the factors of 14.

$14 = 1 \times 14$
$14 = 2 \times 7$

The factors of 14 are 1, 2, 7, and 14.
14 is not a prime number.

 Quick Check

Complete.

9 Identify all the prime numbers in the following set of numbers.

2, 5, 13, 21, 23, 39, 47, 51, 53, 57

Using order of operations to simplify a numerical expression

STEP 1   Work inside parentheses.

STEP 2   Multiply and divide from left to right.

STEP 3   Add and subtract from left to right.

....

1st expression	$(98 + 34) - 6 \times 7$	Perform operations in parentheses.
2nd expression	$132 - 6 \times 7$	Then multiply.
3rd expression	$132 - 42$	Then subtract.
	90	

 Quick Check

Simplify.

10 $(40 - 28) + 8 \times 7$

11 $75 \times (45 \div 5) - 70$

The Number Line

Lesson Objectives

- Represent whole numbers, fractions, and decimals on a number line.
- Interpret and write statements of inequality for two given positive numbers using the symbols > and <.

Learn Represent numbers on a number line.

In this chapter, you will learn about various ways of representing numbers.
A number line can be used to represent the set of **whole numbers** (0, 1, 2, 3, 4, ...).

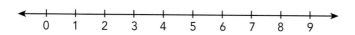

A number line can be horizontal or vertical.

On a horizontal number line, the lesser number always lies to the left of the greater number.

On a vertical number line, the lesser number always lies below the greater number.

Positive numbers are all the numbers greater than 0. On a horizontal number line, they are to the right of 0. On a vertical number line, they are above 0.

The set of positive numbers also includes positive fractions and decimals.

Continue on next page

a) Draw a horizontal number line to represent the whole numbers between 5 and 12.

5 and 12 are not included because the question asks for numbers **between** 5 and 12.

b) Draw a vertical number line to represent the whole numbers from 5 to 12.

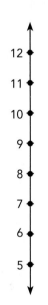

5 and 12 are included because the question asks for numbers **from** 5 to 12.

Learn

Write statements of inequality comparing two whole numbers using the symbols > and <.

You can use a number line to compare whole numbers.

For example, in the number line shown, 35 lies to the right of 33.

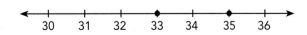

So, 35 is greater than 33.

This can be represented by 35 > 33.

Write the statement "110 is less than 250" using > or <.

110 < 250

Use a number line to help you compare the whole numbers. Then write the statement of inequality.

Guided Practice

Draw a horizontal number line to represent each set of whole numbers.

1 Positive whole numbers less than 5

2 Whole numbers greater than 9 but less than 14

Draw a vertical number line to represent each set of whole numbers.

3 Odd numbers between 1 and 10

4 Positive odd numbers < 15

Learn Represent fractions, mixed numbers, and decimals on a horizontal number line.

a) Represent the fractions $\frac{1}{4}$, $\frac{2}{4}$, and $\frac{3}{4}$ on a number line.

To represent $\frac{1}{4}$s, subdivide each interval between two consecutive whole numbers into four equal intervals using three tick marks.

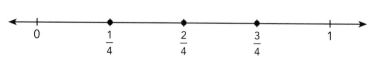

Continue on next page

b) Represent the decimals from 0.1 to 0.9 on a horizontal number line. Use an interval of 0.1 between each decimal.

To represent decimals in tenths, subdivide each interval between two consecutive whole numbers into ten equal intervals.

0 0.1 0.2 0.3 0.4 0.5 0.6 0.7 0.8 0.9 1.0

Guided Practice

Complete each ___?___ with the correct value, and each ▨ ? with > or <.

5 Fill in the missing fractions and mixed numbers on the number line.
Then complete the statements of inequality.

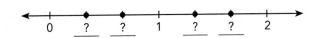

0 ? ? 1 ? ? 2

$\frac{2}{3}$ ▨? 1

2 ▨? $1\frac{1}{3}$

Draw a horizontal number line to represent each set of numbers.

6 Mixed numbers greater than 10 but less than 11
Use an interval of $\frac{1}{4}$ between each pair of mixed numbers.

7 Mixed numbers from 3 to 4, with an interval of $\frac{1}{10}$ between each pair of mixed numbers

8 Decimals between 0 and 1, with an interval of 0.25 between each pair of decimals

9 Decimals greater than 8.0 but less than 12.0
Use an interval of 0.8 between each pair of decimals.

Learn Represent fractions, mixed numbers, and decimals on a vertical number line.

a) Represent the fractions $\frac{1}{5}$, $\frac{2}{5}$, $\frac{3}{5}$, $\frac{4}{5}$ on a vertical number line.

To represent these fractions on the number line, subdivide the interval between 0 and 1 into five smaller intervals.

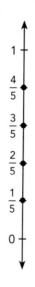

b) Represent the decimals 2.0, 2.2, 2.4, 2.6, …, 4.0 on a vertical number line.

To represent these decimals, subdivide the interval from 2.0 to 4.0 into ten equal intervals of 0.2.

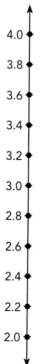

To decide how many tick marks to show on the number line, you can count up by 0.2s, marking them as you go:

2.0, 2.2, 2.4, 2.6, 2.8, 3.0, 3.2, 3.4, 3.6, 3.8, 4.0.

Write statements of inequality comparing two fractions or two decimals using the symbols $>$ and $<$.

You can use a number line to compare fractions and decimals.

a) Compare the two fractions, $\frac{2}{3}$ and $\frac{5}{6}$.

Use a number line to compare $\frac{2}{3}$ and $\frac{5}{6}$.

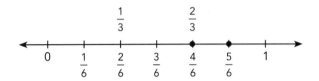

The numbers $\frac{2}{3}$ and $\frac{4}{6}$ are equivalent and are represented by the same point on a number line.

The fraction $\frac{5}{6}$ lies to the right of $\frac{2}{3}$. This means that $\frac{5}{6}$ is greater than $\frac{2}{3}$.

This can be represented as:

$\frac{5}{6} > \frac{2}{3}$.

b) Compare the two decimals, 1.3 and 1.15. Use a number line to help you.

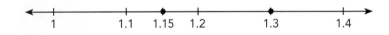

The decimal 1.15 lies to the left of 1.3. This means that 1.15 is less than 1.3.

This can be represented by:

1.15 < 1.3.

Guided Practice

Complete each __?__ with the correct value, and each [?] with > or <.

10 **a)** Fill in the missing decimals on the number line.

b) Compare each pair of decimals using < or >. Use the number line in **a)** to help you.

0.1 [?] 0.05   0.02 [?] 0.07

Draw a vertical number line to represent each set of numbers.

11 Mixed numbers greater than 6 but less than 7

Use an interval of $\frac{1}{6}$ between each pair of mixed numbers.

12 Positive fractions less than 1, with an interval of $\frac{1}{12}$ between each pair of fractions

13 Decimals between 11.4 and 15.0, with an interval of 0.4 between each pair of decimals

14 Decimals greater than 7.2 but less than 9.6
Use an interval of 0.3 between each pair of decimals.

15 Positive decimals less than 7.5, with an interval of 0.75 between each pair of decimals

Compare each pair of numbers using > or <. Use a number line to help you.

16 $3\frac{9}{10}$ **?** $3\frac{3}{10}$

17 2.17 **?** 2.71

18 14.4 **?** 13.38

19 $8\frac{5}{12}$ **?** $\frac{100}{12}$

Learn — **Compare numbers in different forms.** ———————————

Look at these number lines.

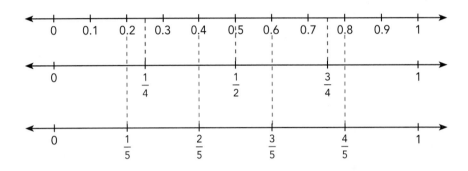

Every whole number, fraction, and decimal can be represented on the number line. A given point on a number line can be written in different forms. For example, $\frac{1}{2} = 0.5$ and $\frac{3}{4} = 0.75$.

You can see that $\frac{1}{4} = 0.25$, $\frac{1}{2} = 0.5$, and $\frac{3}{4} = 0.75$.

You can also see that $\frac{1}{5} = 0.2$, $\frac{2}{5} = 0.4$, $\frac{3}{5} = 0.6$, and $\frac{4}{5} = 0.8$.

· ·

a) Which is greater, $\frac{1}{4}$ or 0.3?

$\frac{1}{4} = 0.25$

0.25 lies to the left of 0.3.

So, $0.3 > \frac{1}{4}$.

b) Which is lesser, 0.62 or $\frac{3}{5}$?

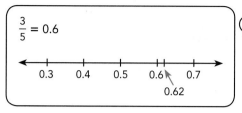

0.6 lies to the left of 0.62.

So, $\frac{3}{5} < 0.62$.

Guided Practice

Complete.

20 Which is greater, $\frac{1}{2}$ or 0.55?

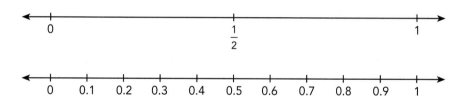

$\frac{1}{2} = \underline{\quad?\quad}$

$\underline{\quad?\quad}$ lies to the $\underline{\quad?\quad}$ of 0.55.

So, 0.55 ⬚? $\frac{1}{2}$.

Compare each ⬚? using > or <. Use a number line to help you.

21 0.2 ⬚? $\frac{1}{4}$

22 $\frac{3}{4}$ ⬚? 0.7

23 0.89 ⬚? $\frac{4}{5}$

24 0.25 ⬚? $\frac{1}{5}$

25 $\frac{2}{5}$ ⬚? 0.3

26 3.26 ⬚? $3\frac{5}{8}$

Copy and complete each number line by filling in the missing values.

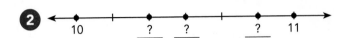

1   ?   24   25   ?   ?   ?

2   10   ?   ?   ?   11

3   5.1   ?   ?   ?   ?   5.2

Draw a horizontal number line to represent each set of numbers.

4 Odd numbers from 11 to 21

5 Positive whole numbers less than 9

6 Whole numbers greater than 12 but less than 18

7 Mixed numbers between 0 and 2, with an interval of $\frac{1}{3}$ between each pair of mixed numbers

8 Decimals from 7.0 to 8.4, with an interval of 0.2 between each pair of decimals

Draw a vertical number line to represent each set of numbers.

9 Even numbers between 20 and 32

10 Positive whole numbers less than 13

11 Whole numbers greater than 6 but less than 16

12 Positive fractions less than 1, with an interval of $\frac{1}{8}$ between each pair of fractions

13 Decimals between 10 and 15, with an interval of 0.75 between each pair of decimals

Compare each pair of numbers using > or <. Use a number line to help you.

14 $2\frac{3}{7}$? $1\frac{9}{7}$

15 $\frac{17}{25}$? $1\frac{7}{25}$

16 $1\frac{4}{5}$? $1\frac{2}{3}$

17 33.61 ? 36.13

18 59.05 ? 59.5

19 98.072 ? 98.027

Draw a horizontal number line from 2 to 3 to represent each set of numbers.

20 $2\frac{4}{5}$, $2\frac{3}{20}$, $2\frac{1}{2}$, $2\frac{11}{20}$, and $2\frac{9}{20}$

21 2.5, 2.125, 2.375, and 2.875

Draw a horizontal number line from 0 to 1 to represent each set of numbers.

22 $\frac{1}{3}$, $\frac{1}{4}$, $\frac{3}{8}$, $\frac{3}{4}$, $\frac{7}{8}$, and $\frac{5}{6}$

23 0.1, 0.25, 0.05, 0.8, 0.75, and 0.95

Compare each pair of numbers using > or <. Use a number line to help you.

24 0.8 ? $\frac{1}{10}$

25 $\frac{1}{5}$? 0.25

26 $\frac{3}{5}$? 0.35

27 0.14 ? $\frac{1}{4}$

28 $\frac{2}{5}$? 0.3

29 0.64 ? $\frac{9}{10}$

30 0.2 ? $\frac{1}{6}$

31 $\frac{7}{8}$? 0.87

Solve.

32 The wingspan of one butterfly is $1\frac{9}{16}$ inches. The wingspan of another butterfly is $1\frac{5}{8}$ inches. Write an inequality comparing the two wingspans.

33 For a class project, Jina made a model of the Empire State Building that was 23.7 centimeters tall. Her friend Caleb made a model that was $23\frac{3}{5}$ centimeters tall. Whose model was taller? How much taller was it?

Prime Factorization

Lesson Objective

- Express a whole number as a product of its prime factors.

Vocabulary

composite number   factor

prime number   prime factor

Learn **Identify composite numbers.**

Another way to represent a whole number is to write it as a product of its **factors**.

Find all the factors of 18.

$18 = 1 \times 18$ $18 = 2 \times 9$ $18 = 3 \times 6$

The factors of 18 are 1, 2, 3, 6, 9, and 18.
The number 18 is an example of a composite number.

> A composite number has more than two different whole-number factors.
>
> 18 has six factors, so it is a composite number.

The number 3 is an example of a **prime number**. A prime number has only two factors, the number itself and 1.

In the list of factors for 18, 2 and 3 are the only prime numbers. 2 and 3 are the prime factors of 18.

Learn **Write a composite number as a product of its prime factors.**

> A composite number can be written as a product using only its **prime factors**. This is known as prime factorization.

For example, you can write 18 as a product using only its prime factors.

$18 = 2 \times 3 \times 3$

Math Note

Finding the prime factorization of a number is not the same as finding the factors of a number. A composite number can be written as the product of different pairs of its factors. But there is one and only one prime factorization for a given composite number.

Express 60 as a product of its prime factors.

Method 1

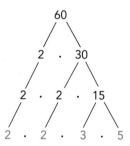

2	60	Divide by prime factor 2.
2	30	Divide by prime factor 2.
3	15	Divide by prime factor 3.
	5	

Start dividing the number by its least prime factor. Continue dividing until the quotient is a prime number.

The prime factors of 60 are 2, 3, and 5.

$60 = 2 \times 2 \times 3 \times 5$

Method 2

```
          60
         /  \
        2  . 30
           /  \
      2 .  2 . 15
     / \   / \  / \
    2 . 2 . 3 . 5
```

Math Note

Another way to write multiplication is to use the multiplication dot.

So, $60 = 2 \cdot 2 \cdot 3 \cdot 5$ means $60 = 2 \times 2 \times 3 \times 5$.

The prime factors of 60 are 2, 3, and 5.

$60 = 2 \cdot 2 \cdot 3 \cdot 5$

Guided Practice

Complete.

1 Express 48 as a product of its prime factors.

Method 1

2	48
?	24
2	?
?	6
	?

$48 = 2 \times \underline{} \times 2 \times \underline{} \times \underline{}$

Method 2

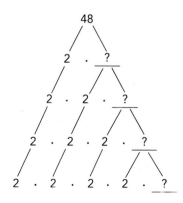

```
              48
             /  \
            2 .  ?
               /  \
          2 .  2 . ?
              /  \
        2 . 2 . 2 . ?
                  / \
      2 . 2 . 2 . 2 . ?
```

$48 = 2 \cdot 2 \cdot 2 \cdot 2 \cdot \underline{}$

Practice 1.2

1 Copy the array of numbers. Circle all the prime numbers.

1	2	3	4	5	6
7	8	9	10	11	12
13	14	15	16	17	18
19	20	21	22	23	24
25	26	27	28	29	30

Express each number as a product of its prime factors.

2 6

3 15

4 36

5 78

6 184

7 360

8 24

9 49

10 81

11 144

12 245

13 510

14 250

15 1,089

16 4,725

17 900

18 27,000

Solve.

19 *Math Journal* Describe the steps for finding the prime factors of 42.

20 400 written as a product of its prime factors is 2 × 2 × 2 × 2 × 5 × 5. Write 800 as a product of its prime factors.

21 Given that 320 written as a product of its prime factors is 2 × 2 × 2 × 2 × 2 × 2 × 5, write 3,200 as a product of its prime factors.

22 2,700 written as a product of its prime factors is 2 × 2 × 3 × 3 × 3 × 5 × 5. Write 270 as a product of its prime factors.

23 It is given that 4,800 can be expressed in terms of its prime factors as 2 × 2 × 2 × 2 × 2 × 2 × 3 × 5 × 5.

   a) Write 1,200 as a product of its prime factors.

   b) Now, write 120 as a product of its prime factors.

1.3 Common Factors and Multiples

Lesson Objectives

- Find the common factors and the greatest common factor of two whole numbers.
- Find the common multiples and the least common multiple of two whole numbers.

Vocabulary

common factor   greatest common factor

common multiple   multiple

least common multiple

Learn — **Identify the common factors of two whole numbers.**

Find the common factors of 12 and 30.

Factors of 12	Factors of 30
12 = 1 × 12	30 = 1 × 30
12 = 2 × 6	30 = 2 × 15
12 = 3 × 4	30 = 3 × 10
	30 = 5 × 6

Identify the factors that are common to both 12 and 30, and circle them.

Factors of 12: ①, ②, ③, 4, ⑥, 12

Factors of 30: ①, ②, ③, 5, ⑥, 10, 15, 30

1, 2, 3, and 6 are all factors of both 12 and 30.

1, 2, 3, and 6 are called the common factors of 12 and 30.

Guided Practice

Complete.

1 Use the lists of factors on the right to find the common factors of 10 and 28.

The factors of 10 are __?__, __?__, __?__, and __?__.

The factors of 28 are __?__, __?__, __?__, __?__, __?__, and __?__.

The common factors of 10 and 28 are __?__ and __?__.

Factors of 10	Factors of 28
10 = 1 × 10	28 = 1 × 28
10 = 2 × 5	28 = 2 × 14
	28 = 4 × 7

Find the common factors of each pair of numbers.

2 16 and 24

3 27 and 35

4 36 and 50

5 40 and 54

Learn Find the **greatest common factor** of two whole numbers.

Find the greatest common factor of 45 and 75.

Method 1

Factors of 45	Factors of 75
45 = 1 × 45	75 = 1 × 75
45 = 3 × 15	75 = 3 × 25
45 = 5 × 9	75 = 5 × 15

Factors of 45: ①, ③, ⑤, 9, ⑮, 45

Factors of 75: ①, ③, ⑤, ⑮, 25, 75

The common factors of 45 and 75 are 1, 3, 5, and 15.

Of these four common factors, 15 is the greatest.

So, 15 is the greatest common factor of 45 and 75.

Method 2

By prime factorization,

45 = ③ · 3 · ⑤

75 = ③ · ⑤ · 5

Identify the prime factors that are common to both 45 and 75, and circle them.

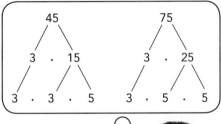

Greatest common factor = 3 · 5

= 15

The greatest common factor of 45 and 75 is 15.

Method 3

3	45, 75
5	15, 25
	3, 5

Divide by common prime factor 3.
Divide by common prime factor 5.
Stop dividing here as 3 and 5 have no common factor other than 1.

3 × 5 = 15

Multiply the common factors.

The greatest common factor of 45 and 75 is 15.

Guided Practice

Complete.

6 Find the greatest common factor of 20 and 32.

Method 1

Factors of 20	Factors of 32
20 = 1 × 20	32 = 1 × 32
20 = 2 × 10	32 = 2 × 16
20 = 4 × 5	32 = 4 × 8

The factors of 20 are __?__, __?__, __?__, __?__, __?__, and __?__.

The factors of 32 are __?__, __?__, __?__, __?__, __?__, and __?__.

The common factors of 20 and 32 are __?__, __?__, and __?__.

The greatest common factor of 20 and 32 is __?__.

Method 2

By prime factorization,

20 = 2 · __?__ · __?__

32 = 2 · __?__ · __?__ · __?__ · __?__

Greatest common factor = 2 · __?__

= __?__

The greatest common factor of 20 and 32 is __?__.

Method 3

$$\begin{array}{r|rr} 2 & 20, & 32 \\ \hline ? & ?, & ? \\ \hline & 5, & 8 \end{array}$$

2 × __?__ = __?__

The greatest common factor of 20 and 32 is __?__.

Find the greatest common factor of each pair of numbers.

7 15 and 27

8 36 and 54

9 48 and 72

10 40 and 100

Hands-On Activity

FIND THE COMMON FACTORS AND THE GREATEST COMMON FACTOR OF TWO NUMBERS

Work in pairs.

STEP 1 Shuffle the number cards and place them face down on a flat surface. Give half the factor cards to each player.

STEP 2 Each player turns over a number card and uses his or her factor cards to show the prime factorization of the number.

STEP 3 The first player states the greatest common factor (GCF) of the two numbers. If the player is correct, the player keeps the two number cards. Players reuse the factor cards on each turn.

Example

| 20 | 42 |

STEP 4 Two new number cards are turned over and the process repeats. This time the second player gets to state the GCF.

STEP 5 Play continues until all number cards have been used. The player with more number cards is the winner.

Learn **Use the greatest common factor with the distributive property.**

Express 12 + 20 as a product of the greatest common factor of the numbers and another sum.

First find the greatest common factor of the two numbers.

$12 = ②\cdot②\cdot 3$

$20 = ②\cdot②\cdot 5$

Greatest common factor of 12 and 20 = $2\cdot 2$

$= 4$

Then write the sum a different way. You know that

$$12 = 4 \cdot 3 \qquad\qquad 20 = 4 \cdot 5$$

So, $12 + 20 = 4 \cdot 3 + 4 \cdot 5$
$$ = 4(3 + 5)$$

The distributive property says that:

$$4(3 + 5) = 4 \cdot 3 + 4 \cdot 5$$

The number lines below show you that $12 + 20$ and $4(3 + 5)$ represent the same number.

Notice that either way, you "end up" at the same place on the number line.

$12 + 20$ is a **jump of 12** plus a **jump of 20**.

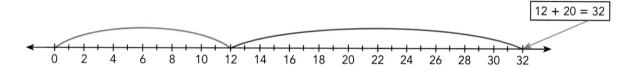

$12 + 20 = 32$

$4(3 + 5)$ is 4 jumps of (**3** + **5**).

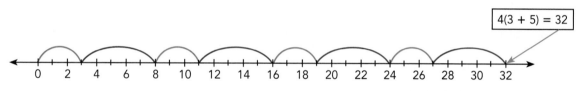

$4(3 + 5) = 32$

Guided Practice

Complete.

11 Express $18 + 45$ as a product of the greatest common factor of the numbers and another sum.

By prime factorization,

$$18 = 2 \cdot \underline{\ ?\ } \cdot \underline{\ ?\ } \qquad\qquad 45 = 3 \cdot \underline{\ ?\ } \cdot \underline{\ ?\ }$$

Greatest common factor of 18 and 45 $= \underline{\ ?\ } \cdot \underline{\ ?\ }$

$$ = \underline{\ ?\ }$$

$$18 + 45 = \underline{\ ?\ } \cdot \underline{\ ?\ } + \underline{\ ?\ } \cdot \underline{\ ?\ }$$
$$ = \underline{\ ?\ } (\underline{\ ?\ } + \underline{\ ?\ })$$

Express the sum of each pair of numbers as a product of the greatest common factor of the numbers and another sum.

12 $35 + 91$

13 $60 + 85$

14 $24 + 64$

Find the common multiples of two whole numbers.

Find the first two common multiples of 8 and 12.

Multiples of 8	Multiples of 12
1 × 8 = 8	1 × 12 = 12
2 × 8 = 16	2 × 12 = 24
3 × 8 = 24	3 × 12 = 36
4 × 8 = 32	4 × 12 = 48
5 × 8 = 40	5 × 12 = 60
6 × 8 = 48	6 × 12 = 72
7 × 8 = 56	7 × 12 = 84
8 × 8 = 64	8 × 12 = 96
9 × 8 = 72	9 × 12 = 108
10 × 8 = 80	10 × 12 = 120
⋮	⋮
⋮	⋮

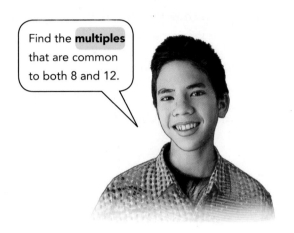

Find the **multiples** that are common to both 8 and 12.

Multiples of 8: 8, 16, (24), 32, 40, (48), 56, 64, (72), 80, ...

Multiples of 12: 12, (24), 36, (48), 60, (72), 84, 96, 108, 120, ...

24, 48, 72, ... are multiples of both 8 and 12.

24, 48, 72, ... are called the common multiples of 8 and 12.

The first two common multiples of 8 and 12 are 24 and 48.

Guided Practice

Complete.

15 Find the first three common multiples of 3 and 5.

The multiples of 3 are $\underline{?}$, $\underline{?}$, $\underline{?}$, $\underline{?}$, $\underline{?}$, $\underline{?}$, $\underline{?}$,

$\underline{?}$, $\underline{?}$, $\underline{?}$, $\underline{?}$, $\underline{?}$, $\underline{?}$, $\underline{?}$, $\underline{?}$, ...

The multiples of 5 are $\underline{?}$, $\underline{?}$, $\underline{?}$, $\underline{?}$, $\underline{?}$, $\underline{?}$,

$\underline{?}$, $\underline{?}$, $\underline{?}$, $\underline{?}$, ...

The first three common multiples of 3 and 5 are $\underline{?}$, $\underline{?}$, and $\underline{?}$.

List the first ten multiples of each pair of numbers. Then find the common multiples of each pair of numbers from the first ten multiples.

16 6 and 12

17 7 and 11

Find the **least common multiple** of two whole numbers.

Find the least common multiple of 6 and 9.

Method 1

Multiples of 6	Multiples of 9
1 × 6 = 6	1 × 9 = 9
2 × 6 = 12	2 × 9 = 18
3 × 6 = 18	3 × 9 = 27
4 × 6 = 24	4 × 9 = 36
5 × 6 = 30	5 × 9 = 45
6 × 6 = 36	6 × 9 = 54
7 × 6 = 42	7 × 9 = 63
8 × 6 = 48	8 × 9 = 72
9 × 6 = 54	9 × 9 = 81
10 × 6 = 60	10 × 9 = 90
⋮	⋮
⋮	⋮

Multiples of 6: 6, 12, (18), 24, 30, (36), 42, 48, (54), 60, …

Multiples of 9: 9, (18), 27, (36), 45, (54), 63, 72, 81, 90, …

The common multiples of 6 and 9 are 18, 36, 54, ….

Out of these common multiples, 18 is the least value.

So, 18 is the least common multiple of 6 and 9.

Method 2

By prime factorization,

$6 = 2 \cdot 3$
$9 = 3 \cdot 3$

Least common multiple $= 2 \cdot 3 \cdot 3$
$= 18$

2 · 3 · 3 is the least product containing 2 · 3 and 3 · 3.
So, 2 · 3 · 3 is the least common multiple of 6 and 9.

The least common multiple of 6 and 9 is 18.

Continue on next page

Method 3

3 | 6, 9   Divide by common prime factor 3.
  ‾‾‾‾‾
    2, 3   Stop dividing as 2 and 3 have no common factor other than 1.

3 × 2 × 3 = 18   Multiply the factors.

The least common multiple of 6 and 9 is 18.

Guided Practice

Complete.

18 Find the least common multiple of 8 and 10.

Method 1

The multiples of 8 are __?__, __?__, __?__, __?__, __?__, __?__,

__?__, __?__, __?__, __?__, ...

The multiples of 10 are __?__, __?__, __?__, __?__, __?__, __?__,

__?__, __?__, __?__, __?__, ...

The common multiples of 8 and 10 are __?__, __?__, ...

The least common multiple of 8 and 10 is __?__.

Method 2

By prime factorization,

$8 = 2 \cdot$ __?__ $\cdot$ __?__ $10 = 2 \cdot$ __?__

Least common multiple $= 2 \cdot$ __?__ $\cdot$ __?__ $\cdot$ __?__

$\qquad\qquad\qquad = $ __?__

The least common multiple of 8 and 10 is __?__.

Method 3

2 | 8,   10
  ‾‾‾‾‾‾‾‾
    __?__, __?__

$2 \times$ __?__ $\times$ __?__ $=$ __?__

The least common multiple of 8 and 10 is __?__.

Find the least common multiple of each pair of numbers.

19 3 and 7   **20** 5 and 12   **21** 4 and 9   **22** 6 and 11

Practice 1.3

Find the common factors of each pair of numbers.

1 18 and 63

2 15 and 75

3 30 and 50

4 64 and 92

5 26 and 78

6 55 and 88

Find the greatest common factor of each pair of numbers.

7 24 and 36

8 30 and 54

9 42 and 98

10 48 and 72

11 65 and 91

12 84 and 100

Find the first five common multiples of each pair of numbers.

13 5 and 6

14 4 and 7

15 9 and 10

16 8 and 11

17 15 and 25

18 7 and 20

Find the least common multiple of each pair of numbers.

19 3 and 10

20 7 and 12

21 5 and 8

22 9 and 11

23 10 and 14

24 18 and 24

Find the greatest common factor of each set of numbers.

25 24, 26, and 84

26 30, 48, and 72

27 36, 24, and 96

28 42, 90, and 81

29 60, 75, and 102

30 63, 105, and 294

Find the least common multiple of each set of numbers.

31 18, 24, and 42

32 21, 33, and 57

33 14, 30, and 70

34 27, 48, and 66

35 55, 75, and 115

36 78, 90, and 140

Find the greatest common factor and the least common multiple of each set of numbers.

37 10, 20, and 25

38 16, 28, and 40

39 54, 81, and 135

40 72, 144, and 216

Solve.

41 Makayla has two types of ropes. She wants to cut the ropes into pieces of the same length for butterfly knots.

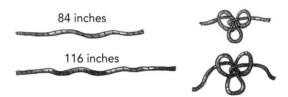

84 inches

116 inches

a) Find the greatest possible length that she can cut for each piece, so that no rope will be left unused.

b) Write the sum of the two lengths and factor out the number you found in part **a)**. What does the number inside the parentheses represent?

42 Giselle buys two types of flowers, 48 pink roses and 56 white lilies. She combines the flowers to make identical bouquets, with no flowers left over.

a) Find the greatest number of bouquets that Giselle can make.

b) Find the number of pink roses and white lilies in each bouquet.

43 A red light flashes every 14 minutes. A blue light flashes every 24 minutes. When will the two lights flash together again, if they last flashed together at 8 A.M.?

44 a) Find the product of 84 and 90.

b) Find the product of the greatest common factor and the least common multiple of 84 and 90.

c) What do you observe about your answers to parts **a)** and **b)**?

d) Choose two other numbers and repeat parts **a)** and **b)**. Do you get the same results?

1.4 Squares and Square Roots

Lesson Objectives

- Find a square of a number.
- Find a square root of a perfect square.

Learn · Find a **square** of a whole number.

a) A square has sides of length 8 centimeters. Find the area of the square.

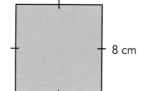
8 cm

Area of the square = 8 × 8
= 64 cm^2

8 × 8 is called the square of 8.
You can write 8 × 8 as 8^2.

8^2 is read as "8 squared".

So, $8^2 = 64$.

The number 2 in 8^2 is called the **exponent**.
The number 8 is called the **base** of the expression.

The square of a whole number is called a **perfect square**.
Since 64 = 8 × 8, 64 is a perfect square.

b) Find the square of 5.

$5^2 = 5 \times 5$
$= 25$

The square of 5 is 25.

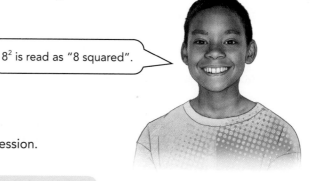

I can relate this to finding the area of a square with sides of length 5 units.

5 units

Guided Practice

Find the square of each number.

1 2

2 6

3 9

4 11

Learn Find a **square root** of a perfect square.

a) A square has an area of 9 square inches. Find the length of each side of the square.

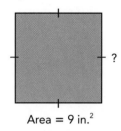

Area = 9 in.²

> **Math Note**
>
> The abbreviation in.² is read "square inches."

You know that

Area of square = length × length.

To find the length of a side of the square, you need to find the number whose square is 9.

Recalling the multiplication facts of 3, you know that

3 × 3 = 9.

So, the length of each side of the square is 3 inches.

3 is called a square root of 9. This can be written as

$\sqrt{9}$ = 3.

You read this as "the square root of 9 equals 3".

> Finding the square root of a number is the inverse of finding the square of a number.

b) Find the square root of 100.

I can relate this to finding the length of the side of a square, given that it has an area of 100 units^2.

? Area = 100 units^2

Method 1

Recalling the multiplication facts of 10, you know that

$$10 \times 10 = 100$$

So, $\sqrt{100} = 10$.

Method 2

By prime factorization,

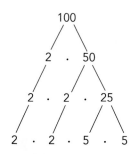

$$100 = 2 \cdot 2 \cdot 5 \cdot 5 \qquad \text{Write the prime factorization.}$$
$$= (2 \cdot 5) \cdot (2 \cdot 5) \qquad \text{Apply the Commutative Property of Multiplication.}$$
$$= (2 \cdot 5)^2 \qquad \text{Rewrite using an exponent.}$$
$$= 10^2$$

So, $\sqrt{100} = 10$.

Guided Practice

Find the square root of each number.

5 25

6 64

7 144

8 196

Practice 1.4

Find the square of each number.

1 3

2 7

3 12

4 10

Find the square root of each number.

5 36

6 81

7 121

8 49

Solve.

9 List the perfect squares that are between 25 and 100.

Find the value of each of the following.

10 35^2

11 56^2

12 64^2

13 $\sqrt{289}$

14 $\sqrt{400}$

15 $\sqrt{484}$

Solve.

16 Given that $41^2 = 1,681$, find the square of 410.

17 Given that $51^2 = 2,601$, find the square root of 260,100.

18 Given that $\sqrt{676} = 26$, evaluate $\sqrt{2,704}$.

19 Given that $\sqrt{1,521} = 39$, evaluate 390^2.

20 Heather wants to make a giant square quilt with sides of length 28 feet. She uses square patches of fabric that have sides of length 4 feet. How many patches of fabric will Heather need to make the giant square quilt?

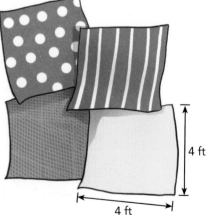

4 ft

4 ft

21 This week, customers at a carpet store pay $3 for a square foot of carpet. Next week the store will be having a sale. During the sale, each square foot of carpet will cost only $2. Neil wants to carpet two square rooms in his house. The floor in one room is 10 feet by 10 feet. The floor in the other room is 14 feet by 14 feet. How much money will Neil save if he waits to buy carpet during the sale?

1.5 Cubes and Cube Roots

Lesson Objectives

- Find a cube of a number.
- Find a cube root of a perfect cube.
- Evaluate numerical expressions involving whole number exponents.

Vocabulary

cube (of a number)   perfect cube

cube root   numerical expression

Find a cube of a whole number.

a) A cube has edges 2 centimeters long. Find its volume.

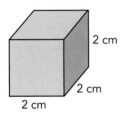

Volume of cube = 2 × 2 × 2

= 8 cm³

2 × 2 × 2 is called the cube of 2.

You can write 2 × 2 × 2 as 2^3.

So, $2^3 = 8$.

The number 3 in 2^3 is the exponent. The number 2 is the base.

> 2^3 is read as "2 cubed".

The cube of a whole number is called a **perfect cube**.
Since 8 = 2 × 2 × 2, 8 is a perfect cube.

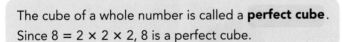

b) Find the cube of 7.

$7^3 = 7 × 7 × 7$

$= 343$

The cube of 7 is 343.

> I can relate this to finding the volume of a cube with edges of length 7 units.

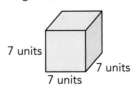

7 units

7 units

7 units

Guided Practice

Find the cube of each number.

 5

 6

3 9

Learn **Find a cube root of a perfect cube.**

a) A cube has a volume of 27 cubic meters. Find the length of each edge of the cube.

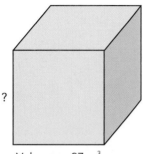

Volume = 27 m³

You know that

Volume of cube = edge × edge × edge.

To find the length of the edge of the cube, you need to find a number whose cube is 27.

You know that

3 × 3 × 3 = 27.

So, the length of each edge of the cube is 3 meters.
3 is called the cube root of 27. This can be written as

$\sqrt[3]{27}$ = 3.

Finding the cube root of a number is the inverse of finding the cube of a number.

b) Find the cube root of 64.

By prime factorization,

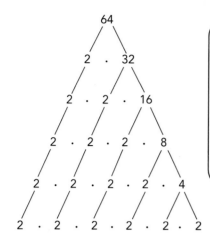

I can relate this to finding the length of an edge of a cube, when I know it has a volume of 64 units³.

Volume = 64 units³

$64 = 2 \cdot 2 \cdot 2 \cdot 2 \cdot 2 \cdot 2$ Write the prime factorization.

$\quad = (2 \cdot 2) \cdot (2 \cdot 2) \cdot (2 \cdot 2)$ Write parentheses.

$\quad = (2 \cdot 2)^3$ Rewrite using an exponent.

$\quad = 4^3$

So, $\sqrt[3]{64} = 4$.

Guided Practice
Find the cube root of each number.

4 216

5 343

6 1,000

 Evaluate numerical expressions that contain exponents.

In order to evaluate expressions with exponents, you need to follow the order of operations.

Order of Operations

STEP 1   Evaluate inside parentheses.

STEP 2   Evaluate exponents.

STEP 3   Multiply and divide from left to right.

STEP 4   Add and subtract from left to right.

Continue on next page

a) Find the value of $3^2 + 4^2$.

$3^2 = 3 \times 3$

$\quad = 9$

$4^2 = 4 \times 4$

$\quad = 16$

So, $3^2 + 4^2 = 9 + 16$ Evaluate terms with exponents first.

$\qquad\qquad = 25$ Then add.

> **Caution** ////////
>
> $3^2 + 4^2$ does not have the same value as $(3 + 4)^2$.

b) Find the value of $7^2 \times 2^2 + 3^3$.

$7^2 \times 2^2 + 3^3 = 49 \times 4 + 27$ Evaluate terms with exponents first.

              Then multiply.

$\qquad\qquad = \;\; 196 + 27$ Finally, add.

$\qquad\qquad = 223$

c) Find the value of $10^3 - 4^2 \times 5^2$.

$10^3 - 4^2 \times 5^2 = 1{,}000 - 16 \times 25$ Evaluate terms with exponents first.

              Then multiply.

$\qquad\qquad = 1{,}000 \;-\; 400$ Finally, subtract.

$\qquad\qquad = 600$

Guided Practice

Complete.

7 Find the values of $5^2 + 5^3$ and $5 \cdot 5 \cdot 5 \cdot 5 \cdot 5$.

$5^2 = \underline{\;?\;} \times \underline{\;?\;}$

$\quad = \underline{\;?\;}$

$5^3 = \underline{\;?\;} \times \underline{\;?\;} \times \underline{\;?\;}$

$\quad = \underline{\;?\;}$

So, $5^2 + 5^3 = \underline{\;?\;} + \underline{\;?\;}$

$\qquad\qquad = \underline{\;?\;}$

$5 \cdot 5 \cdot 5 \cdot 5 \cdot 5 = \underline{\;?\;}$

Find the value of each of the following.

8 $6^3 + 4^2$

9 $7^3 - 4^3$

10 $3^2 \times 5^3 + 9^2$

11 $8^3 \div 4^2 - 5^2$

12 $7^2 + 6^3 \div 2^3$

13 $9^3 - 4^2 \times 3^3$

Practice 1.5

Find the cube of each number.

1 8   **2** 3   **3** 10

Find the cube root of each number.

4 125   **5** 512   **6** 729

Solve.

7 List the perfect cubes that are between 100 and 600.

8 *Math Journal* Find the value of each expression. Then describe any patterns you see.

    a) $2^2 - 1^2$ **b)** $3^2 - 2^2$

    c) $4^2 - 3^2$ **d)** $5^2 - 4^2$

9 Find two consecutive numbers whose squares differ by 17.

Find the value of each of the following.

10 $8^3 + 5^2$ **11** $10^3 - 6^2$

12 $3^3 \times 9^2$ **13** $7^3 \div 3^2$

14 $7^2 + 8^3 - 4^2$ **15** $9^3 - 5^2 + 6^2$

16 $8^3 \times 5^3 \div 5^2$ **17** $10^3 \div 8^2 \times 4^2$

18 $7^3 - 10^2 \div 2^2$ **19** $3^3 + 4^3 \times 6^2$

Find the value of each of the following.

20 17^3 **21** 16^3 **22** 18^3

23 $\sqrt[3]{1,728}$ **24** $\sqrt[3]{8,000}$ **25** $\sqrt[3]{3,375}$

Solve.

26 Given that $11^3 = 1,331$, find the cube of 110.

27 Given that $14^3 = 2,744$, find the cube root of 2,744,000.

28 Given that $\sqrt[3]{4,096} = 16$, evaluate 160^3.

29 Evaluate $13^2 + 20^3 - 18^2$.

30 Evaluate the cube root of $12^3 \times 5^3 \div 8^2$.

31 Find three consecutive numbers whose cubes have a sum of 2,241.

32 A cubic crate with an edge length of 16 feet will be used to contain cubic wooden boxes. Each wooden box has an edge length of 4 feet. How many wooden boxes can the crate contain?

Brain @ Work

Mr. Henderson wants to tile his patio that is rectangular in shape. His patio measures 108 inches by 144 inches. Find the fewest square tiles he can use without cutting any of them. (Hint: First find the largest size tile he can use.)

108 in.

144 in.

Chapter Wrap Up

Concept Map

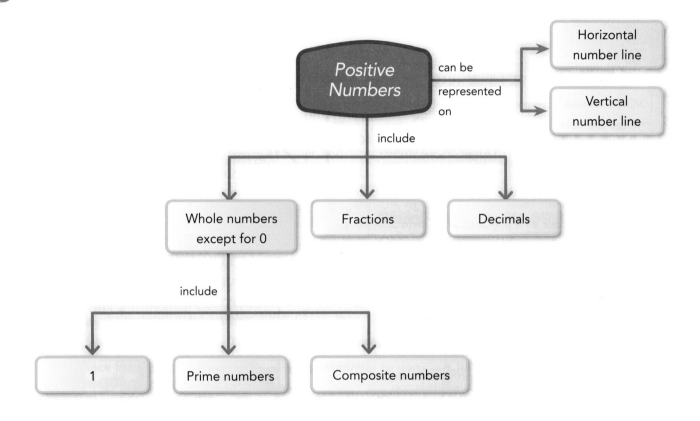

Key Concepts

▶ Positive numbers can be represented on a number line.

▶ You can write a composite number as a product of its prime factors.

▶ The greatest common factor of two or more whole numbers is the greatest factor among all the common factors of the numbers.

▶ The least common multiple of two or more whole numbers is the least multiple among all the common multiples of the numbers.

▶ A perfect square is the square of a whole number. For example, 64 is a perfect square since $64 = 8^2$. 8 is a square root of 64, and this can be written as $\sqrt{64} = 8$.

▶ A perfect cube is the cube of a whole number. For example, 8 is a perfect cube since $8 = 2^3$. 2 is the cube root of 8, and this can be written as $\sqrt[3]{8} = 2$.

Chapter Review/Test

Concepts and Skills

Draw a horizontal number line to represent each set of numbers.

1 Positive whole numbers less than 8

2 Whole numbers greater than 25 but less than 33

3 Mixed numbers from 4 to 6, with an interval of $\frac{1}{4}$ between each pair of mixed numbers

4 Decimals between 3.0 and 3.8, with an interval of 0.2 between each pair of decimals

Express each number as a product of its prime factors.

5 42

6 150

Find the common factors of each pair of numbers.

7 21 and 63

8 35 and 70

Find the greatest common factor of each pair of numbers.

9 8 and 12

10 42 and 32

Find the first three common multiples of each pair of numbers.

11 4 and 5

12 9 and 21

Find the least common multiple of each pair of numbers.

13 6 and 15

14 8 and 11

Find the square of each number.

15 14

16 30

Find the square root of each number.

17 169

18 484

Find the cube of each number.

19 4

20 20

Find the cube root of each number.

21 1,331

22 9,261

Find the value of each of the following.

23 $4^3 + 6^2$

24 $8^3 - 5^2$

25 $5^3 \times 4^3 - 13^2$

26 $8^2 + 10^3 \div 5^2$

Solve.

27 Given that $63^2 = 3,969$, find the square of 630.

28 Given that $\sqrt{1,225} = 35$, evaluate 350^2.

29 Given that $16^3 = 4,096$, find the cube root of 4,096,000.

30 Given that $\sqrt[3]{13,824} = 24$, evaluate 240^3.

Problem Solving
Solve. Show your work.

31 Find two consecutive numbers whose squares differ by 25.

32 Riley is packing 144 pencils, 120 files, and 108 notebooks equally into as many boxes as possible.

    a) Find the greatest number of boxes that Riley could pack the items into.

    b) Find the number of pencils, files, and notebooks in each box.

33 Imelda, Susan, and Clara are driving go-carts around a track. Imelda takes 14 minutes, Susan takes 18 minutes, and Clara takes 10 minutes to drive one lap. Suppose all three of them start together at a point and drive at their same speeds. After how many minutes would all three meet again?

34 How many squares with sides that are 6 inches long are needed to cover a square with a side length of 30 inches without overlapping?

35 A wooden crate is a cube with edge lengths of 18 inches. The crate contains tiny plastic cubes with edge lengths of 3 inches. How many plastic cubes can fit inside the wooden crate?

Negative Numbers and the Number Line

How cold is an iceberg?

Water freezes at 0°C, but the temperature of an iceberg can be much lower than that because icebergs form when the temperature is below 0°C. For example, the temperature in Antarctica, where many icebergs form, is usually below 0°C.

In this chapter, you will learn to use negative numbers to represent temperatures below 0°C. You will also learn how to use negative numbers to solve a variety of real-world problems.

BIG IDEA

▶ Negative numbers are the opposites of positive numbers. For every positive number, there is a corresponding negative number.

Recall Prior Knowledge

Representing positive numbers on a number line

Positive numbers include whole numbers, fractions, and decimals.

Whole numbers represented on a number line:

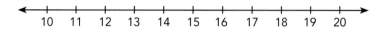

Fractions represented on a number line:

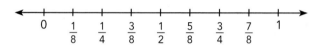

Decimals represented on a number line:

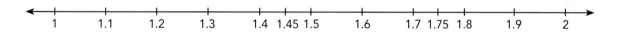

Each of the horizontal number lines shown above can also be represented by one of the vertical number lines below:

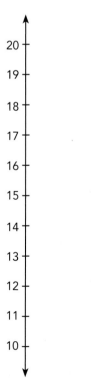

Draw a horizontal number line to represent each set of numbers.

1 Odd numbers from 20 to 30

2 Mixed numbers from 3 to 5, with an interval of $\frac{1}{6}$ between each pair of mixed numbers

3 Decimals between 8.0 and 10.0, with an interval of 0.25 between each pair of decimals

---

Writing statements of inequality for two given positive numbers using the symbols > and <

Compare each pair of numbers using > or <. Use a number line to help you.

a) 0.45 and 0.5

b) $\frac{7}{10}$ and $\frac{2}{5}$

c) $\frac{4}{5}$ and 0.9

a)

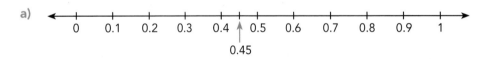

0.45 lies to the left of 0.5. So, 0.45 < 0.5.

b)

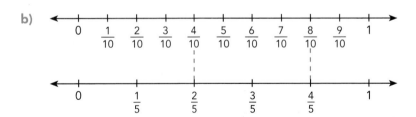

From the number lines, you can see that $\frac{2}{5} = \frac{4}{10}$.

$\frac{7}{10}$ lies to the right of $\frac{4}{10}$. So, $\frac{7}{10} > \frac{2}{5}$.

c) From the number lines, you can see that $\frac{4}{5} = \frac{8}{10} = 0.8$.

0.8 lies to the left of 0.9. So, $\frac{4}{5} < 0.9$.

Quick Check

Compare each pair of numbers using > or <. Use a number line to help you.

4 $\frac{3}{8}$? $\frac{5}{6}$

5 2.14 ? 2.104

6 0.72 ? $\frac{7}{12}$

Negative Numbers

Lesson Objectives

- Use negative numbers to represent real-world quantities.
- Represent, compare, and order positive and negative numbers on a number line.

Vocabulary

negative number

opposite

Learn **Recognize the use of positive and negative numbers in real-world situations.**

Positive and negative numbers can be used to represent many real-world situations.

a) They can be used to represent temperature readings that are above and below zero, as shown in the table. Notice that you use a negative sign before a negative number. You do not need to use a "plus" sign to show that a number is positive.

Time	12 A.M.	4 A.M.	8 A.M.	12 P.M.	4 P.M.	8 P.M.
Temperature (°C)	−5	−12	−8	4	10	2

b) They can be used to represent gains or losses.

For example, in the game of football, −15 can be used to represent a loss of 15 yards, and 30 can be used to represent a gain of 30 yards.

c) They can be used to represent values that are above and below a certain value, such as elevations above or below sea level.

For example, a depression that is 52 feet below sea level can be represented by −52 feet, and a mountain peak that is 7,310 feet above sea level can be represented by 7,310 feet.

> Sea level is considered to be at an elevation of 0 feet.

d) They can be used to represent debits or credits. A debit is an amount someone owes. A credit is an amount owed back to someone.

For example, −$180 means a debit of $180, and $79 means a credit of $79.

Guided Practice

Write a positive or negative number to represent each situation.

1 36°F below zero

2 A debit of $10,540

3 29,035 feet below sea level

4 A gain of 45 yards

Answer the questions.

The table shows the elevations of four locations compared to sea level.

Location	New Orleans, LA	Death Valley, CA	Mount Davidson, CA	Pilot Mountain, NC
Elevation (ft)	−8	−282	928	2,421

5 New Orleans is 8 feet __?__ sea level.

6 Mount Davidson is __?__ feet above sea level.

7 The deepest location among the four locations is __?__ .

8 The highest location among the four locations is __?__ .

9 The location nearest to sea level is __?__ .

Learn **Represent negative numbers on a number line.**

Like positive numbers, negative numbers can also be represented on a number line.

The number line below is extended to represent negative numbers.

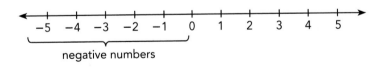

negative numbers

On a horizontal number line, the numbers become greater as you move to the right, and less as you move to the left.

4 is greater than 1.
−4 is less than −1.

A number line that includes negative numbers can be horizontal or vertical, just like a number line that shows only positive numbers.

On a horizontal number line, the negative numbers are placed to the left of zero. The lesser number always lies to the left of the greater number.

On a vertical number line, the negative numbers are placed below zero. The lesser number always lies below the greater number.

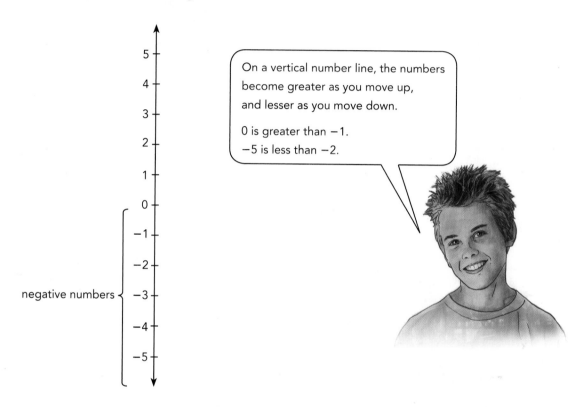

On a vertical number line, the numbers become greater as you move up, and lesser as you move down.

0 is greater than −1.
−5 is less than −2.

negative numbers

Notice that for every positive number, there is a corresponding negative number. For example, for the positive number 3, its corresponding negative number is −3.

On a number line, both 3 and −3 are the same distance from 0, but are on opposite sides of 0. You say that 3 is the **opposite** of −3 and −3 is the opposite of 3.

Zero is neither positive nor negative. Zero is its own opposite.

a) Draw a horizontal number line to represent the numbers from 0 to 6 and their opposites.

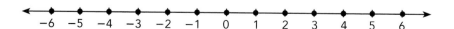

Continue on next page

b) Draw a vertical number line to represent the following set of numbers:
−26, −29, −30, −32, −34.

When you graph a set of numbers, choose a number greater than the greatest number in the set for the last point shown on one end of the number line.

Choose a number less than the least number in the set for the last point shown on the other end of the number line.

Guided Practice

Copy and complete the number line.

10

? −12 ? −10 ? −8 −7 ? −5 −4

Draw a horizontal number line to represent each set of numbers.

11 −8, −5, −4, −2, 2, 5, 7

12 −16, −19, −20, −22, −25

Write the opposite of each number.

13 −14

14 −9

15 −17

16 27

17 −23

18 46

Learn **Write statements of inequality using the symbols > and <.**

Use the number line to compare each pair of numbers using > or <.

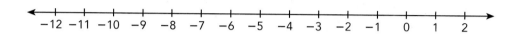

a) −12 ? −10

b) −6 ? −9

c) −8 ? −5

d) 1 ? −4

a) −12 is to the left of −10.
So, −12 < −10.

b) −6 is to the right of −9.
So, −6 > −9.

c) −8 is to the left of −5.
So, −8 < −5.

d) 1 is to the right of −4.
So, 1 > −4.

Caution ////////

When you compare negative and positive numbers, be careful to think about the sign of the numbers.

5 > 3 because 5 is to the right of 3 on a number line. But −5 < 3 because −5 is to the left of 3 on a number line.

Guided Practice

Copy and complete each inequality using > or <.

19 −15 ? −6

20 −20 ? −23

21 −30 ? −3

22 −19 ? 0

23 12 ? −31

24 −75 ? 46

Hands-On Activity

Materials:

- number cards

REPRESENT NEGATIVE NUMBERS ON A NUMBER LINE AND COMPARE TWO NEGATIVE NUMBERS USING > AND <

Work in pairs. Your teacher will give you and your partner a set of number cards with these numbers on them:

−5, −10, −15, −20, −25, −30, −35, −40, −45, −50,
−55, −60, −65, −70, −75, −80, −85, −90, −95, −100

STEP 1 Draw a number line and divide it into ten equal intervals. Label the endpoints −100 and 0. Shuffle the cards and place them face down on a flat surface.

STEP 2 Choose one card and turn it over. Mark the number shown on the card on the drawn number line.

STEP 3 Have your partner choose another card and mark the number shown on the number line.

STEP 4 Work together to write a statement of inequality for the two numbers you represented on the number line.

STEP 5 Repeat **STEP 2** through **STEP 4** using the other number cards.

Learn Interpret and explain statements of order for positive and negative numbers in real-world situations.

a) The table shows the lowest recorded temperature in Alaska for each month from July through December.

Month	Jul	Aug	Sep	Oct	Nov	Dec
Temperature (°F)	16	8	−13	−48	−61	−72

September's lowest recorded temperature of −13°F is lower than August's lowest recorded temperature of 8°F.

To compare these two temperatures using an inequality, you can write −13°F < 8°F.

b) The table shows the elevations of some natural features.

Natural Feature	Elevation (Below Sea Level)
Death Valley, California	−282 feet
Lake Assal, Djibouti	−509 feet
Driskill Mountain, Louisiana	535 feet

The elevation of Death Valley, which is −282 feet, is greater than the elevation of Lake Assal, which is −509 feet.

To compare the two elevations using an inequality, you can write −282 ft > −509 ft.

The elevation of Lake Assal, which is –509 feet, is less than the elevation of Driskill Mountain, which has an elevation of 535 feet.

To compare the two elevations using an inequality, you can write −509 ft < 535 ft.

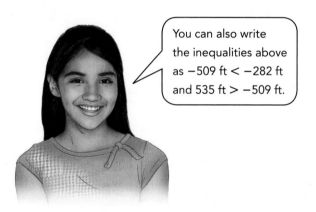

You can also write the inequalities above as −509 ft < −282 ft and 535 ft > −509 ft.

Guided Practice

Write an inequality for each statement using > or <.

25 0°C is warmer than −5°C.

26 The elevation of the Valdes Peninsula, which is −131 feet, is less than the elevation of the Caspian Sea, which is −92 feet.

Write a statement to describe each inequality.

27 −61°F < −47°F

28 −520 feet > −893 feet

Practice 2.1

Write a positive or negative number to represent each situation.

1 438°C above zero

2 164°F below zero

3 8,327 feet below sea level

4 12,316 feet above sea level

5 A loss of 20 yards

6 A credit of $3,401

Copy and complete each number line by filling in the missing numbers.

7

8

Write the opposite of each number.

9 8

10 −5

11 21

12 −29

13 24

14 −106

Draw a horizontal number line to represent each set of numbers.

15 Even negative numbers from −24 to −10

16 The opposites of the whole numbers from 35 to 45

Draw a vertical number line to represent each set of numbers.

17 Odd numbers between −91 and −103

18 Even numbers greater than −6 but less than 12

Use the number line to compare each pair of numbers using > or <.

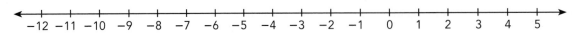

19 −9 ? −2

20 −10 ? −4

21 −5 ? 4

22 2 ? −6

23 −5 ? −12

24 −10 ? 3

Copy and complete each inequality using > or <.

25 −27 ? −3

26 −45 ? 15

27 25 ? −25

28 19 ? −15

29 14 ? −16

30 −81 ? −80

Order the numbers in each set from least to greatest.

31 3, 7, −2, −9, 0, −5

32 −10, 8, 34, −13, 10, −17

Order the numbers in each set from greatest to least.

33 −14, 43, −20, −57, 19, 31

34 98, −101, −76, 125, −92, 113

Answer the questions.

35 Name two numbers that are each 2 units away from −7. Give the opposites of these two numbers.

36 *Math Journal* Is the opposite of a number always negative? Explain.

37 Write an inequality using > or < for the following statement: −22°C is colder than −4°C.

38 Your friend says that the statement 0 < −15 is correct. Explain why the statement is incorrect.

39 The elevation of the deepest part of the Pacific Ocean is −36,200 feet. The elevation of the deepest part of the Indian Ocean is −24,442 feet. Write an inequality to compare the elevations. In which of the two oceans is the deepest part farther from sea level?

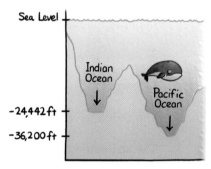

40 The temperature at which a substance boils is called its boiling point. The boiling points of two elements are shown in the table.

Element	Boiling Point (°C)
Oxygen	−183
Nitrogen	−196

Write an inequality to compare the two boiling points. Which element has the greater boiling point?

Write a statement to describe each inequality.

41 −45 feet > −80 feet

42 −436°F < −271°F

Absolute Value

Lesson Objectives

- Understand the absolute value of a number as its distance from 0 on the number line.

- Interpret absolute value as magnitude for a positive or negative quantity in a real-world situation.

Vocabulary

absolute value

ᴸᵉᵃʳⁿ **Write the absolute value of a number.**

The given number line shows the distance of −5 and 5 from 0.

Notice that even though −5 is negative, its distance from 0 is still 5 units.

> The absolute value of a number is the distance of that number from 0 on a number line.
>
> Because distances are always positive, the absolute value of a positive or negative number is always positive.
>
> Absolute value bars are used to show the absolute value of a number.
>
> Examples:
>
> The absolute value of −5 is 5. This can be written as $|-5| = 5$.
>
> The absolute value of 5 is 5. This can be written as $|5| = 5$.

Use the number line to find the absolute value of each of the following numbers.

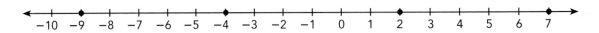

a) $|-9| = 9$ −9 is 9 units from 0.

b) $|7| = 7$ 7 is 7 units from 0.

c) $|-4| = 4$ -4 is 4 units from 0.

d) $|2| = 2$ 2 is 2 units from 0.

Notice that even though -4 is less than 2, the absolute value of -4 is greater than the absolute value of 2.

$|-4| > |2|$

Guided Practice

Use the number line to find the absolute value of each of the following numbers.

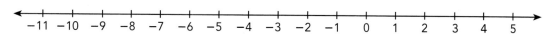

1 $|-10|$ **2** $|3|$ **3** $|-8|$

4 $|1|$ **5** $|-7|$ **6** $|0|$

Write the absolute value of each number.

7 $|-23|$ **8** $|41|$ **9** $|-38|$

10 $|114|$ **11** $|-132|$ **12** $|506|$

Learn   Use absolute values to interpret real-world situations.

a) The figure shows a section from Keith's bank account statement.

Date	Deposit	Withdrawal	Balance
			$280
May 31			
June 15	$40		$320
June 24		$490	-$170

As of May 31, Keith had $280 in his bank account. On June 24, after he withdrew $490, he had −$170 in his bank account.

$|-170| = 170$

This means that Keith had overdrawn $170.

Continue on next page

b) A dog is standing on a cliff, 35 feet above sea level. A dolphin is swimming 6 feet below sea level. An octopus is moving along the seabed, 40 feet below sea level.

You can use positive and negative numbers to show the elevation of the animals relative to sea level.

Dog's elevation = 35 ft
Dolphin's elevation = −6 ft
Octopus's elevation = −40 ft

To decide which animal is farthest from sea level, you do not need to think about whether the animals are above or below sea level. You can use absolute values to compare distances.

Distance of dog from sea level = |35|
$\qquad$ = 35 ft

Distance of dolphin from sea level = |−6|
$\qquad$ = 6 ft

Distance of octopus from sea level = |−40|
$\qquad$ = 40 ft

The octopus is farthest from sea level.

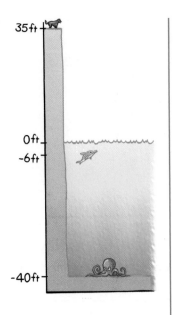

Guided Practice

Answer the questions.

13 Joe owes his sister Lisa $12, and his sister Kelly $18. His brother David owes Joe $20.

a) Joe writes the number −12 to represent the amount he owes Lisa. What numbers should Joe use to represent the other amounts given above?

b) Which person owes the most money?

14 At a parking garage, you can park underground or above ground. The lowest part of the underground parking is 40 feet below ground level. The highest part of the parking garage is 20 feet above ground level. The limousine parking area is 23 feet below ground level.

a) Use positive and negative numbers to represent the locations, with respect to ground level, of the three different parts of the parking garage.

b) Which part of the parking garage is closest to ground level?

Use the number line to find the absolute value of each of the following numbers.

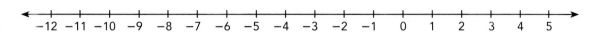

1 |−11| **2** |4| **3** |−6|

Write the absolute value of each number.

4 |35| **5** |−46| **6** |−77|

Copy and complete each inequality using > or <.

7 |−26| ? |30| **8** |−92| ? |−114|

9 |511| ? |−500| **10** |−707| ? |−628|

Answer the questions.

11 Two numbers have an absolute value of 16. Which of the two numbers is greater than 12?

12 *Math Journal* Jesse graphed a point to represent the absolute value of a number on a number line. If the original number is less than −10, describe all the possible values for the point Jesse graphed on the number line. Explain your thinking.

13 The table shows a monthly bank account statement for the period March to July.

Month	March	April	May	June	July
Balance	−$450	−$180	$200	$10	−$240

a) For which months is the account overdrawn?

b) How much was the bank owed in March?

c) In which month was the account overdrawn by the greatest amount?

d) In which month was the account overdrawn by the least amount?

e) How much was the bank owed in total?

14 The table shows some locations with their elevations.

Location	Salton City	Desert Shores	Laguna Salada	Bombay Beach
Elevation (ft)	−124.7	−200.1	−32.8	−226.4

a) Which location is the closest to sea level?

b) Which locations are within 200 feet of sea level?

c) How much farther from sea level is Desert Shores than Salton City?

d) Write the locations in order from the location that is farthest from sea level to the location that is closest to sea level.

15 The table shows the average surface temperature of some planets.

Planet	Earth	Saturn	Uranus	Mars
Average Surface Temperature (°C)	14	−108	−218	−53

a) Which planet has the highest average surface temperature?

b) Which planet has the lowest average surface temperature?

c) On Earth, the boiling temperature of water at sea level is 100°C. Which planet has an average surface temperature that is closest to this temperature?

d) Order the temperatures from lowest to highest.

Brain @ Work

1 You can interpret a negative sign in front of a number as meaning "the opposite of." So, −3 means the opposite of 3.

a) What number is −(−3) the opposite of?

b) What number is −(−3) equal to?

2 On a certain day, the maximum recorded temperature was 15°C and the minimum recorded temperature was −8°C. How many degrees Celsius was the difference between the recorded maximum and recorded minimum temperatures?

Chapter Wrap Up

Concept Map

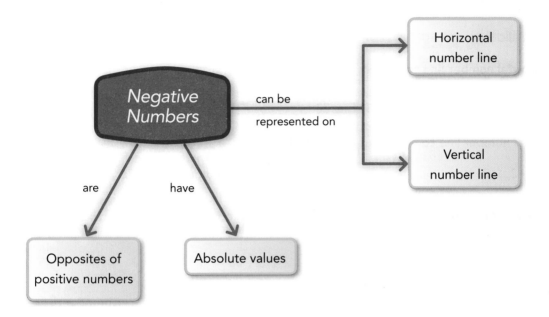

Key Concepts

▶ A negative number is the opposite of its corresponding positive number.
A positive number is the opposite of its corresponding negative number.
For example, 6 and −6 are opposites.

▶ Zero is its own opposite.

▶ Negative numbers can be represented on a number line.

▶ On a horizontal number line, the lesser number always lies to the left of
the greater number.

▶ On a vertical number line, the lesser number always lies below the
greater number.

▶ The absolute value of a number is its distance from 0 on a number line.

▶ The absolute value of a positive or a negative number is positive. The absolute
value of 0 is 0.

Chapter Review/Test

Concepts and Skills

Write the opposite of each number.

1 −47　　　　　　　　　**2** 56　　　　　　　　　**3** −78

Draw a horizontal number line to represent each set of numbers.

4 −41, −37, −34, −30, −28, −25, −22　　　　**5** −133, −129, −126, −122, −119

Draw a vertical number line to represent each set of numbers.

6 −8, −6, −2, 1, 3, 4　　　　　　**7** Odd numbers greater than −40 but less than −28.

Write a positive or negative number to represent each situation.

8 A deposit of $94

9 181°F below zero

10 The plane's altitude is 23,920 feet

11 The elevation of a sunken ship that is 11 meters beneath the ocean's surface

12 A gain of 35 yards

Copy and complete each inequality using > or <.

13 −14 ? −18　　　　　　　　**14** 17 ? −11

15 −34 ? 23　　　　　　　　　**16** −157 ? −145

Order the numbers in each set.

17 Order the numbers from greatest to least:
15, −14, 7, 2, −5, −6, −9

18 Order the numbers from least to greatest:
112, −140, −50, 51, −122, 175, −182

Write an inequality for each of the following statements using > or <.

19 −112°C is warmer than −143°C.

20 The lowest recorded temperature yesterday was −4°C, which is colder than today's lowest recorded temperature of 4°C.

Write the absolute value of each number.

21 |79|

22 |−88|

23 |−102|

Copy and complete each inequality using > or <.

24 |−65| ? |−57|

25 |111| ? |−124|

26 |−153| ? |135|

27 |−209| ? |−278|

Problem Solving

Answer the questions.

28 The Afar Depression is a land formation in Africa. At one location in the Afar Depression, the elevation is −75 meters. At another location, the elevation is −125 meters. Write an inequality to compare the elevations. Which elevation is farther from sea level?

29 The table shows temperature readings taken at the same location at three different times.

Time	12:30 A.M.	4:30 A.M.	8:30 A.M.
Temperature (°C)	−20	−4	12

a) At what time was the location the coldest?

b) Between 12:30 A.M. and 8:30 A.M., the temperature was always rising. Between what two times shown in the table did the temperature reach 0°C?

30 Clarence owes his brother Joe $240, and his best friend Tristan $166. His sister Chloe owes Clarence $275, and his friend Luke owes Clarence $150.

a) Clarence writes the number −240 to represent the amount he owes his brother Joe. What numbers should Clarence use to represent the other amounts given above?

b) Who owes the most money?

c) How much does Clarence owe in total?

d) Which is greater, the amount of money Clarence owes, or the amount of money that people owe him?

CHAPTER 3

Multiplying and Dividing Fractions and Decimals

How much do you know about the construction of your home?

Design and cost are important factors for home builders. Architects have to manage the use of construction materials for the floors, walls, doors, windows, electrical fittings, and more. For example, to build a wooden-framed house, architects need to determine how many joists to use if the joists are $1\frac{1}{3}$ feet apart.

Architects must also calculate the costs of materials and labor. These calculations involve fractions and decimals. In this chapter, you will practice multiplying and dividing with fractions and decimals. The skills you learn will be useful for solving many real-world problems.

BIG IDEA

▶ Whole number concepts can be extended to fractions and decimals when more precise calculations are needed.

Recall Prior Knowledge

Adding and subtracting decimals

$$\begin{array}{r} 3\;.\;8 \\ +\;2\;.\;1 \\ \hline 5\;.\;9 \end{array}$$

$$\begin{array}{r} \overset{1}{7}\;.\;\overset{1}{8}\;6 \\ +\;\;4\;.\;7\;5 \\ \hline 1\;2\;.\;6\;1 \end{array}$$

$$\begin{array}{r} 8\;.\;2\;6 \\ -\;7\;.\;0\;3 \\ \hline 1\;.\;2\;3 \end{array}$$

$$\begin{array}{r} \overset{5}{\cancel{6}}\;.\;\overset{10}{\cancel{1}}\;0 \\ -\;2\;.\;3\;4 \\ \hline 3\;.\;7\;6 \end{array}$$

✔ Quick Check

Add or subtract.

1 5.3 + 6.49

2 6.51 − 2.03

3 9.62 + 7.08

4 8.4 − 7.52

Expressing improper fractions as mixed numbers

$\dfrac{16}{5} = \dfrac{15}{5} + \dfrac{1}{5}$ Rewrite as a sum.

$= 3 + \dfrac{1}{5}$ Write the improper fraction as a whole number.

$= 3\dfrac{1}{5}$ Write the sum as a mixed number.

✔ Quick Check

Express each improper fraction as a mixed number in simplest form.

5 $\dfrac{19}{3}$

6 $\dfrac{26}{4}$

7 $\dfrac{30}{7}$

8 $\dfrac{38}{5}$

9 $\dfrac{50}{8}$

10 $\dfrac{69}{9}$

Expressing mixed numbers as improper fractions

$2\frac{5}{6} = 2 + \frac{5}{6}$ Rewrite as a sum.

$\qquad = \frac{12}{6} + \frac{5}{6}$ Write the whole number as a fraction.

$\qquad = \frac{17}{6}$ Write the sum as an improper fraction.

✔ Quick Check

Express each mixed number as an improper fraction.

11 $3\frac{1}{4}$ **12** $4\frac{3}{7}$ **13** $8\frac{5}{9}$

Multiplying fractions by fractions

Method 1

$\frac{3}{4} \times \frac{2}{9} = \frac{3 \times 2}{4 \times 9}$ Multiply the numerators.
Multiply the denominators.

$\qquad = \frac{6}{36}$ Simplify the product.

$\qquad = \frac{1}{6}$ Write the fraction in simplest form.

Method 2

$\frac{3}{4} \times \frac{2}{9} = \frac{3 \div 3}{4} \times \frac{2}{9 \div 3}$ Divide a numerator and a denominator by the common factor, 3.

$\qquad = \frac{1}{4 \div 2} \times \frac{2 \div 2}{3}$ Divide a numerator and a denominator by the common factor, 2.

$\qquad = \frac{1 \times 1}{2 \times 3}$ Multiply the numerators.
Multiply the denominators.

$\qquad = \frac{1}{6}$

✔ Quick Check

Find each product in simplest form.

14 $\frac{2}{5} \times \frac{7}{8}$ **15** $\frac{10}{11} \times \frac{33}{5}$ **16** $\frac{8}{7} \times \frac{35}{12}$

3.1 Dividing Fractions

Lesson Objective

* Divide a fraction, whole number, or mixed number by a fraction or a mixed number.

Vocabulary

reciprocals   improper fraction

mixed number

Learn   Divide a whole number by a unit fraction.

a) Lee cut 2 pies into pieces that were each $\frac{1}{4}$ of a pie.

How many pieces did Lee cut the 2 pies into?

Number of pieces $= 2 \div \frac{1}{4}$

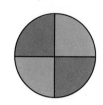

$2 \div \frac{1}{4}$ means: "How many quarters are in 2 wholes?"

The model shows that:

Number of quarters in 1 pie $= 4$

Number of quarters in 2 pies $= 2 \times 4$

So, $2 \div \frac{1}{4} = 2 \times 4$ Write as a multiplication expression.

$\phantom{So, 2 \div \frac{1}{4}} = 8$ Multiply.

Lee cut the 2 pies into 8 pieces.

In one pie, there are 4 quarters. So in two pies, there are $2 \times 4 = 8$ quarters.

Math Note

Two numbers whose product is 1 are called **reciprocals**. In general, dividing by a number is the same as multiplying by the reciprocal of the number.

$2 \div \frac{1}{4} = 2 \times 4$

$\frac{1}{4}$ and **4** are reciprocals.

Continue on next page

b) A bottle contains 2 quarts of cooking oil. A chef uses $\frac{1}{12}$ quart of cooking oil each day. How many days will the bottle of cooking oil last?

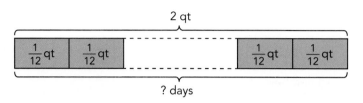

2 qt

$\frac{1}{12}$ qt $\quad$ $\frac{1}{12}$ qt $\quad$ $\frac{1}{12}$ qt $\quad$ $\frac{1}{12}$ qt

? days

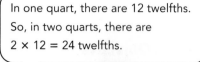

In one quart, there are 12 twelfths. So, in two quarts, there are $2 \times 12 = 24$ twelfths.

$$2 \div \frac{1}{12} = 2 \times 12 \qquad \text{Rewrite using the reciprocal of the divisor.}$$
$$= 24 \qquad \text{Multiply.}$$

The bottle of cooking oil will last 24 days.

Guided Practice

Solve.

1 Rina cut 3 paper squares into a number of equal pieces. Each piece was $\frac{1}{6}$ of a square. Into how many pieces did Rina cut the 3 paper squares?

Number of pieces = $\underline{\quad?\quad} \div \dfrac{?}{?}$

$3 \div \frac{1}{6}$ means: "How many one-sixths are in 3 wholes?"

The model shows that:

Number of one-sixths in 1 paper square = $\underline{\quad?\quad}$

Number of one-sixths in 3 paper squares = $\underline{\quad?\quad} \times \underline{\quad?\quad}$

So, $3 \div \dfrac{1}{6} = \underline{\quad?\quad} \times \underline{\quad?\quad}$

$= \underline{\quad?\quad}$

Dividing by $\frac{1}{6}$ is the same as multiplying by $\underline{\quad?\quad}$.

Rina cut the 3 paper squares into $\underline{\quad?\quad}$ pieces.

Divide.

2 $3 \div \dfrac{1}{5} = \underline{\quad?\quad} \times \underline{\quad?\quad} = \underline{\quad?\quad}$

3 $7 \div \dfrac{1}{4} = \underline{\quad?\quad} \times \underline{\quad?\quad} = \underline{\quad?\quad}$

4 $4 \div \dfrac{1}{2} = \underline{\quad?\quad}$

5 $5 \div \dfrac{1}{3} = \underline{\quad?\quad}$

6 $6 \div \dfrac{1}{5} = \underline{\quad?\quad}$

7 $8 \div \dfrac{1}{8} = \underline{\quad?\quad}$

Hands-On Activity

Materials:

• 5 paper strips

DIVIDING WHOLE NUMBERS BY A FRACTION

Use 5 paper strips of the same size and length. Each strip represents 1 whole.

STEP 1 Take 2 paper strips. Divide each of them into thirds using vertical lines and place them as shown. Then find $2 \div \dfrac{2}{3}$.

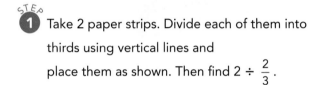

Refer to your model.

Complete:

There are $\underline{\quad?\quad}$ two-thirds in the 2 paper strips.

So, $2 \div \dfrac{2}{3} = \underline{\quad?\quad}$.

STEP 2 Divide each of the other 3 paper strips into fourths using vertical lines and place them as shown. Then find $3 \div \dfrac{3}{4}$.

Refer to your model.

Complete:

There are $\underline{\quad?\quad}$ three-fourths in the 3 paper strips.

So, $3 \div \dfrac{3}{4} = \underline{\quad?\quad}$.

Learn — **Divide a whole number by a proper fraction.**

a) Find $5 \div \frac{2}{3}$.

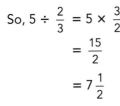

| $\frac{2}{3}$ | $\frac{2}{3}$ | $\frac{2}{3}$ | $\frac{2}{3}$ | $\frac{2}{3}$ | $\frac{2}{3}$ | $\frac{2}{3}$ | $\frac{1}{2}$ of $\frac{2}{3}$ |

Number of two-thirds in 2 wholes = 3

Number of two-thirds in 1 whole = $1\frac{1}{2}$ or $\frac{3}{2}$

Number of two-thirds in 5 wholes = $5 \times \frac{3}{2}$

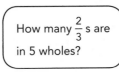

How many $\frac{2}{3}$ s are in 5 wholes?

So, $5 \div \frac{2}{3} = 5 \times \frac{3}{2}$

$= \frac{15}{2}$

$= 7\frac{1}{2}$

$\frac{2}{3}$ and $\frac{3}{2}$ are reciprocals.

So, you are using the fact that dividing a number is the same as multiplying by its reciprocal.

$5 \div \frac{2}{3} = 5 \times \frac{3}{2}$

b) A chef cooks 12 pounds of pasta each day. She uses $\frac{3}{16}$ pound of pasta for each serving she prepares. How many servings of pasta does she prepare each day?

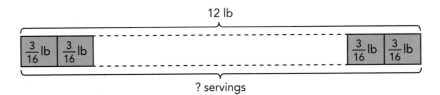

12 lb

| $\frac{3}{16}$ lb | $\frac{3}{16}$ lb | | $\frac{3}{16}$ lb | $\frac{3}{16}$ lb |

? servings

$12 \div \frac{3}{16} = 12 \times \frac{16}{3}$ Rewrite using the reciprocal of the divisor.

$= 64$ Multiply.

She prepares 64 servings of pasta each day.

Check: Calculate the total number of pounds of pasta she cooks.

$64 \times \frac{3}{16} = 12$

The answer is correct.

Guided Practice

Complete.

8 Find $7 \div \dfrac{3}{4}$.

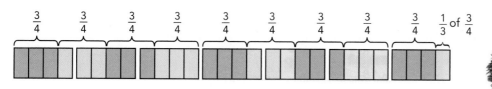

$$\underbrace{\dfrac{3}{4}}\ \underbrace{\dfrac{3}{4}}\ \underbrace{\dfrac{3}{4}}\ \underbrace{\dfrac{3}{4}}\ \underbrace{\dfrac{3}{4}}\ \underbrace{\dfrac{3}{4}}\ \underbrace{\dfrac{3}{4}}\ \underbrace{\dfrac{3}{4}}\ \underbrace{\dfrac{3}{4}}\ \underbrace{\dfrac{1}{3}\text{ of }\dfrac{3}{4}}$$

Number of three-quarters in 3 wholes = 4

Number of three-quarters in 1 whole = $1\dfrac{1}{3}$ or $\dfrac{?}{?}$

Number of three-quarters in 7 wholes = $\underline{\ ?\ } \times \dfrac{?}{?}$

How many $\dfrac{3}{4}$ s are in 7 wholes?

So, $7 \div \dfrac{3}{4} = \underline{\ ?\ } \times \dfrac{?}{?}$

$\qquad\quad = \dfrac{?}{?}$

$\qquad\quad = \underline{\ ?\ }$

Dividing by $\dfrac{3}{4}$ is the same as multiplying by $\dfrac{?}{?}$.

9 Mrs. Johnson bought 6 pizzas. She cut them into many equal pieces for the students in her class. Each piece was $\dfrac{3}{10}$ of a whole pizza. How many students were there in the class if each child received only one piece of pizza?

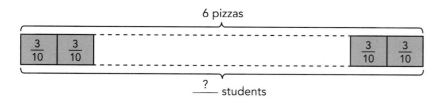

6 pizzas

$\dfrac{3}{10}$ $\dfrac{3}{10}$ $\qquad\qquad$ $\dfrac{3}{10}$ $\dfrac{3}{10}$

$\dfrac{?}{\ }$ students

$6 \div \dfrac{?}{?} = \underline{\ ?\ } \times \dfrac{?}{?}$

$\qquad\quad = \underline{\ ?\ }$

There were $\underline{\ ?\ }$ students in the class.

Divide. Express the quotient in simplest form.

10 $4 \div \dfrac{4}{7}$

11 $6 \div \dfrac{2}{7}$

12 $9 \div \dfrac{3}{8}$

13 $5 \div \dfrac{10}{13}$

14 $10 \div \dfrac{5}{14}$

15 $12 \div \dfrac{9}{10}$

Hands-On Activity

DIVIDING FRACTIONS

Use 2 paper strips of the same size and length. Each strip represents 1 whole.

 STEP 1 Take 1 paper strip and divide it into halves using vertical lines.

Then find $\frac{1}{2} \div \frac{1}{4}$.

Refer to your model.

Complete:

There are ___?___ fourths in a half.

So, $\frac{1}{2} \div \frac{1}{4} =$ ___?___.

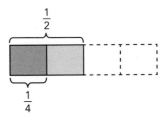

STEP 2 Find $\frac{1}{2} \div \frac{1}{4}$ by multiplication.

$\frac{1}{2} \div \frac{1}{4} = \frac{?}{?} \times \underline{}$ Rewrite using the reciprocal of the divisor.

$= \underline{}$ Multiply.

STEP 3 Divide the other paper strip into one-thirds using vertical lines.

Then find $\frac{2}{3} \div \frac{1}{6}$.

Refer to your model.

Complete:

There are ___?___ one-sixths in $\frac{2}{3}$.

So, $\frac{2}{3} \div \frac{1}{6} =$ ___?___.

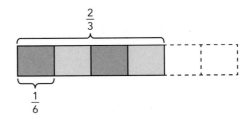

STEP 4 Find $\frac{2}{3} \div \frac{1}{6}$ by multiplication.

$\frac{2}{3} \div \frac{1}{6} = \frac{?}{?} \times \underline{}$ Rewrite using the reciprocal of the divisor.

$= \underline{}$ Multiply.

Learn **Divide a fraction by a fraction.**

a) Mary had $\frac{3}{4}$ of a pizza left over from a party. She cut it into pieces, each of which was $\frac{3}{8}$ of the whole pizza. How many pieces did Mary cut?

Number of pieces $= \frac{3}{4} \div \frac{3}{8}$

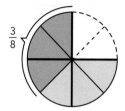

The model shows that there are 2 three-eighths in $\frac{3}{4}$.

So, $\frac{3}{4} \div \frac{3}{8} = 2$.

Another way to show this is:

$$\frac{3}{4} \div \frac{3}{8} = \frac{3}{4} \times \frac{8}{3}$$
$$= 2$$

Division is the inverse of multiplication. So, dividing by $\frac{3}{8}$ is the same as multiplying by $\frac{8}{3}$.

Mary cut the pizza into 2 pieces.

b) A plank is $\frac{4}{5}$ meter in length. A worker cuts it into some pieces, each of which is $\frac{1}{10}$ meter long. Into how many pieces did he cut the plank?

$\frac{4}{5}$ m

| $\frac{1}{10}$ m | $\frac{1}{10}$ m | | | $\frac{1}{10}$ m | $\frac{1}{10}$ m |

$$\frac{4}{5} \div \frac{1}{10} = \frac{4}{5} \times 10 \qquad \text{Rewrite using the reciprocal of the divisor.}$$
$$= 8 \qquad \text{Multiply.}$$

He cut the plank into 8 pieces.

Check: Calculate the total length of the plank.

$$8 \times \frac{1}{10} = \frac{8}{10} = \frac{4}{5} \text{ m}$$

The answer is correct.

Hands-On Activity

A pitcher contains $\frac{4}{5}$ quart of orange juice.

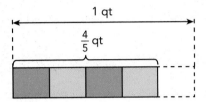

 Copy the model and divide it into tenths using vertical lines.

Complete: $\frac{4}{5}$ qt = $\frac{?}{10}$ qt

 Use the model to answer this question.

Into how many glasses, each containing $\frac{3}{10}$ quart, can the orange juice be poured? __?__

How many quarts of orange juice will be left in the pitcher? $\frac{?}{?}$ qt

 Now find the number of glasses by division.
Express your answer as a mixed number.

Number of glasses = $\frac{4}{5} \div \frac{?}{?}$ Divide.

$= \frac{4}{5} \times \frac{?}{?}$ Rewrite using the reciprocal of the divisor.

$= \frac{?}{?}$ Simplify.

$= \underline{?}$ Write the improper fraction as a mixed number.

The answer $2\frac{2}{3}$ means there are 2 glasses of orange juice, each containing $\frac{3}{10}$ quart, and a remaining glass of orange juice that contains $\frac{2}{3}$ of $\frac{3}{10}$ quart.

How many quarts of orange juice will be left in the pitcher? $\frac{?}{?} \times \frac{?}{?} = \frac{?}{?}$ qt

Guided Practice

Complete.

16 Adam had $\frac{5}{7}$ liter of water. He used the water to fill a few glasses completely.

The capacity of each glass was $\frac{2}{7}$ liter. How many glasses of water did Adam fill?

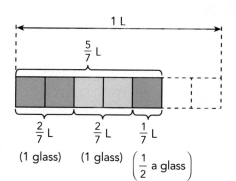

$$\frac{?}{?} \div \frac{?}{?} = \frac{?}{?} \times \frac{?}{?}$$

$$= \frac{?}{?}$$

$$= \underline{\quad?\quad}$$

Adam filled __?__ glasses of water.

17 Lina had $\frac{2}{3}$ of a pizza. She cut it into pieces that were each $\frac{1}{9}$ of the whole pizza. Into how many pieces did she cut it?

$\frac{2}{3}$ of a pizza

| $\frac{1}{9}$ | $\frac{1}{9}$ | | | $\frac{1}{9}$ | $\frac{1}{9}$ |

$$\frac{?}{?} \div \frac{?}{?} = \frac{?}{?} \times \underline{\quad?\quad}$$

$$= \underline{\quad?\quad}$$

She cut it into __?__ pieces.

Divide. Express the quotient in simplest form.

18 $\frac{2}{3} \div \frac{1}{6}$

19 $\frac{3}{5} \div \frac{1}{10}$

20 $\frac{3}{4} \div \frac{1}{2}$

21 $\frac{1}{6} \div \frac{2}{3}$

22 $\frac{5}{8} \div \frac{15}{16}$

23 $\frac{7}{16} \div \frac{5}{12}$

Learn **Divide a fraction by an improper fraction or a mixed number.**

a) Divide $\frac{1}{2}$ by $\frac{7}{3}$.

$\frac{1}{2} \div \frac{7}{3} = \frac{1}{2} \times \frac{3}{7}$ Write as a multiplication expression.

$\quad\quad = \frac{3}{14}$ Multiply.

Check: $\frac{7}{3} \times \frac{3}{14} = \frac{21}{42} = \frac{1}{2}$

The answer is correct.

Division is the inverse of multiplication.
So, dividing by $\frac{7}{3}$ is the same as multiplying by $\frac{3}{7}$.

b) Divide $\frac{3}{4}$ by $1\frac{1}{2}$.

$\frac{3}{4} \div 1\frac{1}{2} = \frac{3}{4} \div \frac{3}{2}$ Write $1\frac{1}{2}$ as an improper fraction.

$\quad\quad = \frac{3}{4} \times \frac{2}{3}$ Rewrite using the reciprocal of the divisor. Divide a numerator and a denominator by the common factor, 3.

$\quad\quad = \frac{1}{4} \times \frac{2}{1}$ Divide a numerator and a denominator by the common factor, 2. Then multiply.

$\quad\quad = \frac{1}{2}$

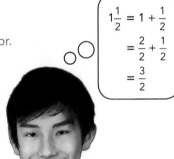

$1\frac{1}{2} = 1 + \frac{1}{2}$
$\quad = \frac{2}{2} + \frac{1}{2}$
$\quad = \frac{3}{2}$

Guided Practice

Complete.

24 Divide $\frac{5}{9}$ by $4\frac{1}{3}$.

$\frac{5}{9} \div 4\frac{1}{3} = \frac{5}{9} \div \frac{?}{?}$

$\quad\quad = \frac{5}{9} \times \frac{?}{?}$

$\quad\quad = \frac{5}{3} \times \frac{?}{?}$

$\quad\quad = \frac{?}{?}$

Caution /////////

Before finding the reciprocal of a whole number or a mixed number, you need to first write it as an improper fraction.

25 Divide $2\frac{3}{5}$ by $1\frac{8}{9}$.

$$2\frac{3}{5} \div 1\frac{8}{9} = \frac{?}{?} \div \frac{?}{?}$$

$$= \frac{?}{?} \times \frac{?}{?}$$

$$= \underline{\quad ? \quad}$$

$2\frac{3}{5}$ and $1\frac{8}{9}$ are both mixed numbers.

Express the mixed numbers as improper fractions.

 # Hands-On Activity

DIVISION INVOLVING WHOLE NUMBERS AND FRACTIONS

Work in pairs.

STEP 1 Find each quotient.

a) $4 \div \frac{2}{5}$ and $\frac{2}{5} \div 4$

b) $\frac{1}{4} \div \frac{2}{3}$ and $\frac{2}{3} \div \frac{1}{4}$

c) $\frac{4}{5} \div \frac{3}{10}$ and $\frac{3}{10} \div \frac{4}{5}$

d) $\frac{5}{8} \div \frac{3}{4}$ and $\frac{3}{4} \div \frac{5}{8}$

STEP 2 What do you observe about the products of each pair of quotients?

STEP 3 Given that $\frac{6}{7} \div 9 = \frac{2}{21}$ and $\frac{10}{11} \div \frac{5}{6} = \frac{12}{11}$, find the following quotients mentally.

a) $9 \div \frac{6}{7}$

b) $\frac{5}{6} \div \frac{10}{11}$

 Math Journal Explain in words the meaning of each division statement.

a) $4 \div \frac{2}{5}$ and $\frac{2}{5} \div 4$

b) $\frac{1}{4} \div \frac{2}{3}$ and $\frac{2}{3} \div \frac{1}{4}$

Divide. Express the quotient in simplest form. Use models to help you.

1 $1 \div \frac{1}{4}$

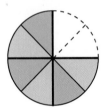

2 $3 \div \frac{3}{5}$

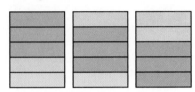

3 $\frac{3}{4} \div \frac{1}{8}$

4 $\frac{2}{3} \div \frac{2}{9}$

Draw a model to find each quotient.

5 $1 \div \frac{1}{5}$

6 $4 \div \frac{8}{9}$

7 $\frac{2}{5} \div \frac{3}{10}$

8 $\frac{3}{4} \div \frac{3}{16}$

Find each quotient. Express your answer in its simplest form.

9 $4 \div \frac{1}{7}$

10 $12 \div \frac{1}{3}$

11 $9 \div \frac{3}{4}$

12 $10 \div \frac{4}{5}$

13 $\frac{1}{2} \div \frac{1}{8}$

14 $\frac{1}{4} \div \frac{1}{2}$

15 $\frac{3}{5} \div \frac{11}{15}$

16 $\frac{2}{3} \div \frac{10}{13}$

17 $\frac{5}{6} \div \frac{7}{12}$

18 $\frac{3}{4} \div \frac{9}{16}$

Find each quotient. Express your answer in its simplest form.

19 $\frac{1}{3} \div \frac{7}{4}$

20 $\frac{1}{2} \div \frac{8}{3}$

21 $\frac{1}{9} \div \frac{14}{3}$

22 $\frac{5}{8} \div \frac{21}{4}$

23 $3\frac{1}{2} \div 2\frac{1}{8}$

24 $5\frac{1}{4} \div 3\frac{1}{2}$

25 $7\frac{3}{5} \div 8\frac{11}{15}$

26 $12\frac{2}{3} \div 5\frac{11}{13}$

Solve. Show your work.

27 6 pizzas were shared equally among a group of children. Each child got $\frac{1}{9}$ of a pizza. How many children were in the group?

28 A rectangle has an area of 15 square meters. It is divided into parts, each with an area of $\frac{3}{8}$ square meter. Into how many parts has the rectangle been divided?

29 How many $\frac{3}{8}$-cup servings are in a pitcher containing $6\frac{3}{4}$ cups of orange juice?

30 Maria buys $8\frac{1}{3}$ pounds of beef to make tacos for a party. She uses $\frac{5}{9}$ pound of beef for each taco. How many tacos can Maria make?

31 A rectangular plot of land has an area of $\frac{1}{8}$ square mile. Its width is $\frac{3}{20}$ mile. What is the length of the plot of land?

32 A farmer has four plots of land, each with an area of 12 acres. He divides them into a number of parts, each with an area of $\frac{8}{9}$ acre. How many parts are there on the four plots of land?

33 The capacity of a large milk carton is $1\frac{1}{2}$ liters. A dozen large cartons are poured into a container and then poured into small cartons that each hold $\frac{3}{10}$ liter. How many small cartons of milk can be filled?

Lesson Objective

- Multiply a decimal by a decimal.

Learn **Multiply tenths by a whole number.**

Multiply 0.4 by 3.

Method 1

A number line can help you to multiply.

$0.4 \times 3 = 3 \times 0.4$

3×0.4 means 3 groups of 0.4.

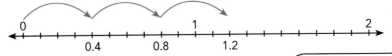

> **Math Note**
>
> **Commutative Property of Multiplication:**
> Two or more numbers can be multiplied in any order.

$3 \times 0.4 = 3 \times 4$ tenths
$\qquad\quad = 12$ tenths
$\qquad\quad = 1.2$

> Multiplication is the same as repeated addition.
>
> $3 \times 0.4 = 0.4 + 0.4 + 0.4$

Method 2

You can multiply using vertical multiplication. Thinking about the place value of each of the factors can help you decide where to place the decimal point in the product.

Step 1 Multiply the number 4 by 3.

$$\begin{array}{r} 4 \\ \times\ 3 \\ \hline 1\,2 \end{array}$$

> Ignore decimal points as you multiply. Then decide where to place the decimal point in the product.

Step 2 You are multiplying 4 tenths (0.4) by 3, so you need to place the decimal point to show that the answer is 12 tenths (1.2).

$$\begin{array}{r} 0.4 \\ \times\ \ 3 \\ \hline 1.2 \end{array}$$ ← 1 decimal place

0.4 ← 1 decimal place

1.2 ← 1 decimal place

Multiply hundredths by a whole number.

Aaron wants to place 7 decals of his favorite bands on a bulletin board. Each decal is 0.15 meter wide. How wide does the bulletin board need to be for all the decals to fit in one row?

7 × 0.15 = ?

Method 1

7 × 0.15 means 7 groups of 0.15.

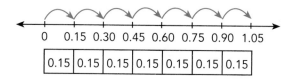

7 × 0.15 = 7 × 15 hundredths
           = 105 hundredths
           = 1.05

The bulletin board needs to be 1.05 meters wide for all the decals to fit in one row.

Method 2

You can multiply using vertical multiplication. Thinking about the place value of each of the factors can help you decide where to place the decimal point in the product.

Step 1 Multiply the number 15 by 7.

$$
\begin{array}{r}
\overset{3}{1}\,5 \\
\times\quad 7 \\
\hline
1\,0\,5
\end{array}
$$

Step 2 You are multiplying 15 hundredths (0.15) by 7, so you need to place the decimal point to show that the answer is 105 hundredths (1.05).

$$
\begin{array}{r}
0.\overset{3}{1}\,5 \quad\longleftarrow\ 2 \text{ decimal places}\\
\times\quad 7 \\
\hline
1.0\,5 \quad\longleftarrow\ 2 \text{ decimal places}
\end{array}
$$

Ignore decimal points as you multiply. Then decide where to place the decimal point in the product.

So, 7 × 0.15 = 1.05.

The bulletin board needs to be 1.05 meters wide for all the decals to fit in one row.

Guided Practice

Complete.

1 Multiply 0.9 by 4.

Method 1

$0.9 \times 4 = 4 \times 0.9$

4×0.9 means __?__ groups of __?__ .

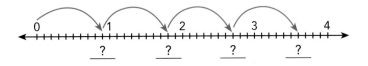

$4 \times$ __?__ $= 4 \times$ __?__ tenths

$\quad\quad = $ __?__ tenths

$\quad\quad = $ __?__

Method 2

Step 1

$$\begin{array}{r} 9 \\ \times\ \ 4 \\ \hline ? \end{array}$$

Step 2

$$\begin{array}{r} 0.9 \\ \times\ \ 4 \\ \hline ? \end{array}$$

2 Multiply 0.025 by 3.

Method 1

$0.025 \times 3 = 3 \times 0.025$

3×0.025 means __?__ groups of __?__ .

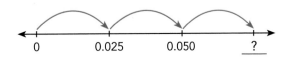

$3 \times 0.025 = 3 \times$ __?__ thousandths

$\quad\quad = $ __?__ thousandths

$\quad\quad = $ __?__

Method 2

Step 1

$$\begin{array}{r} 25 \\ \times\ \ 3 \\ \hline ? \end{array}$$

Step 2

$$\begin{array}{r} 0.025 \\ \times\ \ 3 \\ \hline ? \end{array}$$

Multiply.

3
$$\begin{array}{r} 0.07 \\ \times\ \ 9 \\ \hline ? \end{array}$$

4
$$\begin{array}{r} 0.14 \\ \times\ \ 3 \\ \hline ? \end{array}$$

5
$$\begin{array}{r} 0.045 \\ \times\ \ 7 \\ \hline ? \end{array}$$

Write in vertical form. Then multiply and decide where to place the decimal point.

6 0.32×8

7 9×0.24

8 0.057×6

Multiply tenths by tenths.

A decimal can be expressed as a fraction.

0.5 is equal to $\frac{1}{2}$ and 0.4 is equal to $\frac{2}{5}$.

> 0.5 and 0.4 can be expressed as fractions.
>
> $0.5 = \frac{5}{10} = \frac{1}{2}$
>
> $0.4 = \frac{4}{10} = \frac{2}{5}$

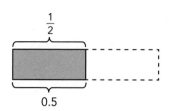
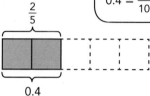

Knowing that decimals can be expressed as fractions can help you think about how to multiply two decimals.

Find 0.4 × 0.5.

Method 1

Think of the decimals as fractions.

$0.4 \times 0.5 = \frac{4}{10} \times \frac{5}{10}$ Express the decimals as fractions.

$= \frac{20}{100}$ Multiply.

$= 0.20$ Express as a decimal.

$= 0.2$

> When you multiply the denominators, you get a denominator of 100. So, the product is 20 hundredths, which can be written as 2 tenths.

Method 2

Step 1 Multiply the number 4 by 5.

$$\begin{array}{r} 4 \\ \times\ 5 \\ \hline 2\,0 \end{array}$$

Step 2 You are multiplying 4 tenths (0.4) by 5 tenths (0.5), so you need to place the decimal point to show that the answer is 20 hundredths (0.20).

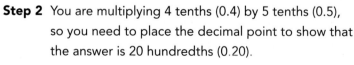

$$\begin{array}{r} 0.4 \quad \longleftarrow \quad \text{1 decimal place} \\ \times\ \ 0.5 \quad \longleftarrow \quad +\ \text{1 decimal place} \\ \hline 0.2\,0 \quad \longleftarrow \quad \text{2 decimal places} \end{array}$$

> Place the decimal point here.

So, 0.4 × 0.5 = 0.20 = 0.2.

Guided Practice

Complete.

9 Find 0.3 × 0.6.

$$0.3 \times 0.6 = \frac{3}{?} \times \frac{?}{?}$$

$$= \frac{?}{?}$$

$$= \underline{\ ?\ }$$

10 Find 0.9 × 0.8.

Step 1

$$
\begin{array}{r}
9 \\
\times\ 8 \\
\hline
? \\
\end{array}
$$

Step 2

$$
\begin{array}{r}
0\,.\,9 \\
\times\quad 0\,.\,8 \\
\hline
? \\
\end{array}
$$

0 . 9 ⟵ _?_ decimal place
×   0 . 8 ⟵ + _?_ decimal place
_?_ ⟵ _?_ decimal places

So, 0.9 × 0.8 = _?_.

Learn **Multiply decimals by decimals with one decimal place.**

a)   Find 2.8 × 0.3.

Step 1 Multiply the number 28 by 3.

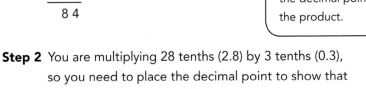

$$
\begin{array}{r}
2 \\
2\,8 \\
\times\quad 3 \\
\hline
8\,4 \\
\end{array}
$$

> Ignore decimal points as you multiply. Then decide where to place the decimal point in the product.

Step 2 You are multiplying 28 tenths (2.8) by 3 tenths (0.3), so you need to place the decimal point to show that the answer is 84 hundredths (0.84).

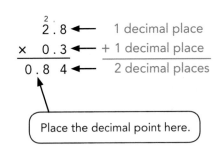

2 . 8 ⟵ 1 decimal place
×   0 . 3 ⟵ + 1 decimal place
0 . 8 4 ⟵ 2 decimal places

Place the decimal point here.

So, 2.8 × 0.3 = 0.84.

Check: $2.8 \times 0.3 = \frac{28}{10} \times \frac{3}{10}$. $10 \times 10 = 100$, so the product will be a fraction with a *hundred* in the denominator.

So, 2.8 × 0.3 = 84 *hundredths*.

b) Find 3.6 × 1.2.

Step 1 Multiply the number 36 by 12.

$$
\begin{array}{r}
\overset{1}{3}\,6 \\
\times\ \ 1\,2 \\
\hline
7\,2 \\
3\,6\,0 \\
\hline
4\,3\,2
\end{array}
$$

Step 2 You are multiplying 36 tenths (3.6) by 12 tenths (1.2), so you need to place the decimal point to show that the answer is 432 hundredths (4.32).

$$
\begin{array}{r}
\overset{1}{3}\,.\,6 \quad \longleftarrow \quad \text{1 decimal place} \\
\times\quad\ 1\,.\,2 \quad \longleftarrow \quad +\ \text{1 decimal place} \\
\hline
7\ \ 2 \\
3\ \ 6\ \ 0 \\
\hline
4\,.\,3\ \ 2 \quad \longleftarrow \quad \text{2 decimal places}
\end{array}
$$

Place the decimal point here.

So, 3.6 × 1.2 = 4.32.

Check: $3.6 \times 1.2 = \dfrac{36}{10} \times \dfrac{12}{10}$. 10 × 10 = 100, so the product will be a fraction with a *hundred* in the denominator.

So, 3.6 × 1.2 = 432 *hundredths*.

Guided Practice

Complete.

11 Find 3.2 × 0.6.

Step 1

$$
\begin{array}{r}
3\ \ 2 \\
\times\ \ \ \ 6 \\
\hline
?
\end{array}
$$

So, 3.2 × 0.6 = ___?___.

Step 2

$$
\begin{array}{r}
3\,.\,2 \quad \longleftarrow \quad \underline{\ ?\ } \text{ decimal place} \\
\times\ 0\,.\,6 \quad \longleftarrow \quad +\ \underline{\ ?\ } \text{ decimal place} \\
\hline
?\quad \longleftarrow \quad \underline{\ ?\ } \text{ decimal places}
\end{array}
$$

Write in vertical form. Then multiply and decide where to place the decimal point.

12 4.3 × 5.7

Learn Multiply decimals with one or more decimal places.

Find 0.56 × 1.2.

Step 1 Multiply the number 56 by 12.

$$
\begin{array}{r}
\overset{1}{5}\,6 \\
\times\ \ 1\,2 \\
\hline
1\,1\,2 \\
5\,6\,0 \\
\hline
6\,7\,2
\end{array}
$$

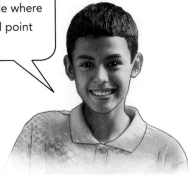

Ignore decimal points as you multiply. Then decide where to place the decimal point in the product.

Step 2 You are multiplying 56 hundredths (0.56) by 12 tenths (1.2), so you need to place the decimal point to show that the answer is 672 thousandths (0.672).

$$
\begin{array}{r}
\overset{1}{0}.\overset{1}{5}\,6 \quad \longleftarrow \quad \text{2 decimal places} \\
\times\ \ \ \ 1\,.\,2 \quad \longleftarrow \quad + \text{ 1 decimal place} \\
\hline
1\ \ 1\ \ 2 \\
0\ \ 5\ \ 6\ \ 0 \\
\hline
0\,.\,6\ 7\ 2 \quad \longleftarrow \quad \text{3 decimal places}
\end{array}
$$

Place the decimal point here.

So, 0.56 × 1.2 = 0.672.

Guided Practice

Complete.

13 Find 0.89 × 0.4.

Step 1

$$
\begin{array}{r}
8\,9 \\
\times\ \ 4 \\
\hline
?
\end{array}
$$

So, 0.89 × 0.4 = ___?___.

Step 2

$$
\begin{array}{r}
0\,.\,8\,9 \quad \longleftarrow \quad \underline{\ ?\ } \text{ decimal places} \\
\times\ \ \ \ 0\,.\,4 \quad \longleftarrow \quad + \underline{\ ?\ } \text{ decimal place} \\
\hline
? \quad \longleftarrow \quad \underline{\ ?\ } \text{ decimal places}
\end{array}
$$

Write in vertical form. Then multiply and decide where to place the decimal point.

14 0.43 × 1.5

Hands-On Activity

Materials:

- graph paper
- ruler

STEP 1 Draw four 10 × 10 squares on graph paper.

STEP 2 Mark each side from 0 to 1 as shown.

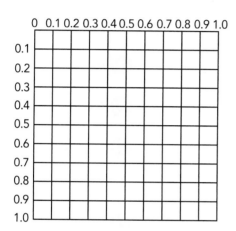

STEP 3 **a)** Find two decimals that give a product of 0.12.

$$\underline{\quad?\quad} \times \underline{\quad?\quad} = 0.12$$

Show and shade 0.12 on the grids in two different ways.

Example

0.2 × 0.6 = 0.12

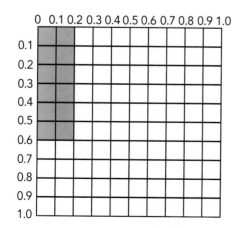

b) Find two decimals that give a product of 0.36.
Show and shade 0.36 on the grids in two different ways.

Practice 3.2

Complete.

1 0.3 × 4 is the same as __?__ groups of __?__.   **2** 7 × 0.8 is the same as __?__ groups of __?__.

Write a multiplication statement that represents each number line.

3

4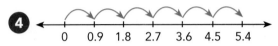

Write in vertical form. Then multiply.

5 0.9 × 12   **6** 0.47 × 5   **7** 0.063 × 9

8 0.85 × 11   **9** 0.1 × 0.2   **10** 0.2 × 0.3

11 0.4 × 0.4   **12** 0.6 × 0.7   **13** 0.7 × 0.9

Multiply mentally.

14 0.7 × 8   **15** 0.9 × 9   **16** 0.9 × 11

17 0.7 × 0.4   **18** 0.8 × 0.6   **19** 0.3 × 0.9

20 0.7 × 0.7   **21** 0.5 × 0.9   **22** 0.8 × 0.9

23 0.15 × 6   **24** 0.22 × 4   **25** 0.25 × 3

26 0.032 × 5   **27** 0.041 × 8   **28** 0.055 × 9

Write in vertical form. Then multiply.

29 1.2 × 0.6   **30** 0.89 × 1.2   **31** 2.3 × 1.5

32 3.4 × 6.7   **33** 4.9 × 6.3   **34** 5.8 × 7.8

35 0.46 × 1.3   **36** 0.705 × 0.5   **37** 0.597 × 0.21

38 *Math Journal* Your friend knows how to find the product $\frac{57}{100} \times \frac{3}{10}$.
However, your friend does not know how to find the product 0.57 × 0.3.
Write an explanation that will help your friend understand how to multiply the
two decimals.

3.3 Dividing Decimals

Lesson Objective

- Divide a whole number or a decimal by a decimal.

 Divide a whole number by a decimal with one decimal place.

a) Jamie and his friend live 1 mile apart on the same street. Each block on this street is 0.2 mile long. How many blocks apart do the two friends live?

$1 \div 0.2 = ?$

Method 1

The division expression $1 \div 0.2$ means "How many 0.2s are in 1 whole?"

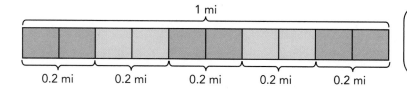

1 mi

0.2 mi 0.2 mi 0.2 mi 0.2 mi 0.2 mi

The model shows the division of 1 mile into five equal parts of 0.2 mile.

The model shows that:

$1 \div 0.2 = 5$

The two friends live 5 blocks apart.

Method 2

$1 \div 0.2 = 1 \div \dfrac{2}{10}$ Express the decimal as a fraction.

$= 1 \times \dfrac{10}{2}$ Rewrite using the reciprocal of the divisor.

$= \dfrac{10}{2}$ Multiply.

$= 5$ Simplify.

b) Find $16 \div 0.4$.

$16 \div 0.4 = 16 \div \dfrac{4}{10}$ Express the decimal as a fraction.

$= 16 \times \dfrac{10}{4}$ Rewrite using the reciprocal of the divisor.

$= \dfrac{4 \times 10}{1}$ Divide by the common factor, 4.

$= 40$ Simplify.

Guided Practice

Complete.

1 Find 1 ÷ 0.5.

Method 1

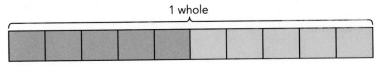

1 whole

The model shows that:

1 ÷ 0.5 = __?__

Method 2

$1 \div 0.5 = 1 \div \dfrac{?}{?}$

$= 1 \times \dfrac{?}{?}$

$= \underline{}$

How many 0.5s are in 1 whole?

2 Find 48 ÷ 0.3.

$48 \div 0.3 = 48 \div \dfrac{?}{?}$

$= 48 \times \dfrac{?}{?}$

$= \underline{}$

Learn **Divide a whole number by hundredths.**

Find 96 ÷ 0.12.

The division expression 96 ÷ 0.12 means "How many 0.12s are in 96?"

96

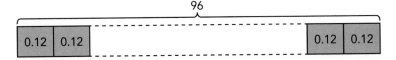

Division is the inverse of multiplication. Use the reciprocal of the divisor to find the answer.

$96 \div 0.12 = 96 \div \dfrac{12}{100}$ Express the decimal as a fraction.

$= 96 \times \dfrac{100}{12}$ Rewrite using the reciprocal of the divisor.

$= 8 \times 100$ Divide by the common factor, 12.

$= 800$ Multiply.

Guided Practice

Complete.

3 Complete the model to show the division expression 98 ÷ 0.14.

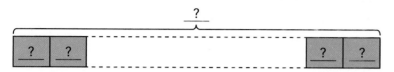

Divide.

4 $75 \div 0.15 = ? \div \dfrac{?}{?}$

$\quad\quad\quad = ? \times \dfrac{?}{?}$

$\quad\quad\quad = \underline{\ ?\ }$

5 $156 \div 0.13 = ? \div \dfrac{?}{?}$

$\quad\quad\quad\quad = ? \times \dfrac{?}{?}$

$\quad\quad\quad\quad = \underline{\ ?\ }$

Learn — Divide tenths by tenths.

Find 0.8 ÷ 0.2.

The division expression 0.8 ÷ 0.2 means "How many 0.2s are in 0.8?"
The number line below can be used to answer this question.

Each small interval represents 0.2.
There are 4 intervals.

So, 0.8 ÷ 0.2 = 4.

There are four 0.2s in 0.8.

Guided Practice

Complete.

6 Find 0.9 ÷ 0.3.

The division expression 0.9 ÷ 0.3 means "How many __?__s are in __?__?"

Each small interval represents __?__.

There are __?__ intervals.

So, 0.9 ÷ 0.3 = __?__.

There are __?__ 0.3s in 0.9.

Divide hundredths by hundredths.

Find 0.56 ÷ 0.04.

The division expression 0.56 ÷ 0.04 means "How many 0.04s are in 0.56?"
There will be many intervals if you try to show this on a number line.

0   0.04 0.08 0.12   ...   0.56

Besides using a number line, you can use other methods to find the answer.

Method 1

$0.56 = \dfrac{56}{100}$ and $0.04 = \dfrac{4}{100}$

$0.56 \div 0.04 = \dfrac{56}{100} \div \dfrac{4}{100}$ Express the decimals as fractions.

$\qquad\qquad = \dfrac{56}{100} \times \dfrac{100}{4}$ Rewrite using the reciprocal of the divisor.

$\qquad\qquad = \dfrac{56}{4}$ Divide by the common factor, 100.

$\qquad\qquad = 14$ Divide.

Method 2

$0.56 \div 0.04 = \dfrac{0.56}{0.04}$ Express the quotient as a fraction.

$\qquad\qquad = \dfrac{56}{4}$ Multiply both the numerator and denominator
by 100 to make the divisor a whole number.

$\qquad\qquad = 14$ Divide.

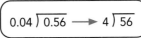

$0.04 \overline{)0.56} \longrightarrow 4 \overline{)56}$

Math Note

When you multiply a number by 100,
you move the decimal point two
places to the right.

$0.56 \times 100 = 56$

$0.04 \times 100 = 4$

Guided Practice

Complete.

7 Find 0.72 ÷ 0.03.

Method 1

$$0.72 = \frac{?}{100} \quad \text{and} \quad 0.03 = \frac{?}{?}$$

$$0.72 \div 0.03 = \frac{?}{100} \div \frac{?}{?} \qquad \text{Express the decimals as fractions.}$$

$$= \frac{?}{?} \times \frac{?}{?} \qquad \text{Rewrite using the reciprocal of the divisor.}$$

$$= \frac{?}{?} \qquad \text{Divide by the common factor, 100.}$$

$$= \underline{?} \qquad \text{Divide.}$$

Method 2

$$0.72 \div 0.03 = \frac{0.72}{?} \qquad \text{Express the quotient as a fraction.}$$

$$= \frac{?}{?} \qquad \begin{array}{l}\text{Multiply both the numerator and denominator} \\ \text{by 100 to make the divisor a whole number.}\end{array}$$

$$= \underline{?} \qquad \text{Divide.}$$

Learn **Divide hundredths by tenths.**

Find 0.96 ÷ 0.4.

Method 1

$$0.96 = \frac{96}{100} \quad \text{and} \quad 0.4 = \frac{4}{10}$$

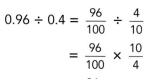
Note that the denominators are different.

$$0.96 \div 0.4 = \frac{96}{100} \div \frac{4}{10} \qquad \text{Express the decimals as fractions.}$$

$$= \frac{96}{100} \times \frac{10}{4} \qquad \text{Rewrite using the reciprocal of the divisor.}$$

$$= \frac{24}{10} \qquad \begin{array}{l}\text{Divide by the common factor, 4.} \\ \text{Divide by the common factor, 10.}\end{array}$$

$$= 2.4 \qquad \text{Divide.}$$

Method 2

$$0.96 \div 0.4 = \frac{0.96}{0.4} \qquad \text{Express the quotient as a fraction.}$$

$$= \frac{9.6}{4} \qquad \begin{array}{l}\text{Multiply both the numerator and denominator} \\ \text{by 10 to make the divisor a whole number.}\end{array}$$

$$= 2.4 \qquad \text{Divide.}$$

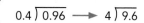
$$0.4\overline{)0.96} \longrightarrow 4\overline{)9.6}$$

Guided Practice

Complete.

8 Find $0.78 \div 0.6$.

Method 1

$$0.78 = \frac{?}{?} \quad \text{and} \quad 0.6 = \frac{?}{?}$$

$$0.78 \div 0.6 = \frac{?}{?} \div \frac{?}{?}$$ Express the decimals as fractions.

$$= \frac{?}{?} \times \frac{?}{?}$$ Rewrite using the reciprocal of the divisor.

$$= \frac{?}{?}$$ Divide by the common factor, 10.

$$= \underline{\quad?\quad}$$ Divide.

Method 2

$$0.78 \div 0.6 = \frac{0.78}{?}$$ Express the quotient as a fraction.

$$= \frac{?}{?}$$ Multiply both the numerator and denominator by 10 to make the divisor a whole number.

$$= \underline{\quad?\quad}$$ Divide.

$$0.6\overline{)0.78} \longrightarrow 6\overline{)\ ?\ }$$

9 Find $6.75 \div 0.3$.

Method 1

$$6.75 = \frac{?}{?} \quad \text{and} \quad 0.3 = \frac{?}{?}$$

$$6.75 \div 0.3 = \frac{?}{?} \div \frac{?}{?}$$ Express the decimals as fractions.

$$= \frac{?}{?} \times \frac{?}{?}$$ Rewrite using the reciprocal of the divisor.

$$= \frac{?}{?}$$ Divide by the common factor, 10.

$$= \underline{\quad?\quad}$$ Divide.

Method 2

$$6.75 \div 0.3 = \frac{?}{?}$$ Express the quotient as a fraction.

$$= \frac{?}{?}$$ Multiply both the numerator and denominator by 10 to make the divisor a whole number.

$$= \underline{\quad?\quad}$$ Divide.

Practice 3.3

Write a division expression that represents each model.

1

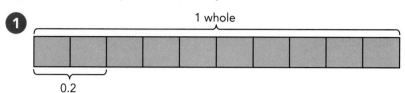

1 whole

0.2

2

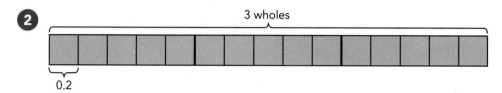

3 wholes

0.2

Divide.

3 2 ÷ 0.4

4 4 ÷ 0.5

5 5 ÷ 0.2

6 8 ÷ 0.8

7 9 ÷ 0.3

8 7 ÷ 0.4

9 12 ÷ 0.3

10 42 ÷ 0.7

11 55 ÷ 0.5

12 69 ÷ 0.2

13 86 ÷ 0.5

14 93 ÷ 0.4

15 1 ÷ 0.02

16 3 ÷ 0.06

17 6 ÷ 0.15

18 7 ÷ 0.35

19 8 ÷ 0.32

20 9 ÷ 0.72

Draw a model to show each division expression.

21 2 ÷ 0.5

22 5 ÷ 0.2

Divide.

23 36 ÷ 0.36

24 49 ÷ 0.14

25 56 ÷ 0.28

26 72 ÷ 0.20

27 81 ÷ 0.54

28 256 ÷ 0.64

29 749 ÷ 0.7

30 972 ÷ 0.8

31 96 ÷ 0.16

32 545 ÷ 0.25

33 0.6 ÷ 0.3

34 0.64 ÷ 0.04

35 0.78 ÷ 0.06

36 0.85 ÷ 0.5

37 0.025 ÷ 0.5

38 0.816 ÷ 0.34

39 4.5 ÷ 0.2

40 8.82 ÷ 0.6

Real-World Problems: Fractions and Decimals

Lesson Objective

- Solve problems involving fractions and decimals.

Learn **Multiply decimals to solve real-world problems.**

At a supermarket, a pound of almonds costs $3.90. If Jen wants to buy 4.5 pounds of almonds, how much will she have to pay?

4.5 × $3.90 = $17.55

Jen will have to pay $17.55 for the almonds.

4.5 × 3.90 is the same as 4.5 × 3.9.

Check for reasonableness: Estimate the value of 4.5 × 3.9.

4.5 is close to 5 and 3.9 is close to 4, so the answer should be close to 5 × 4.
5 × 4 = 20

The estimate shows the answer 17.55 is reasonable.

Guided Practice

Solve.

1 The cost of carpeting a square yard is $8.60. How much does it cost to carpet 9.7 square yards?

9.7 × $? = $?

9.7 × ? is the same as 9.7 × ? .

It costs $? to carpet 9.7 square yards.

Divide decimals to solve real-world problems.

A caterer sliced 6.5 ounces of cheese into pieces that weighed 0.5 ounce each. How many pieces of cheese did the caterer slice?

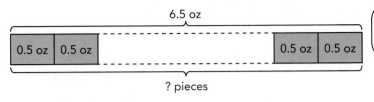

6.5 oz

| 0.5 oz | 0.5 oz | | 0.5 oz | 0.5 oz |

? pieces

How many 0.5s are in 6.5?

$6.5 \div 0.5 = 65 \div 5$
$\qquad\quad = 13$

The caterer sliced 13 pieces of cheese.

Guided Practice

Solve.

2 A roll of cloth 12 meters long is cut into smaller pieces of the same size. Each piece is 0.75 meter long. How many small pieces of cloth can be cut from the 12-meter roll?

$\underline{\quad?\quad}$ m

| $\underline{?}$ m | $\underline{?}$ m | | $\underline{?}$ m | $\underline{?}$ m |

$\underline{\quad?\quad}$ pieces

$12 \; \boxed{?} \; \underline{\quad?\quad} = \underline{\quad?\quad}$

$\underline{\quad?\quad}$ small pieces of cloth can be cut from the 12-meter roll.

3 Rosie buys 2.24 pounds of sliced ham to make sandwiches. She uses 0.16 pound for a sandwich. How many sandwiches can Rosie make?

$\underline{\quad?\quad} \div \underline{\quad?\quad} = \underline{\quad?\quad}$

Rosie can make $\underline{\quad?\quad}$ sandwiches.

4 Bryce has $12.75. She wants to buy gifts for friends at a souvenir shop. If each souvenir costs $0.85, how many souvenirs can Bryce buy?

$\$\underline{\quad?\quad} \; \boxed{?} \; \$\underline{\quad?\quad} = \underline{\quad?\quad}$

Bryce can buy $\underline{\quad?\quad}$ souvenirs.

Learn **Divide a whole number by a fraction to solve two-step problems.**

Chris works at a bakery. He bakes 14 loaves of banana bread. He sells 8 whole loaves to customers. Then he cuts the remaining loaves into slices so he can sell the slices to customers. If each slice is $\frac{1}{7}$ of a loaf, how many slices can Chris sell?

14 − 8 = 6 loaves

Chris cuts 6 loaves of bread into slices.

$6 \div \frac{1}{7} = 6 \times 7$
$\qquad = 42$

Chris can sell 42 slices.

Now I need to find how many $\frac{1}{7}$s are in 6 loaves.

Guided Practice
Solve.

5. A paper artist uses 18 paper rectangles for a collage. He uses 6 of them for the border of the artwork. He then cuts the remaining paper rectangles into equal strips, each $\frac{1}{4}$ of a paper rectangle. How many strips of paper does he cut?

$\underline{\ ?\ } - \underline{\ ?\ } = \underline{\ ?\ }$ pieces

He uses $\underline{\ ?\ }$ paper rectangles to cut into strips of paper.

Now I need to find how many $\underline{\ ?\ }$ of a paper rectangle can be cut.

$\underline{\ ?\ } \div \dfrac{?}{?} = \underline{\ ?\ } \times \underline{\ ?\ }$
$\qquad = \underline{\ ?\ }$

He cuts $\underline{\ ?\ }$ strips of paper.

6. Sophie buys a roll of string that is 20 meters long. She uses 3 meters of string to tie a parcel. She then cuts the remaining string into equal pieces, each $\frac{1}{2}$ meter long. How many pieces does Sophie cut?

$\underline{\ ?\ } \div \dfrac{?}{?} = \underline{\ ?\ } \times \underline{\ ?\ }$
$\qquad = \underline{\ ?\ }$

Sophie cuts $\underline{\ ?\ }$ pieces.

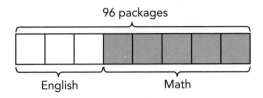

Divide a whole number by a fraction to solve multi-step problems.

A school district buys 96 packages of highlighters. $\frac{3}{8}$ of the packages go to the English department, and the rest to the math department. The math department gives $\frac{2}{3}$ of each package to each math teacher working in the school district. How many math teachers will receive highlighters?

```
              96 packages
        ┌──────────────────┐
┌───┬───┬───┬───┬───┬───┬───┬───┐
│   │   │   │░░░│░░░│░░░│░░░│░░░│
└───┴───┴───┴───┴───┴───┴───┴───┘
└──────┬──────┘└───────┬────────┘
    English          Math
```

First, find the number of packages that go to the math department.

Remainder ⟶ $1 - \frac{3}{8} = \frac{5}{8}$

$\frac{5}{8} \times 96 = 5 \times 12$

$\qquad = 60$

60 packages of highlighters go to the math department.

Then, find the number of math teachers.

This is another way to do it.

The model shows that:

8 units ⟶ 96 packages

1 unit ⟶ 96 ÷ 8 = 12 packages

5 units ⟶ 5 × 12 = 60 packages

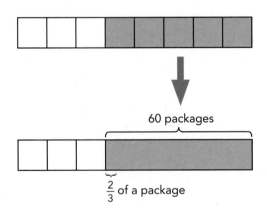

```
┌───┬───┬───┬───┬───┬───┬───┬───┐
│   │   │   │░░░│░░░│░░░│░░░│░░░│
└───┴───┴───┴───┴───┴───┴───┴───┘

                ↓

              60 packages
        ┌──────────────────┐
┌───┬───┬───┬──────────────────┐
│   │   │   │░░░░░░░░░░░░░░░░░░░│
└───┴───┴───┴──────────────────┘
          └┬┘
       $\frac{2}{3}$ of a package
```

The math department gives $\frac{2}{3}$ of each package to each math teacher.

$60 \div \frac{2}{3} = 60 \times \frac{3}{2}$

$\qquad\quad = 90$

90 math teachers will receive highlighters.

Guided Practice

Solve.

7 Andrea buys 75 cups of cranberry-apple juice for a party. She uses $\frac{2}{5}$ of the juice to make punch. She then uses the remaining juice to pour single servings that are $\frac{5}{6}$ cup each. How many single servings does Andrea pour?

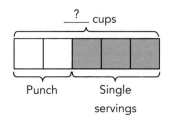

? cups

Punch   Single servings

This is another way to do it.

___?___ units ⟶ ___?___ cups

1 unit ⟶ ___?___ ÷ ___?___ = ___?___ cups

___?___ units ⟶ ___?___ × ___?___ = ___?___ cups

First, find the number of cups remaining.

Remainder ⟶ $\frac{?}{} - \frac{?}{?} = \frac{?}{?}$

$\frac{?}{?} \times \frac{?}{} = \frac{?}{}$

There are __?__ cups of cranberry-apple juice remaining.

Then, find the number of single servings.

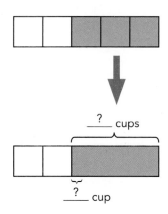

? cups

? cup

The remaining juice is poured into single servings that are $\frac{5}{6}$ cup each.

$\frac{?}{} \div \frac{?}{?} = \frac{?}{} \times \frac{?}{?}$

$= \underline{?}$

Andrea pours __?__ single servings.

Kathy has 9 sticks of modeling clay. She cuts the sticks into thirds and shares the pieces equally with some children. Each child gets $\frac{2}{3}$ of a stick.

a) How many children are there altogether?

$$9 \div \frac{2}{3} = 9 \times \frac{3}{2}$$
$$= \frac{27}{2}$$
$$= 13\frac{1}{2}$$

There are 13 children altogether.

> When you divide 9 by $\frac{2}{3}$, you get $13\frac{1}{2}$. Why is $13\frac{1}{2}$ not the answer to the question, "How many children are there altogether?"

b) What fraction of a stick of clay is left?

$$13 \times \frac{2}{3} = \frac{26}{3}$$
$$= 8\frac{2}{3}$$
$$9 - 8\frac{2}{3} = \frac{1}{3}$$

$\frac{1}{3}$ of a stick of clay is left.

c) What is the total amount of modeling clay each child will get if the remainder is divided evenly and added to the clay each child already has?

Method 1

$$\frac{1}{3} \div 13 = \frac{1}{3} \times \frac{1}{13}$$
$$= \frac{1}{39}$$

Each child will get an additional $\frac{1}{39}$ of a stick.

$$\frac{2}{3} + \frac{1}{39} = \frac{26}{39} + \frac{1}{39}$$
$$= \frac{27}{39}$$
$$= \frac{9}{13}$$

Each child will get $\frac{9}{13}$ of a stick of clay in total.

Method 2

$$9 \div 13 = \frac{9}{13}$$

Each child will get $\frac{9}{13}$ of a stick of clay in total.

Guided Practice

Solve.

8 Meredith bakes 5 pumpkin pies. She cuts the pies into quarters and distributes the pieces equally among her neighbors. Each neighbor receives $\frac{3}{4}$ of a pie.

a) How many neighbors does Meredith distribute the pies to?

$$5 \div \frac{3}{4} = \underline{\quad?\quad} \times \frac{?}{?}$$
$$= \underline{\quad?\quad}$$

Meredith distributes the pies to __?__ neighbors.

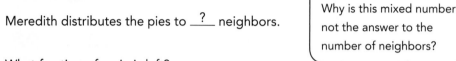

When you divide 5 by $\frac{3}{4}$, you get a mixed number. Why is this mixed number not the answer to the number of neighbors?

b) What fraction of a pie is left?

$$\underline{\quad?\quad} \times \frac{3}{4} = \underline{\quad?\quad}$$
$$5 - \underline{\quad?\quad} = \underline{\quad?\quad}$$

__?__ of a pie is left.

c) What is the total amount of pie each neighbor will receive if the remainder is divided evenly and distributed to each neighbor?

$$5 \div \underline{\quad?\quad} = \underline{\quad?\quad}$$

Each neighbor will receive __?__ of a pie in total.

9 Some bottles containing $\frac{2}{5}$ gallon of water each are used to fill a 7-gallon container. How many of these bottles are needed to fill the container with water to its brim?

$$7 \div \frac{2}{5} = \underline{\quad?\quad} \times \frac{?}{?}$$
$$= \underline{\quad?\quad}$$

When you divide 7 by $\frac{2}{5}$, you get a mixed number. Why is this mixed number not the number of bottles needed to fill the container?

__?__ bottles are needed to fill the container with water to its brim.

Divide a fraction by a whole number to solve real-world problems.

Lucile collects U.S. stamps and foreign stamps. $\frac{1}{4}$ of them are foreign stamps.

She divides the U.S. stamps equally between two friends, Michelle and Nadia. If Lucile has 72 U.S. and foreign stamps altogether, how many stamps does Nadia receive from Lucile?

Method 1

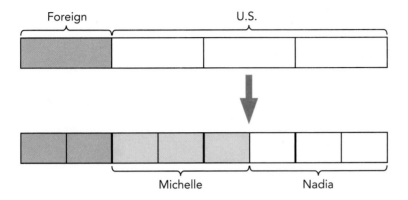

The model shows that:

Nadia receives $\frac{3}{8}$ of the total number of stamps.

8 units ⟶ 72 stamps
1 unit ⟶ 72 ÷ 8 = 9 stamps
3 units ⟶ 3 × 9 = 27 stamps

Nadia receives 27 stamps.

Method 2

U.S. stamps ⟶ $1 - \frac{1}{4} = \frac{3}{4}$

$\frac{3}{4} = \frac{6}{8}$

$\frac{6}{8} \div 2 = \frac{6}{8} \times \frac{1}{2}$

$\qquad = \frac{3}{8}$

Nadia and Michelle each receives $\frac{3}{8}$ of the total number of stamps.

$\frac{3}{8} \times 72 = 27$

Nadia receives 27 stamps.

Guided Practice

Solve.

10 Lilian has a part-time job. Each month, she spends $\frac{1}{3}$ of her earnings on clothes,

saves $\frac{3}{8}$ of the remainder, and spends the rest of her earnings on food.

a) What fraction of her earnings does she spend on food?

b) If she earns $540, how much does she spend on food each month?

Method 1

a)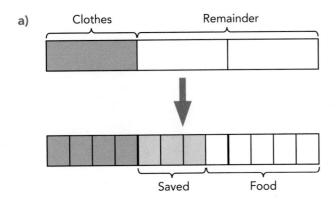

The model shows that:

She spends $\frac{?}{?}$ of her earnings on food.

b) ___?___ units ⟶ $540

       1 unit ⟶ $___?___ ÷ ___?___ = $___?___

   ___?___ units ⟶ ___?___ × $___?___ = $___?___

She spends $___?___ on food each month.

Method 2

a) $1 - \frac{1}{3} = \frac{?}{?}$ (remainder)

    $\frac{3}{8} \times \frac{?}{?} = \frac{?}{?}$ (saved)

    $\frac{?}{?} - \frac{?}{?} = \frac{?}{?}$ (spent on food)

She spends $\frac{?}{?}$ of her earnings on food.

b) $\frac{?}{?} \times \$540 = \$\underline{?}$

She spends $___?___ on food each month.

^{earn} **Divide a fraction by a fraction to solve real-world problems.**

Steven uses $\frac{2}{3}$ of his garden to plant tomatoes and another $\frac{1}{9}$ of it to plant lettuce.

He then divides the rest of his garden into several small plots of land. The area of

each small plot of land is $\frac{1}{18}$ of the area of his entire garden.

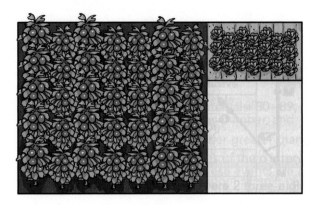

a)   How many small plots of land are there?

First, find the fraction of Steven's land that he divides into small plots.

Fraction of land divided = 1 − Fraction used for lettuce and tomatoes

$$= 1 - \left(\frac{2}{3} + \frac{1}{9}\right) \qquad \text{Substitute.}$$

$$= 1 - \frac{7}{9} \qquad \text{Add inside parentheses.}$$

$$= \frac{2}{9} \qquad \text{Simplify.}$$

Then, find how many $\frac{1}{18}$ s are in this fraction.

$$\frac{2}{9} \div \frac{1}{18} = \frac{2}{9} \times 18$$
$$= 4$$

There are 4 small plots of land.

b)   If the total area of Steven's garden is 90 square yards, what is the area of each
small plot of land?

$$\frac{1}{18} \times 90 = 5$$

The area of each small plot of
land is 5 square yards.

> The area of each small plot
> is $\frac{1}{18}$ of 90 square yards.
>
> Remember that
> $\frac{1}{18}$ of 90 = $\frac{1}{18} \times 90$.

Guided Practice

Solve.

11 $\frac{2}{3}$ of a square is colored green. Asha cuts this green part into a number of pieces so that each piece is $\frac{1}{9}$ of the whole square.

a) Find the number of pieces Asha has.

$$\frac{?}{?} \div \frac{?}{?} = \frac{?}{?} \times \underline{\quad?\quad}$$

$$= \underline{\quad?\quad}$$

Asha has __?__ pieces.

b) If the area of the square is 45 square inches, what is the area of each piece?

Area of green part $= \dfrac{?}{?} \times 45 = \underline{\quad?\quad}$ in.^{2}

Area of each piece $= \underline{\quad?\quad} \div \underline{\quad?\quad} = \underline{\quad?\quad}$ in.^{2}

The area of each piece is __?__ square inches.

12 $\frac{3}{5}$ of the students in a class were boys. The teacher divided the boys equally into groups so that each group of boys had $\frac{1}{10}$ of the number of students in the class. The teacher then divided the girls equally into groups such that each group of girls had $\frac{1}{5}$ of the number of students in the class.

a) Find the number of groups of boys and the number of groups of girls.

Number of groups of boys $= \dfrac{?}{?} \div \dfrac{?}{?}$ 　　　　Number of groups of girls $= \dfrac{?}{?} \div \dfrac{?}{?}$

$\qquad\qquad\qquad\quad = \dfrac{?}{?} \times \underline{\quad?\quad}$ 　　　　$\qquad\qquad\qquad\quad = \dfrac{?}{?} \times \underline{\quad?\quad}$

$\qquad\qquad\qquad\quad = \underline{\quad?\quad}$ 　　　　$\qquad\qquad\qquad\quad = \underline{\quad?\quad}$

There were __?__ groups of boys and __?__ groups of girls.

b) If there were 16 girls in the class, how many boys were there in each group?

$\frac{2}{5}$ of the class ⟶ 16 students

$\frac{1}{5}$ of the class ⟶ __?__ students

$\frac{3}{5}$ of the class ⟶ __?__ students

$\underline{\quad?\quad} \div 6 = \underline{\quad?\quad}$

There were __?__ boys in each group.

Practice 3.4

Solve. Show your work.

1. An ounce of pine nuts costs $1.40. If Ellen buys 2.5 ounces of pine nuts, how much will she have to pay?

2. 25 pints of apple juice are poured into $\frac{1}{2}$-pint bottles. How many bottles can be filled with apple juice?

3. 40 pounds of sugar are repackaged into packets of $\frac{1}{16}$ pound each. How many packets of sugar are there?

4. Tom used $\frac{5}{8}$ yard of ribbon to tie weights on the tail of his kite. He cut the length of ribbon into equal pieces that were $\frac{1}{12}$ yard long. How many pieces, each $\frac{1}{12}$ yard long, did Tom cut from the $\frac{5}{8}$-yard ribbon?

$\frac{1}{12}$ yard

5. A carpenter has a 6-foot long board. He wants to cut the board into pieces that are $\frac{4}{5}$ foot long.

   a) How many pieces of length $\frac{4}{5}$ foot can the carpenter cut from the board?

   b) What length of the original board will be left after the carpenter has cut all the pieces that are $\frac{4}{5}$ foot long?

6. A candle maker has $4\frac{1}{2}$ pounds of clear wax. He wants to cut the wax into pieces that are $\frac{2}{3}$ pound each.

   a) How many $\frac{2}{3}$-pound pieces can he divide the wax into?

   b) How much wax is left over?

7. A roll of ribbon was 9 meters long. Kevin cut 8 pieces of ribbon, each of length 0.8 meter, to tie some presents. He then cut the remaining ribbon into some pieces, each of length 0.4 meter.

   a) How many pieces of ribbon, each 0.4 meter in length, did Kevin have?

   b) What was the length of ribbon left over?

8 Mike has a large tropical fish collection. He gives $\frac{2}{3}$ of his fish to a local high school. Then he gives $\frac{2}{5}$ of the remaining fish to an elementary school. In the end, he has 30 fish left. How many fish did Mike have at first?

9 A costume designer has 40 yards of red fabric to make costumes for a musical in which 8 performers will wear red dresses and 14 people will wear red scarves. The costume maker uses $3\frac{1}{2}$ yards for each dress, and $\frac{3}{4}$ yard for a scarf.

a) After making the dresses and scarves, the costume designer uses the leftover fabric to make some sashes for the dresses. If each sash uses $\frac{1}{4}$ yard of fabric, how many sashes can be made?

b) The costume designer decides to make the sashes a little smaller, so that each of the 8 dresses can have a sash. What fraction of a yard of fabric should the costume maker use to make each sash?

10 Jack read $\frac{1}{6}$ of a book on Monday and another $\frac{1}{3}$ of it on Tuesday. He took another 4 days to finish reading the book. He read the same number of pages on each of the 4 days.

a) What fraction of the book did he read on each of the 4 days?

b) If he read 40 pages on each of these 4 days, find the number of pages in the book.

11 The school librarian has $100 to spend on some books for the school. She wants to order many copies of the same book so an entire classroom can read the book. Each copy costs $3.95. Shipping for the books will be $6.95.

a) How many copies can the librarian order?

b) Describe how you can use estimation to decide if your answer to part **a)** is reasonable.

12 Jason cycled for 3 hours. He cycled $7\frac{1}{2}$ miles each hour for the first two hours and the distance he cycled for the third hour was $\frac{1}{4}$ of the total distance he cycled in 3 hours. What was the total distance Jason cycled in 3 hours?

13 The length of a field was 20 yards. Mr. Matsumoto planted a row of peas every $\frac{3}{4}$ yard.

    a) How many rows of peas did Mr. Matsumoto plant?

    b) What was the remaining length of field?

14 A sign in an elevator says the elevator can lift up to 450 kilograms. John has 10 boxes that weigh 13.75 kilograms each, and a number of additional boxes that weigh 15.5 kilograms each. If he puts the 10 boxes on the elevator, how many of the additional boxes can be lifted in the same load?

15 Ken had a number of colored marbles in a bag. $\frac{1}{4}$ of the marbles were red, $\frac{2}{3}$ of the remaining marbles were blue, and the rest were yellow. Given that there were 120 red and yellow marbles altogether, how many marbles were there in the bag?

16 Rachel used $\frac{3}{8}$ of her money to buy some blouses and $\frac{2}{5}$ of the remainder to buy 2 pairs of pants. A pair of pants costs 3 times as much as a blouse. How many blouses did she buy?

17 Sheila went shopping and spent $120 on a coat. She then used $\frac{2}{3}$ of the remaining money to buy a dress. She was left with $\frac{1}{5}$ of her original amount of money. How much did Sheila have at first?

Brain @ Work

Alex, Beth and Carol share a sum of money. Alex receives 0.7 of the sum of money. Beth and Carol receive the rest of the money. If Beth receives $\frac{5}{12}$ of the money shared by both her and Carol, and Carol receives $847, how much money does Alex get?

Chapter Wrap Up

Concept Map

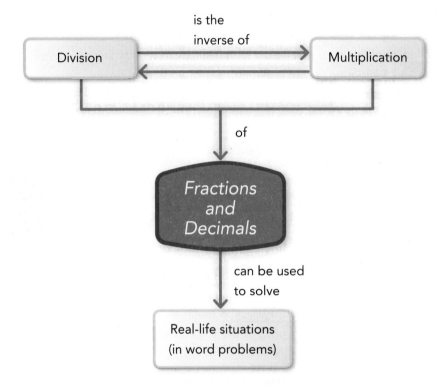

Key Concepts

▶ To divide any number by a fraction, you can multiply the number by the reciprocal of the fraction.

▶ You learned two methods for multiplying decimals. Thinking about the place value of decimal factors can help you think about the place value of the product.

• Express both decimals as fractions. Multiply, and then express the result as a decimal.

• Multiply the numerical values of the decimals. Then use what you know about the place value of the factors to place the decimal point.

▶ You learned two methods for dividing a decimal by a decimal.

• Express both decimals as fractions. Divide, and then express the result as a decimal.

• Rewrite the division expression as a fraction. Multiply to make the divisor a whole number. Then divide the numerator by the denominator.

Chapter Review/Test

Concepts and Skills

Divide.

1 $15 \div \frac{1}{3}$

2 $24 \div \frac{1}{6}$

3 $\frac{3}{8} \div \frac{3}{4}$

4 $\frac{7}{12} \div \frac{1}{3}$

Multiply.

5 0.3×8

6 6×0.7

7 0.28×6

8 7×0.068

9 0.3×0.6

10 0.5×0.8

11 5.7×0.4

12 9.3×0.89

Divide.

13 $6 \div 0.6$

14 $8 \div 0.4$

15 $35 \div 0.7$

16 $88 \div 0.2$

17 $5 \div 0.25$

18 $8 \div 0.16$

19 $96 \div 0.16$

20 $396 \div 0.36$

21 $0.87 \div 0.03$

22 $0.98 \div 0.7$

Problem Solving

Solve. Show your work.

23 In January, Jane volunteered at a hospital for a total of 12 hours. She spent $\frac{4}{5}$ hour at the hospital every time she volunteered. How many times did Jane volunteer in January?

24 Paul is making loaves of raisin bread to sell at a fundraising event. The recipe calls for $\frac{1}{3}$ cup of raisins for each loaf, and Paul has $3\frac{1}{4}$ cups of raisins.

a)   How many loaves can Paul make?

b)   How many cups of raisins will he have left over?

25 Jane has a dog that eats 0.8 pound of dog food each day. She buys a 40-pound bag of dog food. How many days will this bag of dog food last?

26 Mervin had some cartons of milk. He sold $\frac{2}{5}$ of the cartons of milk in the morning. He then sold $\frac{3}{4}$ of the remainder in the afternoon. 24 more cartons of milk were sold in the afternoon than in the morning. How many cartons of milk did Mervin have at first?

27 Alice baked a certain number of pies. She gave $\frac{1}{8}$ of the pies to her friends and $\frac{1}{4}$ of the remainder to her neighbor. She was left with 63 pies. How many pies did Alice bake at first?

28 At a concert, $\frac{2}{5}$ of the people were men. There were 3 times as many women as children. If there were 45 more men than children, how many people were there at the concert?

29 $\frac{3}{4}$ of the students in a school were girls and the rest were boys. $\frac{2}{3}$ of the girls and $\frac{1}{2}$ of the boys attended the school carnival. Find the total number of students in the school if 330 students did not attend the carnival.

30 At a baseball game, there were three times as many males as females. $\frac{5}{6}$ of the males were boys and the rest were men. $\frac{2}{3}$ of the females were girls and the rest were women. Given that there were 121 more boys than girls, how many adults were there at the baseball game?

31 Mr. Thomas spent $1,600 of his savings on a television set and $\frac{2}{5}$ of the remainder on a refrigerator. He had $\frac{1}{3}$ of his original amount of savings left.

a) What was Mr. Thomas's original savings?

b) What was the cost of the refrigerator?

32 Sue buys 8.5 pounds of chicken to make tacos. She uses 0.3 pound of chicken for each taco.

a) How many tacos can Sue make?

b) How many pounds of chicken are left over?

Cumulative Review Chapters 1–3

Concepts and Skills

Draw a horizontal number line to represent each set of numbers. (Lesson 1.1)

1 Mixed numbers from 3 to 7, with an interval of $\frac{1}{3}$ between each pair of mixed numbers

2 Decimals between 4.2 and 5.4, with an interval of 0.3 between each pair of decimals

Express each number as a product of its prime factors. (Lesson 1.2)

3 84

4 240

Find the greatest common factor of each pair of numbers. (Lesson 1.3)

5 16 and 60

6 63 and 96

Find the least common multiple of each pair of numbers. (Lesson 1.3)

7 9 and 12

8 15 and 18

Find the square root of each number. (Lesson 1.4)

9 256

10 676

Find the cube root of each number. (Lesson 1.5)

11 1,728

12 5,832

Find the value of each of the following. (Lesson 1.5)

13 $5^3 - 11^2 + 7^3$

14 $4^3 \div 8^2 \times 12^3$

Solve. (Lesson 1.5)

15 Given that $56^2 = 3,136$, find the square of 112.

16 Given that $13^3 = 2,197$, find the cube root of 17,576.

Draw a vertical number line to represent each set of numbers. (Lessons 1.3, 2.1)

17 Multiples of 3 between 81 and 110

18 Even numbers greater than -37 but less than -25

Write a positive or negative number to represent each situation. (Lesson 2.1)

19 Getting a pay raise of $320 per year

20 214°F below zero

21 Riding an elevator down 15 floors

Copy and complete each inequality using > or <. (Lesson 2.1)

22 121 ? −388

23 −795 ? 347

24 −78 ? −132

25 −234 ? −243

Write an inequality for each of the following statements using > or <. (Lesson 2.1)

26 185°F is colder than 209°F.

27 Town A, which is 84 kilometers from Town B, is farther from Town B than Town C, which is 76 kilometers from Town B.

Copy and complete each inequality using > or <. (Lesson 2.2)

28 |−356| ? |368|

29 |232| ? |−324|

30 |264| ? |246|

31 |−311| ? |−389|

Divide. (Lesson 3.1)

32 $28 \div \frac{1}{5}$

33 $42 \div \frac{2}{3}$

34 $\frac{3}{8} \div 12$

35 $\frac{5}{14} \div \frac{10}{21}$

Multiply. (Lesson 3.2)

36 0.3 × 3.8

37 6.3 × 4.7

38 0.28 × 474

39 8.23 × 9.107

Divide. (Lesson 3.3)

40 72 ÷ 0.3

41 8.1 ÷ 0.3

42 2.88 ÷ 1.2

43 128 ÷ 0.02

Problem Solving

Solve. Show your work.

44 Alison paid $21.75 for a number of packs of rice crackers. Three packs of rice crackers cost $1.45. How many packs of rice crackers did Alison buy? If she were to buy 60 packs of the same rice crackers, would $30 be enough to pay for them? (Chapter 3)

45 Find two consecutive numbers whose cubes differ by 169. (Chapter 1)

46 Two light houses flash their lights every 30 seconds and 40 seconds respectively. Given that they last flashed together at 10:40 A.M., when will they next flash together? (Chapter 1)

47 $\frac{7}{8}$ of a rectangle is colored red. Damien cuts this red part into a number of pieces so that each piece is $\frac{1}{24}$ of the whole rectangle. Find the number of red pieces Damien has. (Chapter 3)

48 Jon spent $\frac{1}{3}$ of his allowance on baseball cards, $\frac{1}{4}$ on baseball souvenirs, and $\frac{3}{8}$ on a baseball ticket. If he had $5 left, how much allowance did he have to start with? (Chapter 3)

49 A baker baked some loaves of bread. 240 loaves were sold by the end of the day. The baker was then left with $\frac{9}{25}$ of the number of loaves that were baked. How many loaves of bread did the baker bake on that day? (Chapter 3)

50 Tickets to a performance are available at $45 for the front row seats and $25 for the back row seats. There are 18 front rows with 39 seats in each row, and 27 back rows with 4 seats in each row. If $\frac{5}{6}$ of all the front row seats and $\frac{7}{9}$ of the back row seats are sold, how much is the total ticket sales? (Chapter 3)

51 A charitable organization packed 195 bags of rice, 325 blankets, and 455 bottles of water equally into boxes. (Chapter 1)

  a) Find the greatest possible number of boxes that the items can be packed into.

  b) Find the number of bags of rice, blankets, and bottles of water in each box.

Ratio

How can math help you cook?

Have you ever seen a recipe for a loaf of bread? The recipe tells you how much of each type of ingredient to use. You might need 1 cup of buttermilk and 3 cups of flour to make a loaf of bread. The ratio 1 to 3 describes the relationship between the number of cups of buttermilk and the number of cups of flour in the bread.

Now, suppose you want to make 5 loaves of bread. You need to increase the number of cups of buttermilk and the number of cups of flour you use. In this chapter, you will learn how to use ratios to solve problems like "scaling up" the amounts of ingredients in a recipe.

BIG IDEA

▶ You can use a ratio to compare two quantities, and you can use ratios to solve problems.

Recall Prior Knowledge

Expressing fractions as equivalent fractions by multiplication

$\frac{5}{7} = \frac{5 \times 2}{7 \times 2} = \frac{10}{14}$ Multiply both the numerator and denominator by the same number, 2.

$\frac{5}{7} = \frac{5 \times 3}{7 \times 3} = \frac{15}{21}$ Multiply both the numerator and denominator by the same number, 3.

$\frac{5}{7} = \frac{10}{14} = \frac{15}{21}$

So, $\frac{5}{7}$, $\frac{10}{14}$, and $\frac{15}{21}$ are equivalent fractions.

✓ Quick Check

Express each fraction as two equivalent fractions using multiplication.

1 $\frac{3}{4}$

2 $\frac{7}{9}$

3 $\frac{6}{11}$

Expressing fractions as equivalent fractions by division

$\frac{18}{36} = \frac{18 \div 3}{36 \div 3} = \frac{6}{12}$ Divide both the numerator and denominator by the common factor, 3.

$\frac{18}{36} = \frac{18 \div 6}{36 \div 6} = \frac{3}{6}$ Divide both the numerator and denominator by the common factor, 6.

$\frac{18}{36} = \frac{6}{12} = \frac{3}{6}$

So, $\frac{18}{36}$, $\frac{6}{12}$, and $\frac{3}{6}$ are equivalent fractions.

✓ Quick Check

Express each fraction as two equivalent fractions using division.

4 $\frac{16}{56}$

5 $\frac{21}{63}$

6 $\frac{35}{140}$

Writing equivalent fractions

Find the unknown numerator or denominator in each pair of equivalent fractions.

a) $\dfrac{4}{7} = \dfrac{?}{42}$

$\dfrac{4}{7} = \dfrac{4 \times 6}{7 \times 6}$

$\quad = \dfrac{24}{42}$

b) $\dfrac{5}{12} = \dfrac{35}{?}$

$\dfrac{5}{12} = \dfrac{5 \times 7}{12 \times 7}$

$\quad = \dfrac{35}{84}$

✓ Quick Check

Find the unknown numerator or denominator in each pair of equivalent fractions.

7 $\dfrac{3}{8} = \dfrac{?}{56}$

8 $\dfrac{7}{9} = \dfrac{21}{?}$

9 $\dfrac{?}{11} = \dfrac{30}{55}$

10 $\dfrac{6}{?} = \dfrac{42}{84}$

Writing fractions in simplest form

$\dfrac{12}{16} = \dfrac{12 \div 4}{16 \div 4}$ Divide both the numerator and denominator by the greatest common factor, 4.

$\quad = \dfrac{3}{4}$

✓ Quick Check

Express each fraction in simplest form.

11 $\dfrac{5}{45}$

12 $\dfrac{18}{63}$

13 $\dfrac{22}{55}$

Converting measurements given in one unit of measure to another

Find the unknown measurement.

$\underline{\ ?\ }$ in. = 3 ft

1 ft = 12 in.

3 ft = 3 × 12 = 36 in.

5.2 km = $\underline{\ ?\ }$ m

1 km = 1,000 m

5.2 km = 1,000 × 5.2 = 5,200 m

✅ Quick Check

Find the unknown measurement.

14 ___?___ cm = 4 m

15 9.8 kg = ___?___ g

16 6 ft = ___?___ yd

17 10 L = ___?___ mL

18 ___?___ yd = 72 in.

19 5 lb = ___?___ oz

Interpreting a comparison bar model

Find the values of A and B.

a)

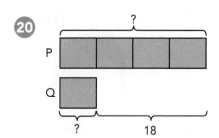

2 units ⟶ 12

1 unit ⟶ $\frac{12}{2}$ = 6

Value of A:
5 units ⟶ 5 × 6 = 30

Value of B:
3 units ⟶ 3 × 6 = 18

b)

5 units ⟶ 35

1 unit ⟶ $\frac{35}{5}$ = 7

Value of A:
3 units ⟶ 3 × 7 = 21

Value of B:
2 units ⟶ 2 × 7 = 14

✅ Quick Check

Find the values of P and Q.

20

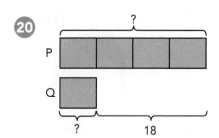

21

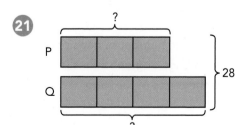

Lesson Objectives

- Write ratios to compare two quantities.
- Interpret ratios given in fraction form.
- Use a ratio to find what fraction one quantity is of another or how many times as great one is as the other.

Learn   Understand the meaning of ratio.

You can compare numbers or quantities by comparing their sizes.

Compare 7 and 4.

7

4

7 is greater than 4.

Compare 5 centimeters and 9 centimeters.

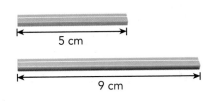

5 cm

9 cm

5 centimeters is shorter than 9 centimeters.

Another way to compare numbers or quantities is to use a ratio.
The numbers or quantities you are comparing form the **terms** of a ratio.
Suppose there are 7 bags of orange cubes and 4 bags of green cubes.
Each bag has an equal number of cubes.

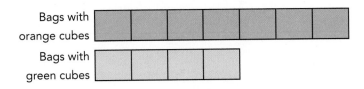

Bags with orange cubes

Bags with green cubes

So, the ratio of the number of bags of orange cubes to the number of bags of green cubes is 7 : 4.
7 and 4 are the terms of the ratio.

The ratio does not give the actual number of cubes. Because each bag has an equal number of cubes, the ratio 7 : 4 also means that there are 7 orange cubes for every 4 green cubes.

When two quantities, such as the lengths of two rods, have the same units, you can write a ratio without units to compare the quantities.

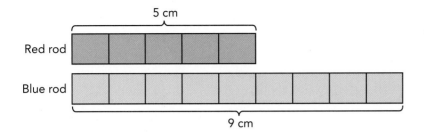

5 centimeters and 9 centimeters have the same unit.
So, the ratio of the length of the red rod to the length of the blue rod
is 5 cm : 9 cm, or 5 : 9. The terms of the ratio are 5 and 9.

If you want to use a ratio to compare two quantities that have different units, such as meters and centimeters, you must first express the quantities using the same unit.

For example, 3 centimeters and 4 meters have different units.
4 meters can be expressed as 400 centimeters.

1 m = 100 cm

3 cm : 4 m = 3 cm : 400 cm
            = 3 : 400

Caution ///////

You cannot compare two quantities using a ratio if they cannot be expressed as the same unit.

For example, 3 centimeters and 4 kilograms cannot be expressed as the same unit.

Guided Practice

Complete.

1 The ratio of the number of CDs to the number of CD sleeves is __?__ : __?__ .

2 Mrs. Carter buys 4 bags of apples and 7 bags of oranges.
Each bag has an equal number of fruits.

The ratio of the number of apples to the number of oranges is __?__ : __?__ .

3 Desiree has a cat that weighs 12 pounds and a dog that weighs 13 pounds.

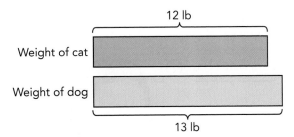

a) The ratio of the weight of the cat to the weight of the dog is __?__ : __?__ .

b) The ratio of the weight of the dog to the weight of the cat is __?__ : __?__ .

State whether each of the following can be expressed as a ratio.

4 6 kg and 84 kg   **5** 72 ft and 2 yd   **6** 3 oz and 30 in.

Complete.

7 13 cm : 2 m = 13 cm : __?__ cm   Think: 1 m = 100 cm, so 2 m = __?__ cm.

  = __?__ : __?__

8 5 kg : 13 g = __?__ g : __?__ g   Think: 1 kg = 1,000 g, so 5 kg = __?__ g.

  = __?__ : __?__

9 9 mL : 7 L = __?__ mL : __?__ mL   Think: 1 L = 1,000 mL, so 7 L = __?__ mL.

  = __?__ : __?__

Learn Use a part-part or a part-whole model to show ratios.

There were 55 adults and 32 children at a party.

a) Find the ratio of the number of adults to the number of children at the party. Use a part-part model.

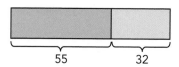

The number of adults and the number of children are parts of a whole.

The ratio of the number of adults to the number of children at the party is 55 : 32.

b) Find the ratio of the number of children to the total number of people at the party. Use a part-whole model.

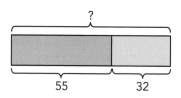

The total number of people forms the whole.

Total number of people at the party = 55 + 32
= 87

So, the ratio of the number of children to the total number of people at the party is 32 : 87.

Guided Practice

Complete.

10 John keeps 17 angelfish and 24 guppies.

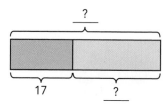

a) Find the ratio of the number of angelfish to the number of guppies.

The ratio of the number of angelfish to the number of guppies is __?__ : __?__ .

b) Find the ratio of the number of guppies to the total number of fish.

Total number of fish = __?__ + __?__

= __?__

The ratio of the number of guppies to the total number of fish is __?__ : __?__ .

Lesson 4.1 Comparing Two Quantities   **121**

11 Alex has a string 72 centimeters long. He cuts it into two pieces. The length of the shorter piece is 31 centimeters. What is the ratio of the length of the longer piece to the total length of the string?

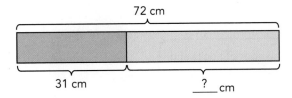

72 cm

31 cm

__?__ cm

$72 - \underline{} = \underline{}$

The length of the longer piece is __?__ centimeters.

__?__ cm : __?__ cm = __?__ : __?__

The ratio of the length of the longer piece to the total length of the string

is __?__ : __?__.

12 The total amount of money Pamela and Rachel saved in a week was $45. Pamela saved $13.

a) Find the amount of money Rachel saved.

b) Find the ratio of the total amount of money Pamela and Rachel saved to the amount of money Rachel saved.

Learn **Write and interpret ratios as fractions.**

You can also write ratios as fractions.

a) Two out of three animals in a pet store are birds.
You can write the ratio of the number of birds to the number of animals
as 2 to 3, 2 : 3, or $\frac{2}{3}$.

Use a part-whole model.

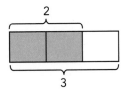

2

3

Notice that when you write the ratio as $\frac{2}{3}$, you can also see that $\frac{2}{3}$ of the animals are birds.

Number of groups of birds = 2
Total number of groups of animals = 3

b) The birds in the pet store are parakeets and canaries. There are 3 parakeets and 7 canaries. Find the ratio of the number of parakeets to the number of canaries.

Use a part-part model.

$$\underbrace{}_{3} \qquad \underbrace{}_{7}$$

Number of parakeets = 3
Number of canaries = 7

The ratio of the number of parakeets to the number of canaries is 3 : 7.

Notice that the ratio $\frac{3}{7}$ does not tell you what fraction of the birds are parakeets or canaries. Instead, it tells you that there are 3 parakeets for every 7 canaries.

Total number of birds = 3 + 7 = 10

So, the ratio of the number of parakeets to the total number of birds is 3 : 10 or $\frac{3}{10}$.

Similarly, the ratio of the number of canaries to the total number of birds is 7 : 10 or $\frac{7}{10}$.

Guided Practice

Complete. You may draw a model to help you.

13 The ratio of the number of white parrots to the number of green parrots is 7 : 8. Write a ratio to describe the number of green parrots to the total number of parrots.

Total number of parrots = $\underline{}^{?}$ + $\underline{}^{?}$ = $\underline{}^{?}$ units

The ratio of the number of green parrots to the total number of parrots

is $\underline{}^{?}$: $\underline{}^{?}$ or $\frac{?}{?}$.

Solve. You may draw a model to help you.

14 The ratio of the number of male teachers to the number of female teachers in a school is 5 : 9.

   a) What fraction of the teachers are females?

   b) What fraction of the teachers are males?

Learn **Use ratios to find how many times one number or quantity is as great as another.**

The height of a giraffe and the height of a horse are represented in the model.

Height of giraffe

Height of horse

   a) How many times the height of the horse is the height of the giraffe?

$$\frac{\text{Height of giraffe}}{\text{Height of horse}} = \frac{6}{3} = \frac{2}{1}$$

The height of the giraffe is 2 times the height of the horse.

   b) How many times the height of the giraffe is the height of the horse?

$$\frac{\text{Height of horse}}{\text{Height of giraffe}} = \frac{3}{6} = \frac{1}{2}$$

The height of the horse is $\frac{1}{2}$ times the height of the giraffe.

Guided Practice

Complete.

15 The height of a coconut tree is 48 feet and the height of a papaya tree is 12 feet.

   a) How many times the height of the papaya tree is the height of the coconut tree?

$$\frac{\text{Height of cococut tree}}{\text{Height of papaya tree}} = \frac{?}{?}$$

The height of the coconut tree is __?__ times the height of the papaya tree.

   b) How many times the height of the coconut tree is the height of the papaya tree?

$$\frac{\text{Height of papaya tree}}{\text{Height of cococut tree}} = \frac{?}{?}$$

The height of the papaya tree is __?__ times the height of the coconut tree.

Practice 4.1

Write two ratios to compare the quantities.

1

2 Catherine has 23 video game disks and Dylan has 37 video game disks.

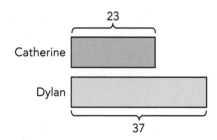

3 In a school, there are 8 classes in the sixth grade and 7 classes in the seventh grade. Each class has an equal number of students.

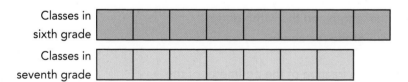

State whether each of the following can be expressed as a ratio.

4 6 cm and 60 g

5 54 kg and 54 m

6 12 g and 45 kg

7 87 ft and 93 yd

Solve. Show your work.

8 There are 123 students in a drama club. 65 of them are girls.

    a) What is the ratio of the number of boys to the number of girls?

    b) What is the ratio of the number of boys to the total number of students?

9 There were 37 clarinet players and 150 trumpet players who tried out for a music competition.

   a) Find the ratio of the number of clarinet players to the number of trumpet players.

   b) Find the ratio of the number of trumpet players to the total number of players.

10 Carl had $43 when he entered the museum gift shop. After spending some money, he had $18 left.

   a) Find the amount of money Carl spent.

   b) Find the ratio of the amount of money Carl spent to the amount of money he had when he entered the gift shop.

11 Kelvin's monthly allowance is $42 and Mike's monthly allowance is $63. How many times Mike's monthly allowance is Kelvin's monthly allowance?

12 The ratio of the weight of vegetables sold to the weight of fruits sold is 45 : 144.

   a) How many times the weight of vegetables sold is the weight of fruits sold?

   b) What fraction of the total weight of vegetables and fruits sold is the weight of vegetables sold?

13 The ratio of the length to the width of a rectangle is 5 : 2.

   a) Express the difference between the length and the width of the rectangle as a fraction of the length of the rectangle.

   b) Express the width of the rectangle as a fraction of the perimeter of the rectangle.

Math Journal **Describe a situation that each ratio could represent.**

14 5 : 16

15 98 : 3

16 1,000 : 1

4.2 Equivalent Ratios

Lesson Objectives

- Write equivalent ratios.
- Write ratios in simplest form.
- Compare ratios.

Vocabulary

equivalent ratios   simplest form

Learn   Equivalent ratios show the same comparisons of numbers and quantities.

Linus has 8 red marbles and 12 blue marbles.

The ratio of the number of red marbles to the number of blue marbles is 8 : 12.

Linus groups 2 marbles of the same color into each group.

There are 4 groups of red marbles and 6 groups of blue marbles.
The ratio of the number of groups of red marbles to the number of groups of
blue marbles is 4 : 6.

Next, he groups 4 marbles of the same color into each group.

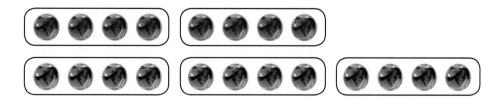

There are 2 groups of red marbles and 3 groups of blue marbles.
The ratio of the number of groups of red marbles to the number of groups of
blue marbles is 2 : 3.

Continue on next page

Notice that Linus is not changing the number of red marbles or the number of blue marbles. He is only regrouping the marbles.

8 red marbles : **12 blue marbles**   8 red marbles : **12 blue marbles**

Divide into groups   Divide into groups
of 2 marbles.   of 4 marbles.

4 groups of 2 : **6 groups** of 2   2 groups of 4 : **3 groups** of 4

The ratios 8 : 12, 4 : 6, and 2 : 3 are equivalent ratios.

Guided Practice

Complete.

1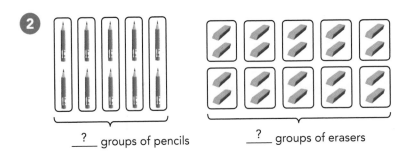

The ratio of the number of pencils to the number of erasers

is ___?___ : ___?___.

2

___?___ groups of pencils   ___?___ groups of erasers

The ratio of the number of groups of pencils to the number of groups

of erasers is ___?___ : ___?___.

3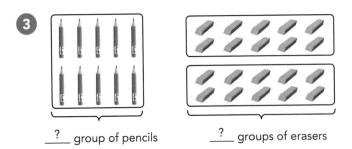

___?___ group of pencils   ___?___ groups of erasers

The ratio of the number of groups of pencils to the number of groups

of erasers is ___?___ : ___?___.

4   10 pencils : 20 erasers   10 pencils : 20 erasers

Divide into   Divide into
groups of 2.   groups of 10.

__?__ groups of 2 : __?__ groups of 2   __?__ group of 10 : __?__ groups of 10

The ratios __?__ : __?__ , __?__ : __?__ , and __?__ : __?__ are equivalent ratios.

Learn   **Use the greatest common factor to write ratios in simplest form.**

You can write a ratio in simplest form by dividing the terms by their greatest common factor.

a)   Express the ratio 50 : 20 in simplest form.

$÷ 10$ $\overset{50 : 20}{\underset{=\ 5 : 2}{}}$ $÷ 10$ Divide each term by the greatest common factor, 10.

b)   Express the ratio 8 cm : 3 m in simplest form.

First, express the two quantities as the same unit. Then simplify the ratio.

8 cm : 3 m = 8 cm : 300 cm   Think: 1 m = 100 cm, so 3 m = 300 cm.
= 8 : 300   Write ratio without units.
= 8 ÷ 4 : 300 ÷ 4   Divide each term by the greatest common factor, 4.
= 2 : 75   Simplify.

Guided Practice

Complete.

5 Express the ratio 12 : 64 in simplest form.

$÷ \underline{?}$ $\overset{12\ :\ 64}{\underset{=\ \underline{?}\ :\ \underline{?}}{}}$ $÷ \underline{?}$

6 Express the ratio 7 kg : 21 g in simplest form.

7 kg = __?__ g

7 kg : 21 g = __?__ g : __?__ g

= __?__ ÷ __?__ : __?__ ÷ __?__

= __?__ : __?__

Learn Equivalent ratios have the same ratio in simplest form.

a)

P

Q

$P : Q = 1 : 2$

R

S

$R : S = 2 : 4$

÷ 2   ÷ 2

$= 1 : 2$

Two ratios are equivalent when each ratio can be expressed as the same ratio in simplest form.

The ratios 1 : 2 and 2 : 4 are equivalent ratios.
Each ratio can be expressed in simplest form as 1: 2.

b) Are the ratios 3 : 4 and 6 : 9 equivalent?

3 : 4 is in simplest form.

6 : 9 = 2 : 3   Divide each term by the greatest common factor, 3.

3 : 4 and 2 : 3 are not the same ratio.
So, 3 : 4 and 6 : 9 are not equivalent ratios.

c) Are the ratios 1 : 4 and 12 : 3 equivalent?

1 : 4 is in simplest form.

12 : 3 = 4 : 1   Divide each term by the
                       greatest common factor, 3.

1 : 4 and 4 : 1 are not the same ratio.
So, 1 : 4 and 12 : 3 are not equivalent ratios.

Math Note

The order of the terms in a ratio is important.

So, 2 : 5 is not the same as 5 : 2.

Guided Practice

State whether each pair of ratios are equivalent.

7 7 : 8 and 8 : 7

8 5 : 9 and 15 : 27

9 12 : 13 and 24 : 39

10 4 : 24 and 8 : 48

Martha plans to bake some loaves of bread. The recipe for one loaf of bread uses 3 tablespoons of sunflower seeds and 4 tablespoons of cranberries.

If Martha plans to make more loaves of bread, she can find an equivalent ratio of the number of tablespoons of sunflowers seeds to the number of tablespoons of cranberries by multiplying both terms of the ratio by the same number.

× 2 3 : 4 × 2   Multiply by a factor of 2.
= 6 : 8

× 3 3 : 4 × 3   Multiply by a factor of 3.
= 9 : 12

× 4 3 : 4 × 4   Multiply by a factor of 4.
= 12 : 16

× 5 3 : 4 × 5   Multiply by a factor of 5.
= 15 : 20

3 : 4, 6 : 8, 9 : 12, 12 : 16, and 15 : 20 are equivalent ratios.

So, $\frac{3}{4} = \frac{6}{8} = \frac{9}{12} = \frac{12}{16} = \frac{15}{20}$.

For 5 loaves of bread, Martha will use 15 tablespoons of sunflower seeds and 20 tablespoons of cranberries.

Guided Practice

Complete.

11 Use multiplication to find three ratios equivalent to 7 : 8.

× 2 7 : 8 × 2   × ? 7 : 8 × ?   × ? 7 : 8 × ?
= ? : ?   = ? : ?   = ? : ?

7 : 8, ? : ? , ? : ? , and ? : ? are equivalent ratios.

So, $\frac{7}{8} = \frac{?}{?} = \frac{?}{?} = \frac{?}{?}$.

^{Learn} **Find equivalent ratios by division.**

Tasty Catering has a recipe for lentil soup that uses 18 cups of lentils and 54 cups of tomatoes.

To use this recipe to make less soup, you can find the ratio of the number of cups of lentils to the number of cups of tomatoes. Then you can use division to find an equivalent ratio.

First, find the common factors of the terms. Then divide the terms by the common factors.

Excluding 1, the common factors of 18 and 54 are 2, 3, 6, 9, and 18.

÷ 2 18 : 54 ÷ 2   Divide by the common factor 2.
= 9 : 27

÷ 3 18 : 54 ÷ 3   Divide by the common factor 3.
= 6 : 18

÷ 6 18 : 54 ÷ 6   Divide by the common factor 6.
= 3 : 9

÷ 9 18 : 54 ÷ 9   Divide by the common factor 9.
= 2 : 6

÷ 18 18 : 54 ÷ 18   Divide by the common factor 18.
= 1 : 3

> Excluding 1, there are five common factors.
> So, you can use division to find five whole number ratios that are equivalent to 18 : 54.

18 : 54, 9 : 27, 6 : 18, 3 : 9, 2 : 6, and 1 : 3 are equivalent ratios.

So, $\frac{18}{54} = \frac{9}{27} = \frac{6}{18} = \frac{3}{9} = \frac{2}{6} = \frac{1}{3}$.

Tasty Catering can use 1 cup of lentils to 3 cups of tomatoes to make lentil soup.

Guided Practice

Complete.

12 Use division to find all the whole number ratios that are equivalent to 24 : 96.

> Excluding 1, what are the common factors of 24 and 96?

Learn

Find the missing term of a pair of equivalent ratios.

Given three terms in a pair of equivalent ratios, you can find the missing term.

Find the missing terms in these equivalent ratios.

a) $4 : 5 = 12 : ?$

First, find the multiplying factor. Then multiply the second term by the multiplying factor.

Method 1

$4 \times 3 = 12$

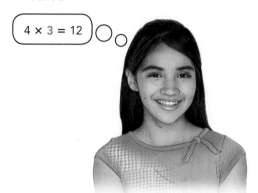

Method 2

$12 \div 4 = 3$

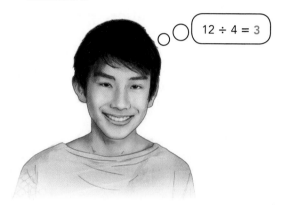

$\times 3 \quad \overset{\mathbf{4 : 5}}{\underset{= \mathbf{12 : 15}}{\curvearrowright}} \quad \times 3$

So, the multiplying factor is **3**.

$3 \times 5 = 15$

b) $42 : 54 = 7 : ?$

First, find the common factor. Then divide the second term by the common factor.

Method 1

$42 \div 6 = 7$
$54 \div 6 = 9$

Method 2

$42 \div 7 = 6$

$\div 6 \quad \overset{\mathbf{42 : 54}}{\underset{= \mathbf{7 : 9}}{\curvearrowright}} \quad \div 6$

So, the common factor is **6**.

$54 \div 6 = 9$

Guided Practice

Find the missing term in each pair of equivalent ratios.

13 $\times$ ___?___ $\overset{6:7}{\curvearrowright}$ $\times$ ___?___

$= 30 : $ ___?___

14 $\div$ ___?___ $\overset{28:42}{\curvearrowright}$ $\div$ ___?___

$= $ ___?___ $: 6$

15 $48 : 64 = $ ___?___ $: 8$

16 $4 : 9 = 36 : $ ___?___

^{earn} **Work with tables of ratios.**

a) Students in the school musical are going to sell tickets. Each student is expected to sell 3 youth tickets and 5 adult tickets. The students use a table to predict how many tickets will be sold. How many tickets will be sold if 50 students sell tickets?

Number of Students	Number of Youth Tickets	Number of Adult Tickets
1	3	5
2	6	10
3	9	15
4	12	20

Notice that the ratio of the number of youth tickets to the number of adult tickets is the same for all the rows in the table. All the ratios can be written in simplest form as 3 : 5.

$\div 2$ $\overset{6:10}{\curvearrowright}$ $\div 2$ Divide by the common factor 2.

$= 3 : 5$

$\div 3$ $\overset{9:15}{\curvearrowright}$ $\div 3$ Divide by the common factor 3.

$= 3 : 5$

$\div 4$ $\overset{12:20}{\curvearrowright}$ $\div 4$ Divide by the common factor 4.

$= 3 : 5$

You can use the ratio 3 : 5 to find how many tickets will be sold if more students sell tickets.

Number of Students	Number of Youth Tickets	Number of Adult Tickets	
1	3	5	
2	6	10	Multiply by 2.
3	9	15	Multiply by 3.
4	12	20	Multiply by 4.
...	...	...	...
50	150	250	Multiply by 50.

So, if 50 students sell tickets, 150 youth tickets and 250 adult tickets will be sold.

b) The student council is selling bouquets of daisies and tulips. The ratio of the number of daisies to the number of tulips is the same for all the bouquets. You can use ratios to find the missing information in the table.

Number of Bouquets	Number of Daisies	Number of Tulips
1	?	?
2	24	12
3	?	18

First, find the number of daisies and tulips in 1 bouquet.

When there are 2 bouquets, the ratio of the number of daisies to the number of tulips is 24 : 12 = 2 : 1.

In 2 bouquets, there are twice as many of each type of flowers as there are in 1 bouquet. So, divide by 2 to find the number of flowers in 1 bouquet.

Daisies : Tulips

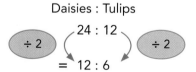

24 : 12

÷ 2   ÷ 2

= 12 : 6

There are 12 daisies and 6 tulips in 1 bouquet.

Continue on next page

Then find the number of daisies and tulips in 3 bouquets.

In 3 bouquets, there are 3 times as many flowers as there are in 1 bouquet. So, multiply the terms of the ratio 12 : 6 by 3.

Daisies : Tulips

× 3 $\quad$ 12 : 6 $\quad$ × 3

= 36 : 18

There are 36 daisies and 18 tulips in 3 bouquets.

Check that the ratio of the number of daisies to the number of tulips in the bouquets is 2 : 1.

1 bouquet	2 bouquets	3 bouquets
12 : 6 = 2 : 1	24 : 12 = 2 : 1	36 : 18 = 2 : 1

Guided Practice

Solve.

17 Selena and Drew each has a summer job. The table shows the amount of money they earn, based on the number of hours they work.

Number of Days	Selena's Earnings ($)	Drew's Earnings ($)
1	31	33
2	62	66
3	93	99

a) Express the ratio of Selena's earnings to Drew's earnings in simplest form.

b) If Selena works 4 days, she will earn $ _?_ .

If Selena works 30 days, she will earn $ _?_ .

c) If Drew works 4 days, he will earn $ _?_ .

If Drew works 30 days, he will earn $ _?_ .

18 A school organized a paper recycling competition. The table shows the amount of oil and the amount of water saved by recycling paper.

Weight of Paper Recycled (ton)	Amount of Oil Saved (gal)	Amount of Water Saved (gal)
1	380	?
2	?	14,000
3	1,140	?
4	?	?

a) How many gallons of water will be saved if 1 ton of paper is recycled?

b) Express the ratio of the amount of oil saved to the amount of water saved in simplest form.

c) How many gallons of oil will be saved if 2 tons of paper are recycled?

d) How many gallons of water will be saved if 3 tons of paper are recycled?

e) How many gallons of oil and water will be saved if 4 tons of paper are recycled?

Check that the ratio of the amount of oil saved to the amount of water saved is __?__ : __?__ in simplest form.

1 ton of recycled paper
380 : __?__ = __?__ : __?__

2 tons of recycled paper
__?__ : 14,000 = __?__ : __?__

3 tons of recycled paper
1,140 : __?__ = __?__ : __?__

4 tons of recycled paper
__?__ : __?__ = __?__ : __?__

Practice 4.2

Express each ratio in simplest form.

1 13 : 39

2 16 : 40

3 25 : 15

4 56 : 21

5 30 : 54

6 72 : 48

7 26 cm : 4 m

8 9 kg : 36 g

9 35 min : 2 h

State whether each pair of ratios are equivalent.

10 11 : 17 and 17 : 11

11 7 : 11 and 21 : 33

12 15 : 35 and 25 : 45

13 15 : 20 and 20 : 25

14 38 : 19 and 2 : 1

15 12 : 8 and 18 : 12

Find the missing term in each pair of equivalent ratio.

16 7 : 9 = 49 : ___?___

17 12 : 5 = 144 : ___?___

18 4 : 15 = 48 : ___?___

19 7 : 13 = 77 : ___?___

20 45 : 36 = ___?___ : 12

21 30 : 48 = ___?___ : 8

22 72 : 84 = ___?___ : 7

23 121 : 88 = ___?___ : 8

Find the equivalent ratios.

24 Use multiplication to find three ratios equivalent to 8 : 12.

25 Use division to find all the whole number ratios equivalent to 168 : 56.

Copy and complete.

26 A manufacturer's instruction states that 3 cups of cleaning agent should be diluted with 5 cups of water before use. Copy and complete the table.

Amount of Cleaning Agent (cups)	3	9	12	?	?
Amount of Water (cups)	5	?	?	35	45

Find the missing term of each pair of equivalent ratio.

27 63 : 27 = 49 : ___?___

28 81 : 18 = 36 : ___?___

29 24 : 96 = 5 : ___?___

30 72 : 24 = 15 : ___?___

31 60 : 144 = ___?___ : 60

32 125 : 80 = ___?___ : 48

33 90 : 15 = ___?___ : 7

34 98 : 112 = 63 : ___?___

Solve.

35 Judy uses 5 ounces of lemonade concentrate for every 9 ounces of orange juice concentrate to make a fruit punch.

a) Find the ratio of the number of ounces of orange juice concentrate to the number of ounces of lemonade concentrate she uses.

b) If Judy uses 36 ounces of orange juice concentrate to make the fruit punch, how many ounces of lemonade concentrate does she use?

c) If Judy uses 45 ounces of lemonade concentrate to make the fruit punch, how many ounces of orange juice concentrate does she use?

36 In a science experiment, Farah mixed a salt solution and vinegar in the ratio 3 : 7.

a) If she used 262.8 milliliters of salt solution, how much vinegar did she use?

b) If 0.56 liter of vinegar was used, how much salt solution did she use?

37 A fruit seller packs different fruits into baskets of the same size. The ratio of the weight of bananas to the weight of apples to the weight of pears is the same for all the baskets. The table shows the different weights of fruits in the baskets. Copy and complete the table.

Number of Baskets	Weight of Fruits (lb)		
	Bananas	**Apples**	**Pears**
1	?	6	?
2	8	?	?
3	12	18	15

4.3 Real-World Problems: Ratios

Lesson Objective

- Solve real-world problems involving ratios.

Learn **Draw models to solve problems involving ratios.**

Megan prepares a fruit punch using apple juice and orange juice in the ratio 4 : 3.

a) If the total volume of the fruit punch is 630 milliliters, find the volume of apple juice Megan uses.

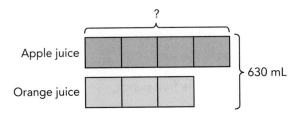

Volume of apple juice : Volume of orange juice = 4 : 3
Total volume of fruit punch = 4 + 3 = 7 units
7 units ⟶ 630 mL
1 unit ⟶ $\frac{630}{7}$ = 90 mL
4 units ⟶ 4 × 90 = 360 mL

Megan uses 360 milliliters of apple juice.

b) If Megan uses 520 milliliters of apple juice to make the fruit punch, find the volume of orange juice she uses.

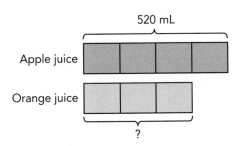

Volume of apple juice : Volume of orange juice = 4 : 3
4 units ⟶ 520 mL
1 unit ⟶ $\frac{520}{4}$ = 130 mL
3 units ⟶ 3 × 130 = 390 mL

Megan uses 390 milliliters of orange juice.

Guided Practice

Solve.

1 A box contains baseball and football cards. The number of baseball cards to the number of football cards is in the ratio 5 : 1.

a) If the total number of cards is 1,380, find the number of each type of cards.

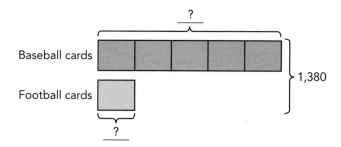

Total number of units = ___?___ + ___?___ = ___?___

___?___ units ⟶ 1,380

1 unit ⟶ $\dfrac{?}{?}$ = ___?___

The number of football cards is ___?___.

5 units ⟶ ___?___ × ___?___ = ___?___

The number of baseball cards is ___?___.

b) Suppose the number of baseball cards is 950, find the number of football cards.

950

Baseball cards

Football cards

?

___?___ units ⟶ ___?___

1 unit ⟶ $\dfrac{?}{?}$ = ___?___

The number of football cards is ___?___.

Jenny prepares a ceramic glaze mixture of feldspar, red iron oxide, and silica in the ratio 5 : 2 : 3. The mass of the mixture is 1 kg 200 g. Find the mass of each ingredient used to prepare the mixture.

1 kg 200 g = 1,200 g

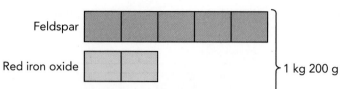

Total number of units = 5 + 2 + 3

$\qquad\qquad\qquad$ = 10

10 units $\longrightarrow$ 1,200 g

1 unit $\longrightarrow$ $\frac{1,200}{10}$ = 120 g

2 units $\longrightarrow$ 2 × 120 = 240 g

The mass of the red iron oxide is 240 grams.

3 units $\longrightarrow$ 3 × 120 = 360 g

The mass of the silica is 360 grams.

5 units $\longrightarrow$ 5 × 120 = 600 g

The mass of the feldspar is 600 grams.

Add the mass of each ingredient to check that the total is 1 kg 200 g.

240 g + 360 g + 600 g = 1,200 g or 1 kg 200 g

Guided Practice

Solve.

2 A school raised $18,000 at a charity event. The money raised was shared among three charities, A, B, and C, in the ratio 1: 2: 3. How much money did each charity receive?

Total number of units = $\underline{\quad?\quad}$ + $\underline{\quad?\quad}$ + $\underline{\quad?\quad}$

$\qquad\qquad\qquad\quad$ = $\underline{\quad?\quad}$

$\underline{\quad?\quad}$ units $\longrightarrow$ $\$\underline{\quad?\quad}$

1 unit $\longrightarrow$ $\$\frac{?}{?}$ = $\$\underline{\quad?\quad}$

A received $\$\underline{\quad?\quad}$.

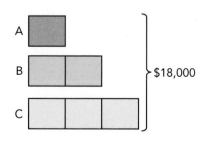

2 units $\longrightarrow$ __?__ × __?__ = $ __?__

B received $ __?__.

3 units $\longrightarrow$ __?__ × __?__ = $ __?__

C received $ __?__.

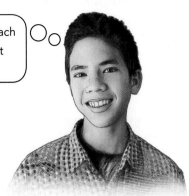

Add the amount of money each charity received to check that the total is $18,000.

3 The number of coins collected by Xavier, Yohann, and Zachary is in the ratio 2 : 5 : 8. Yohann collected 85 coins.

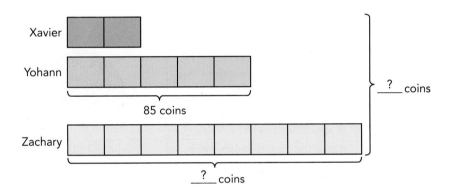

Xavier

Yohann

85 coins

Zachary

__?__ coins

__?__ coins

a) Find the number of coins Zachary collected.

5 units $\longrightarrow$ __?__ coins

1 unit $\longrightarrow$ $\dfrac{?}{?}$ = __?__ coins

__?__ units $\longrightarrow$ __?__ × __?__ = __?__ coins

Zachary collected __?__ coins.

b) Find the number of coins collected by the three boys altogether.

Total number of units = __?__ + __?__ + __?__

= __?__

__?__ units $\longrightarrow$ __?__ × __?__ = __?__ coins

The three boys collected __?__ coins altogether.

The ratio of the number of CDs Brad has to the number of CDs Keith has is 2 : 3.
The ratio of the number of CDs Keith has to the number of CDs Simone has is 6 : 11.
Brad has 24 CDs. How many CDs do Keith and Simone have altogether?

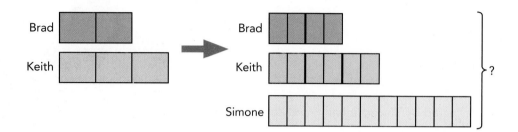

Brad : Keith = 2 : 3   Keith : Simone = 6 : 11

×2   ×2

= 4 : 6

> Use equivalent ratios to rewrite 2 : 3 as 4 : 6. Then the term that represents Keith's CDs is the same in the ratio that compares Brad's CDs to Keith's CDs as it is in the ratio that compares Keith's CDs to Simone's CDs.

So, Brad : Keith : Simone = 4 : 6 : 11.

Method 1

4 units ⟶ 24 CDs

1 unit ⟶ $\frac{24}{4}$ = 6 CDs

6 units ⟶ 6 × 6 = 36 CDs

Keith has 36 CDs.

11 units ⟶ 11 × 6 = 66 CDs
Simone has 66 CDs.

36 + 66 = 102
The total number of CDs Keith and Simone have is 102.

Method 2

Total number of units Keith and Simone have = 6 + 11
                                            = 17

4 units ⟶ 24 CDs

1 unit ⟶ $\frac{24}{4}$ = 6 CDs

17 units ⟶ 17 × 6 = 102 CDs

The total number of CDs Keith and Simone have is 102.

Guided Practice

Solve.

4 At Stacey's middle school, students either ride bikes to school, walk, or take a bus. The ratio of the number of students who ride bikes to the number who walk is 3 : 4. The ratio of the number of students who walk to the number who take a bus is 12 : 7. There are 560 students in all.

a) Find the number of students who ride bikes to school.

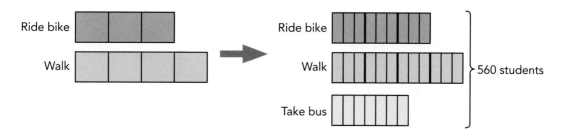

Ride bike : Walk = ___?___ : 4   Walk : Take bus = 12 : ___?___

× ___?___   × ___?___

= ___?___ : ___?___

So, Ride bike : Walk : Take bus = ___?___ : ___?___ : ___?___ .

Total number of units = ___?___ + ___?___ + ___?___

= ___?___

___?___ units ⟶ 560 students

1 unit ⟶ $\frac{?}{?}$ = ___?___ students

9 units ⟶ ___?___ × ___?___ = ___?___ students

The number of students who ride bikes is ___?___ .

b) Find the number of students who walk to school.

___?___ units ⟶ ___?___ × ___?___ = ___?___ students

The number of students who walk is ___?___ .

c) Find the number of students who take a bus to school.

___?___ units ⟶ ___?___ × ___?___ = ___?___ students

The number of students who take a bus is ___?___ .

Draw models to solve before-and-after problems.

Sam had some U.S. and foreign stamps. The ratio of the number of U.S. stamps to the number of foreign stamps was 3 : 4. He bought 21 more U.S. stamps and the ratio became 9 : 8.

Before

The ratio of the number of U.S. stamps to the number of foreign stamps was 3 : 4.

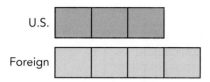

After

The ratio of the number of U.S. stamps to the number of foreign stamps became 9 : 8.

The length of the model for foreign stamps does not change. The model for foreign stamps is divided into 8 units.

The model for U.S. stamps is divided into units of the same size and additional units are added to make the total length 9 units.

The additional units represent the 21 additional stamps Sam bought.

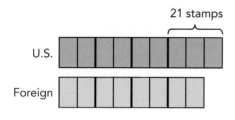

There is no change in the number of foreign stamps.

a) How many foreign stamps did Sam have?

3 units ⟶ 21 stamps

1 unit ⟶ $\frac{21}{3}$ = 7 stamps

8 units ⟶ 8 × 7 = 56 stamps

Sam had 56 foreign stamps.

b) How many U.S. stamps did Sam have in the end?

9 units ⟶ 9 × 7 = 63 stamps

Sam had 63 U.S. stamps in the end.

Guided Practice

Solve.

5 Claire keeps some green and red plates in a cabinet. The ratio of the number of green plates to the number of red plates is 2 : 1. She adds 18 more red plates in the cabinet and the ratio becomes 4 : 5.

Before

The ratio of the number of green plates to the number of red plates is
__?__ : __?__.

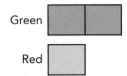

After

The ratio of the number of green plates to the number of red plates becomes
__?__ : __?__.

The length of the model for __?__ plates does not change. The model for __?__ plates is divided into __?__ units.

The model for red plates is divided into units of the same size and additional units are added to make the total length __?__ units.

The additional units represent the __?__ red plates Claire adds in the cabinet.

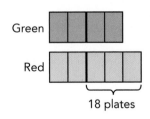

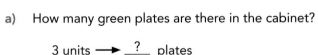
18 plates

> There is no change in the number of green plates.

a) How many green plates are there in the cabinet?

$$3 \text{ units} \longrightarrow \underline{\quad?\quad} \text{ plates}$$

$$1 \text{ unit} \longrightarrow \frac{?}{?} = \underline{\quad?\quad} \text{ plates}$$

$$\underline{\quad?\quad} \text{ units} \longrightarrow \underline{\quad?\quad} \times \underline{\quad?\quad} = \underline{\quad?\quad} \text{ plates}$$

There are __?__ green plates in the cabinet.

b) How many red plates are there in the cabinet in the end?

$$\underline{\quad?\quad} \text{ units} \longrightarrow \underline{\quad?\quad} \times \underline{\quad?\quad} = \underline{\quad?\quad} \text{ plates}$$

There are __?__ red plates in the cabinet in the end.

Practice 4.3

Solve. Show your work.

1 A rope is cut into three pieces P, Q, and R. The lengths of the pieces are in the ratio 3 : 5 : 7. If the rope is 33 feet 9 inches long, find the lengths of P, Q, and R.

2 Alice, Bernice, and Cheryl shared some stamps in the ratio 8 : 9 : 18. Alice received 184 stamps. Find the number of stamps that Bernice and Cheryl each received.

3 Alan, Gil, and Deb's point score in a video game was in the ratio 2 : 3 : 4. Deb scored 114,400 points.

  a) How many points did Gil score?

  b) How many points did they score in all?

4 Lara has three cats: Socks, Princess, and Luna. The ratio of Socks's weight to Princess's weight is 4 : 5. The ratio of Princess's weight to Luna's weight is 6 : 7. What is the ratio of Socks's weight to Luna's weight?

5 Danny poured 78 liters of water into containers X, Y, and Z. The ratio of the volume of water in Container X to the volume of water in Container Y is 5 : 2. The ratio of the volume of water in Container Y to the volume of water in Container Z is 8 : 11.

  a) How much water was poured into Container X?

  b) How much more water was poured into Container X than Container Z?

6 The ratio of the number of mystery books to the number of science fiction books is 4 : 3. The ratio of the number of science fiction books to the number of biographies is 4 : 5. If there are 48 science fiction books, find the total number of books.

7 In a music room, the ratio of the number of clarinets to the number of flutes was 3 : 4. After the school bought another 24 flutes, the ratio became 3 : 8. How many clarinets were there in the music room?

8 In a school gym, the ratio of the number of boys to the number of girls was 4 : 3. After 160 boys left the gym, the ratio became 4 : 5. How many girls were there in the gym?

9 The ratio of the number of men to the number of women on a bus was 2 : 3. At a bus stop, 4 women got off and the ratio became 4 : 5.

a) How many men were on the bus?

b) How many women were on the bus in the end?

10 The number of chickens to the number of ducks on a farm was 6 : 5. After 63 ducks were sold, there were 3 times as many chickens as ducks left.

a) How many chickens were there on the farm?

b) How many chickens and ducks were there altogether on the farm in the end?

11 The ratio of the volume of fruit juice to the volume of smoothies served at a party was $4\frac{1}{2}$: 2.4. There were 35 liters more fruit juice served than smoothies. Find the volume of smoothies served.

12 A piece of ribbon is cut into two shorter pieces in the ratio 2.8 : 1.25. The difference in the length of the two shorter pieces is 80.6 centimeters. What is the length of the original piece of ribbon?

13 *Math Journal* The ratio of the number of beads collected by Jane to the number of beads collected by Jill is 7 : 3. Jane gave some beads to Jill. Is it possible for both Jane and Jill to have the same number of beads after Jane gave some beads to Jill? Explain why you think so.

14 Today the ratio of Elinor's age to her mother's age is 3 : 8. After 15 years, the ratio will become 6 : 11.

a) Find Elinor's age today.

b) Find her mother's age after 15 years.

15 The ratio of Mike's savings to Nick's savings was 4 : 3. After Mike saved another $120 and Nick saved another $60, the ratio became 8 : 5. What was their combined savings before each of them saved the additional money?

Brain @ Work

1   *ABCD* is a rectangle. *BD* is a straight line that cuts the rectangle into equal halves. The ratio of the area of P to the area of Q is 2 : 5, and the ratio of the area R to the area of S is 4 : 3. The area of S is 9 square centimeters.

a)   Find the ratio of the area of R to the area of the rectangle.

b)   Find the area of the rectangle.

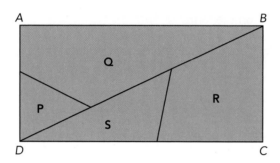

2   A farmer raises chickens and sheep on his farm. The ratio of the total number of legs of the chickens to the total number of legs of the sheep is 4 : 7.
Find the minimum number of chickens and sheep on his farm.
Copy and complete the table to solve the problem.
(Hint: Make a list and solve the problem using guess and check.)

Number of Chickens	Number of Legs of Chickens	Number of Sheep	Number of Legs of Sheep	Number of Legs of Chickens : Number of Legs of Sheep
1	2	1	4	2 : 4 = 1 : 2
?	?	?	?	?
?	?	?	?	?

Chapter Wrap Up

Concept Map

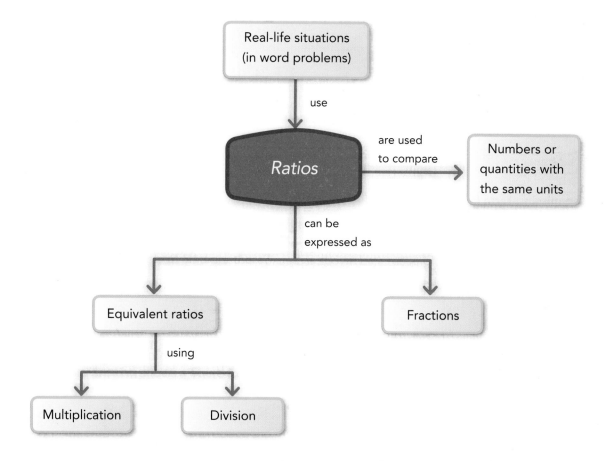

Key Concepts

▶ A ratio compares two or more numbers or quantities.

▶ When two quantities have the same units, you can compare them using a ratio without units.

▶ The ratio of two numbers, such as 3 and 4, can be written in three ways:
3 to 4, 3 : 4, or $\frac{3}{4}$.

▶ A ratio can be expressed as another equivalent ratio by
  • multiplying the terms of the ratio by the same multiplying factor.
  • dividing the terms of the ratio by a common factor.

▶ Given two equivalent ratios, you can find an unknown term given the other three terms.

Chapter Review/Test

Concepts and Skills

Write each ratio in simplest form.

1 8 : 24

2 36 : 9

3 6 : 20

4 24 : 15

5 14 : 49

6 45 : 30

7 27 : 72

8 64 : 56

Find the missing term in each pair of equivalent ratios.

9 1 : 3 = 6 : ___?___

10 4 : 7 = ___?___ : 21

11 25 : 15 = ___?___ : 3

12 54 : 36 = 18 : ___?___

13 4 : ___?___ = 20 : 25

14 ___?___ : 9 = 48 : 72

15 28 : ___?___ = 4 : 6

16 ___?___ : 36 = 21 : 12

Problem Solving

Solve. Show your work.

17 The city has 28 fire engines and 36 fire trucks. Find the ratio of the number of fire engines to the number of fire trucks in simplest form.

18 Of the 80 students who signed up for after school clubs, 16 students signed up for the art club, and the rest signed up for other clubs. Find the ratio of the number of students who signed up for the art club to the number of students who signed up for other clubs. Give your answer in simplest form.

19 On Saturday, Alison used her cell phone for 36 minutes. On Sunday, she used her cell phone for 18 minutes more than on Saturday. Find the ratio of the number of minutes Alison used on Saturday to the total number of minutes on Saturday and Sunday. Give your answer in simplest form.

20 Daniel is 12 years old. Elliot is 15 years older than Daniel. Frank is 3 years younger than Elliot. Find the ratio of Daniel's age to Frank's age. Give your answer in simplest form.

21 The ratio of the number of left-handed batters to the number of right-handed batters is 5 : 8. There are 45 left-handed batters.

a) How many right-handed batters are there?

b) Find the ratio of the number of left-handed batters to the total number of batters. Give your answer in simplest form.

22 Mrs. Johnson gave a sum of money to her son and daughter in the ratio 5 : 6. Her daughter received $2,400. How much did Mrs. Johnson give away in all?

23 The ratio of the number of boys to the number of girls in a school is 5 : 7. If there are 600 students in the school, how many girls are there?

24 The murals in a school are painted by its grade 6 and grade 7 students. The number of mural painters from grade 6 and the number of mural painters from grade 7 is the same for each mural in the school. Copy and complete the table.

Number of Murals	Number of Grade 6 Students	Number of Grade 7 Students
1	5	?
2	?	14
3	15	21
4	?	?

25 A sum of money was shared among Aaron, Ben, and Charles in the ratio 2 : 5 : 7. If Charles's share was $1,180 more than Aaron's share, what was the original sum of money shared?

26 The ratio of the number of beads Karen had to the number of beads Patricia had was 2 : 5. After Patricia bought another 75 beads, the ratio became 4 : 15. How many beads did each girl have at first?

27 Mr. Young had some bottles of apple juice and orange juice. The ratio of the number of bottles of apple juice to the number of bottles of orange juice was 3 : 2. After he sold 64 bottles of apple juice, the ratio became 1 : 6. How many bottles of apple juice and orange juice did Mr. Young have altogether in the end?

Rates

Who is the better goal scorer?

Soccer is one of the world's most popular sports. People everywhere have opinions about who are the best players.

Look at the illustration below. Assume that Player 29 scored 15 goals in 10 matches and Player 11 scored 25 goals in 20 matches. Which of the two players do you think is a better goal scorer?

One way to decide is to find and compare the number of goals scored per match by each of the two players. The number of goals per match is an example of a rate.

In this chapter, you will learn about applications of rates in the real world. Some rates you may have seen before include unit prices for food and gas, postal rates, and parking fees.

BIG IDEA

▶ You can use a rate to compare one quantity to another quantity, and use rates to solve problems.

Recall Prior Knowledge

Multiplying whole numbers

Find 324 × 72.

$$\begin{array}{r} \overset{1\ 2}{3}2\,4 \\ \times\quad 7\,2 \\ \hline 6\,4\,8 \\ 2\,2{,}6\,8\,0 \\ \hline 2\,3{,}3\,2\,8 \end{array}$$

324 × 2 = 648
324 × 70 = 22,680

☑ Quick Check

Multiply.

1 268 × 13

2 54 × 471

3 532 × 48

4 75 × 698

Multiplying fractions or mixed numbers by a whole number

$\dfrac{2}{15} \times 3 = \dfrac{2}{15 \div 3} \times (3 \div 3)$ Divide the denominator of the fraction and the whole number by the common factor, 3.

$\qquad\quad = \dfrac{2}{5} \times 1$ Multiply.

$\qquad\quad = \dfrac{2}{5}$

$2\dfrac{3}{5} \times 4 = \dfrac{13}{5} \times 4$ Express the mixed number as an improper fraction.

$\qquad\quad = \dfrac{52}{5}$ Multiply.

$\qquad\quad = 10\dfrac{2}{5}$ Express the improper fraction as a mixed number.

☑ Quick Check

Find each product. Express the product in simplest form.

5 $4 \times \dfrac{5}{32}$

6 $\dfrac{7}{12} \times 36$

7 $3\dfrac{2}{7} \times 5$

8 $9\dfrac{1}{2} \times 8$

Multiplying fractions

$\dfrac{4}{9} \times \dfrac{3}{16} = \dfrac{4 \div 4}{9} \times \dfrac{3}{16 \div 4}$ Divide a numerator and a denominator by the common factor, 4.

$= \dfrac{1}{9 \div 3} \times \dfrac{3 \div 3}{4}$ Divide a numerator and a denominator by the common factor, 3.

$= \dfrac{1}{3} \times \dfrac{1}{4}$ Multiply.

$= \dfrac{1}{12}$

✓ Quick Check

Find each product. Express the product in simplest form.

9 $\dfrac{2}{7} \times \dfrac{63}{84}$

10 $\dfrac{11}{18} \times \dfrac{3}{44}$

Dividing with fractions and whole numbers

$\dfrac{3}{4} \div 27 = \dfrac{3}{4} \times \dfrac{1}{27}$ Rewrite using the reciprocal of the divisor.

$= \dfrac{3 \div 3}{4} \times \dfrac{1}{27 \div 3}$ Divide a numerator and a denominator by the common factor, 3.

$= \dfrac{1}{4} \times \dfrac{1}{9}$ Multiply.

$= \dfrac{1}{36}$

✓ Quick Check

Find each quotient. Express the quotient in simplest form.

11 $\dfrac{6}{7} \div 30$

12 $72 \div \dfrac{9}{10}$

13 $\dfrac{7}{9} \div 49$

14 $56 \div \dfrac{8}{11}$

Dividing fractions

$$\frac{5}{8} \div \frac{35}{72} = \frac{5}{8} \times \frac{72}{35}$$ Rewrite using the reciprocal of the divisor.

$$= \frac{5 \div 5}{8} \times \frac{72}{35 \div 5}$$ Divide a numerator and a denominator by the common factor, 5.

$$= \frac{1}{8 \div 8} \times \frac{72 \div 8}{7}$$ Divide a numerator and a denominator by the common factor, 8.

$$= \frac{1}{1} \times \frac{9}{7}$$ Multiply.

$$= \frac{9}{7}$$ Express the improper fraction as a mixed number.

$$= 1\frac{2}{7}$$

✔ Quick Check

Find each quotient. Express the quotient in simplest form.

15 $\dfrac{4}{9} \div \dfrac{36}{135}$

16 $\dfrac{77}{92} \div \dfrac{11}{42}$

Finding the quantity represented by a number of units

If 4 units represent 132 centimeters, find the value of 9 units.

4 units ⟶ 132 cm

1 unit ⟶ $\dfrac{132}{4}$ = 33 cm

9 units ⟶ 9 × 33 = 297 cm

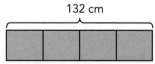

132 cm

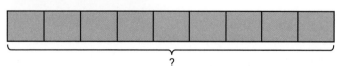

?

✔ Quick Check

Find the value of each set.

17   If 7 units represent 98 liters, find the value of 15 units.

18   If 13 units represent 143 square meters, find the value of 24 units.

Finding ratios

You can use a ratio to compare two quantities expressed as the same unit.

Find the ratio of length 47 centimeters to 2 meters.

$$47 \text{ cm} : 2 \text{ m}$$
$$= 47 \text{ cm} : 200 \text{ cm}$$
$$= \quad 47 : 200$$

cm and m are different units.
Express 2 m as 200 cm.

This ratio can be expressed in three ways:

47 : 200, 47 to 200, and $\dfrac{47}{200}$.

When you divide or multiply the terms of a ratio by the same number, you obtain equivalent ratios.

12 : 18, 6 : 9, and 2 : 3 are equivalent ratios.
2 : 3 is in simplest form.

6 : 7, 12 : 14, and 18 : 21 are equivalent ratios.
6 : 7 is in simplest form.

☑ Quick Check

Express each ratio in simplest form.

19 4 km : 370 m

20 66 L : 120 mL

21 15 in. : 5 ft

22 270 qt : 105 gal

Find two ratios equivalent to each ratio.

23 4 : 9

24 5 : 13

5.1 Rates and Unit Rates

Lesson Objective

- Solve unit rate problems including unit pricing and constant speed.

Learn — **Meaning of rates**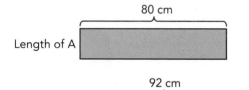

You can use a ratio to compare two quantities that have the same units.

A is 80 centimeters long. B is 92 centimeters long.
A and B are two lengths with the same unit.

80 cm

Length of A

The ratio of the length of A to the length of B is 80 : 92 or 40 : 46 or 20 : 23.

92 cm

Length of B

There is no need to include units in the ratio of the lengths because the units are the same.

You can use a rate to compare two quantities with different units, such as money and time.

For example, if Sarah earns $23 in one hour, you can use the rate $23 per hour, or $\frac{\$23}{1\text{ hour}}$ to describe how much money she earns in one hour.

This rate can also be written as $23/h.

The rate $23/h is an example of a unit rate. A **unit rate** compares a quantity to one unit of a different quantity.

$23 per hour means $23 for each hour.

Math Note

The symbol / means *per*.

Guided Practice

State whether each statement is expressed as a unit rate.

1 A monkey plucked 4 coconuts per minute.

2 Mary paid $2 for a bottle of orange juice.

3 A basketball team scored 294 points in 6 games.

4 Douglas reads 3 books in a week.

Learn **Express and compute unit rates in terms of time and other quantities.**

Nick fills 24 bottles in 8 minutes. At what rate are the bottles being filled with water?

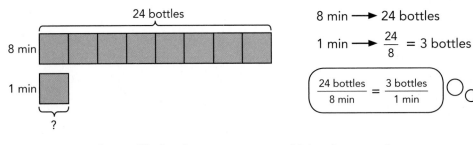

8 min ⟶ 24 bottles

1 min ⟶ $\frac{24}{8}$ = 3 bottles

$$\frac{24 \text{ bottles}}{8 \text{ min}} = \frac{3 \text{ bottles}}{1 \text{ min}}$$

The bottles are being filled with water at a rate of 3 bottles per minute.

Guided Practice

Solve.

5 A photocopy machine can print 405 copies in 9 minutes. What is the rate at which the machine prints the copies?

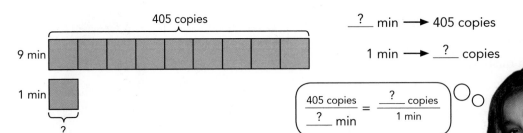

___?___ min ⟶ 405 copies

1 min ⟶ ___?___ copies

$$\frac{405 \text{ copies}}{\underline{\;?\;} \text{ min}} = \frac{\underline{\;?\;} \text{ copies}}{1 \text{ min}}$$

The machine prints the copies at a rate of ___?___ copies per ___?___ .

Learn Find a unit rate.

A school buys 2.75 acres of land for a new athletic field. What is the cost per acre if the school pays $275,000 for the land?

Cost per acre = Total cost ÷ Total number of acres

$= \$275,000 \div 2.75$

$= \$\dfrac{275,000}{2.75}$

$= \$\dfrac{27,500,000}{275}$

$= \$100,000$

> **Math Note**
>
> Multiply both the numerator and denominator of the fraction by the same number to make the divisor a whole number.

The unit cost of the piece of land is $100,000 per acre.

Guided Practice

Solve.

6 A sports center buys 1.25 acres of land for a new swimming complex. What is the cost per acre if the sports center pays $100,000 for the land?

Cost per acre = Total cost ÷ Total number of acres

$= \$100,000 \div \underline{\ ?\ }$

$= \$\dfrac{100,000}{?}$

$= \$\dfrac{?}{?}$

$= \$\underline{\ ?\ }$

The unit cost of the piece of land is $\underline{\ ?\ }$ per acre.

7 A few years ago, when the fuel tank in Sally's car was completely empty, she paid $63 to fill the tank with 22.5 gallons of gasoline. What was the cost per gallon?

Cost per gallon = Cost of gasoline ÷ Volume of gasoline filled

$= \$\underline{\ ?\ } \div \underline{\ ?\ }$

$= \$\underline{\ ?\ }$

The unit cost of the gasoline was $\underline{\ ?\ }$ per gallon.

The table shows the costs of some fruits purchased at a farm stand.

Type of Fruit	Amount Purchased	Amount Paid	Cost Per Pound
Mango	2.00 lb	$2.60	?
Pear	2.50 lb	$3.50	?
Orange	2.25 lb	$2.70	?

Which fruit costs the most per pound?

To find out which fruit costs the most per pound, you can divide to find the unit cost for each fruit.

Cost of mangoes per pound = Cost of mangoes ÷ Weight of mangoes
= $2.60 ÷ 2
= $1.30

The unit cost of the mangoes is $1.30 per pound.

Cost of pears per pound = Cost of pears ÷ Weight of pears
= $3.50 ÷ 2.5
= $1.40

The unit cost of the pears is $1.40 per pound.

Cost of oranges per pound = Cost of oranges ÷ Weight of oranges
= $2.70 ÷ 2.25
= $1.20

The unit cost of the oranges is $1.20 per pound.

Comparing the unit costs of the three types of fruits, the unit cost of the pears is the greatest.

Unit cost of oranges < Unit cost of mangoes < Unit cost of pears
$1.20   < $1.30   < $1.40

So, the pears cost the most per pound.

Guided Practice

Solve.

 The table shows the costs of some food items Billy bought from a supermarket.

Type of Food	Amount Purchased	Amount Paid	Cost Per Pound
Potatoes	5 lb	$4.00	?
Carrots	5 lb	$3.00	?
Onions	2 lb	$2.50	?

Which type of food costs the most per pound?

Cost of potatoes per pound = Cost of potatoes ÷ Weight of potatoes

$$= \$ \underline{} \div \underline{}$$

$$= \$ \underline{}$$

The unit cost of the potatoes is $ \underline{} per pound.

Cost of carrots per pound = Cost of carrots ÷ Weight of carrots

$$= \$ \underline{} \div \underline{}$$

$$= \$ \underline{}$$

The unit cost of the carrots is $ \underline{} per pound.

Cost of onions per pound = Cost of onions ÷ Weight of onions

$$= \$ \underline{} \div \underline{}$$

$$= \$ \underline{}$$

The unit cost of the onions is $ \underline{} per pound.

Comparing the unit costs of the food items, the unit cost of the $\underline{}$ is the greatest.

Unit cost of $\underline{}$ < Unit cost of $\underline{}$ < Unit cost of $\underline{}$

$ $\underline{}$ < $ $\underline{}$ < $ $\underline{}$

So, the $\underline{}$ cost the most per pound.

Learn **Find the speed or rate of travel of a moving object.**

Speed is a rate that compares distance traveled to the time taken to travel that distance.
It is defined as the distance traveled per unit time.

$$\text{Speed} = \frac{\text{Distance}}{\text{Time}}$$

Look at the example.

Daryl rode from Town A to Town B.
In 1 hour, he rode 40 miles.
Gavin also drove in the same direction.
In 1 hour, he drove 50 miles.

> Daryl rode at a speed of 40 miles per hour.
>
> Gavin drove at a speed of 50 miles per hour.

....

a) A car traveled a distance of 120 miles in 2 hours. Find the speed of the car.

Method 1

```
        120 mi
      ┌─────────┐
2 h   │    │    │
      └────┴────┘
1 h   │    │
      └────┘
        ?
```

2 h ⟶ 120 mi

1 h ⟶ $\frac{120}{2}$ = 60 mi

The speed of the car was 60 miles per hour.

Method 2

$$\text{Speed} = \frac{\text{Distance}}{\text{Time}}$$
$$= \frac{120}{2}$$
$$= 60 \text{ mi/h}$$

> $\frac{120 \text{ mi}}{2 \text{ h}} = \frac{60 \text{ mi}}{1 \text{ h}}$

The speed of the car was 60 miles per hour.

b) Joyce is climbing up a steep trail. She climbs $\frac{3}{4}$ mile in $\frac{1}{2}$ hour.

Find her climbing speed in miles per hour.

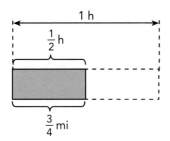

$$\text{Speed} = \text{Distance} \div \text{Time}$$
$$= \frac{3}{4} \div \frac{1}{2}$$
$$= \frac{3}{4} \times 2$$
$$= 1\frac{1}{2} \text{ mi/h}$$

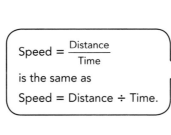

Speed $= \dfrac{\text{Distance}}{\text{Time}}$

is the same as

Speed = Distance ÷ Time.

Joyce's climbing speed is $1\frac{1}{2}$ miles per hour.

Guided Practice

Solve.

9 A truck traveled a distance of 280 kilometers in 4 hours. Find the speed of the truck.

Method 1

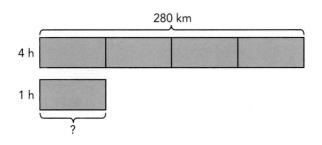

4 h ⟶ __?__ km

1 h ⟶ $\dfrac{?}{?}$ = __?__ km

The speed of the truck is __?__ kilometers per hour.

Method 2

Speed of truck $= \dfrac{\text{Distance}}{\text{Time}}$

$= \dfrac{?}{?}$

$=$ __?__ km/h

The speed of the truck is __?__ kilometers per hour.

10 A car travels $\frac{1}{4}$ kilometer in $\frac{1}{2}$ minute. Find the speed of the car in kilometers per minute.

Solve. Show your work.

1 A machine can print 300 T-shirts in 10 minutes. How many T-shirts can the machine print in 1 minute?

2 Alisa types 900 words in 20 minutes. What is her typing speed in words per minute?

3 A 2-liter bottle is filled completely with water from a faucet in 10 seconds. How much water is filled into the bottle each second?

4 Bill is paid $200 for 5 days of work. How much is he paid per day?

5 Janice swims 450 meters in 5 minutes. Find her swimming speed in meters per minute.

6 A garden snail moves $\frac{1}{6}$ foot in $\frac{1}{3}$ hour. Find the speed of the snail in feet per hour.

7 *Math Journal* A plumber pays $3.60 for 60 centimeters of pipe. Explain how the plumber can use the unit cost of the pipe to find the cost of buying 100 meters of the same kind of pipe. Show the calculations the plumber needs to make.

8 Rovan can make 48 tarts per hour. Copy and complete the table.

Number of Hours	Number of Tarts
1	48
2	?
3	?
4	?
5	?
6	?

a) At this rate, how many tarts can Rovan make in 6 hours?

b) At this rate, how long will she take to make 120 tarts?

9 A sprinkler system is designed to water $\frac{5}{8}$ acre of land in $\frac{1}{4}$ hour. How many acres of land can it water in 1 hour?

10 The table shows the costs of three types of meat John bought at a supermarket. Copy and complete the table.

Type of Meat	Amount Purchased	Amount Paid	Cost Per Pound
Beef	2.0 lb	$7.20	?
Pork	2.5 lb	$8.10	?
Chicken	3.5 lb	$9.80	?

Which type of meat costs the least per pound?

11 *Math Journal* The table shows the data about distances and times for three sprinters.

Sprinter	Distance Ran	Time Taken
Sebastian	60 m	6.34 s
Steve	100 m	10.23 s
Smith	150 m	14.98 s

Who is the fastest sprinter? Justify your answer.

12 A supermarket sells the three brands of rice shown in the table below.

Brand	Mass of Rice	Price
A	500 g	$1.20
B	5 kg	$9.80
C	10 kg	$18.90

Raimondo wants to buy 30 kilograms of rice.

a) Which brand of rice should he buy to get the best deal, assuming that all three brands are of the same quality?

b) How much will he save if he buys the cheapest brand of rice as compared to the most expensive one?

Real-World Problems: Rates and Unit Rates

Lesson Objective

- Solve problems involving rates and unit rates.

Vocabulary

average speed

Learn **Solve simple word problems involving rates and unit rates.**

A machine can pack 70 boxes of spaghetti in 5 minutes.
At this rate, how many boxes of spaghetti can it pack in 8 minutes?

The machine can pack the same number of boxes every minute.

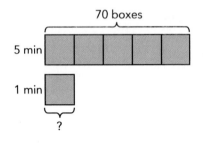

$$5 \text{ min} \longrightarrow 70 \text{ boxes}$$

$$1 \text{ min} \longrightarrow \frac{70}{5} = 14 \text{ boxes}$$

The unit rate is 14 boxes per minute.

The machine can pack 14 boxes of spaghetti in 1 minute.

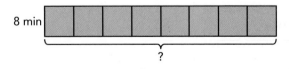

$$8 \text{ min} \longrightarrow 8 \times 14 = 112 \text{ boxes}$$

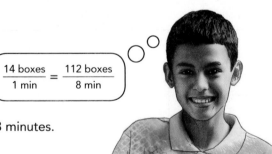

$$\frac{14 \text{ boxes}}{1 \text{ min}} = \frac{112 \text{ boxes}}{8 \text{ min}}$$

The machine can pack 112 boxes of spaghetti in 8 minutes.

Guided Practice

Solve.

1 A unicycle wheel makes 196 revolutions in 7 minutes.

a) At this rate, how many revolutions does it make in 1 minute?

The unicycle wheel makes the same number of revolutions every minute.

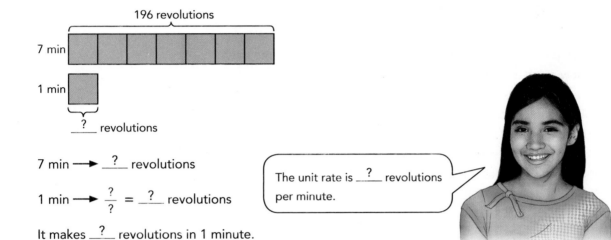

7 min ⟶ __?__ revolutions

1 min ⟶ $\dfrac{?}{?}$ = __?__ revolutions

The unit rate is __?__ revolutions per minute.

It makes __?__ revolutions in 1 minute.

b) At this rate, how many revolutions does the unicycle wheel make in 15 minutes?

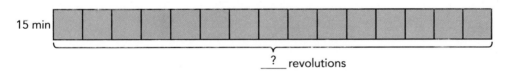

__?__ revolutions

__?__ min ⟶ __?__ × __?__ = __?__ revolutions

The unicycle makes __?__ revolutions in 15 minutes.

2 Megan babysits for 5 hours and earns $60.

a) At this rate, how much does she earn in 1 hour?

__?__ hours ⟶ $__?__

1 hour ⟶ $__?__ ÷ __?__ = $__?__

She earns $ __?__ in 1 hour.

b) At this rate, how much will Megan earn if she babysits for 14 hours?

14 hours ⟶ __?__ × $__?__ = $__?__

Megan will earn $__?__ if she babysits for 14 hours.

Read a table to find the information to solve multi-step rate problems.

The table shows the fees at a parking lot.

First Hour	Free
Second Hour	$1.75
After the Second Hour	$2.50 per hour

Ben parked his car there from 9 A.M. to 2 P.M. on the same day. How much did he pay for parking?

Total number of hours = 5 h
Parking fee for first hour = $0
Parking fee for second hour = $1.75
Parking fee for last three hours = 3 × $2.50
$$= \$7.50$$

Total parking fee = $0 + $1.75 + $7.50
$$= \$9.25$$

Ben paid $9.25 for parking.

Guided Practice

Solve.

3 The table shows the charges for renting a bicycle.

Tom rented a bicycle from 10 A.M. to 2 P.M. ON the same day. How much did he pay for renting the bicycle?

First Hour	$3.00
For Every Additional $\frac{1}{2}$ Hour	$2.50

Total number of hours = ___?___ h

Charge for first hour = $___?___

Charge for each additional 1 hour = 2 × Cost for each additional $\frac{1}{2}$ hour

$$= 2 \times \$\underline{\quad?\quad}$$

$$= \$\underline{\quad?\quad}$$

Charge for last three hours = ___?___ × $___?___

$$= \$\underline{\quad?\quad}$$

Total charge = $___?___ + $___?___

$$= \$\underline{\quad?\quad}$$

Tom paid $___?___ for renting the bicycle.

Learn **Solve multi-step word problems involving comparison of unit rates.**

Andy needs new batteries for his video game controller. He is trying to decide between two brands.

A package of two Brand A batteries costs $3.20. The manufacturer claims the batteries will last for 20 hours.

A package of two Brand B batteries cost $2.80. The manufacturer claims the batteries will last for 14 hours.

Which battery should Andy buy? Explain why you think so.

First, find the number of hours of battery time Andy will get per dollar.

Brand A:

$3.20 $\longrightarrow$ 20 h

$1 $\longrightarrow$ $\dfrac{20}{3.20}$ = 6.25 h

Andy will get 6.25 hours of battery time per dollar.

Brand B:

$2.80 $\longrightarrow$ 14 h

$1 $\longrightarrow$ $\dfrac{14}{2.80}$ = 5 h

Andy will get 5 hours of battery time per dollar.

With Brand A, Andy gets 6.25 hours of battery time per dollar. With Brand B, he gets 5 hours of battery time per dollar. Because 6.25 hours > 5 hours, Brand A is a better buy, and he should buy Brand A.

Guided Practice

Solve.

4 Chloe scored 87 points in 5 basketball games, and Fiona scored 45 points in 2 basketball games. Which of the two players scored more points per game? Explain.

Chloe:

5 games $\longrightarrow$ __?__ points

1 game $\longrightarrow$ __?__ ÷ 5 = __?__ points

Chloe scored __?__ points per game.

Fiona:

2 games $\longrightarrow$ __?__ points

1 game $\longrightarrow$ __?__ ÷ __?__ = __?__ points

Fiona scored __?__ points per game.

Comparing the number of points each player scored per game, __?__ scored a higher number of points per game.

So, __?__ scored more points per game.

Mr. Anthony drives his truck at a speed of 45 kilometers per hour .

a) At this speed, how far does he travel in 2 hours?

In 1 hour, Mr. Anthony travels 45 kilometers.

In 2 hours, Mr. Anthony travels 45 × 2 = 90 kilometers.

b) At this speed, how far does he travel in 5 hours?

In 5 hours, Mr. Anthony travels **45 × 5 = 225 kilometers.**

Speed　Time　Distance

Distance = Speed × Time

D

S　T

D = S × T

Math Note

The formula relating distance, speed, and time is often written as:

Distance = Rate × Time

A racing car can travel at a speed of 175 kilometers per hour. How far can the racing car travel in 3 hours?

Method 1

1 h ⟶ 175 km
3 h ⟶ 3 × 175 = 525 km

The racing car can travel 525 kilometers in 3 hours.

Method 2

Distance = Speed × Time
       = 175 × 3
       = 525 km

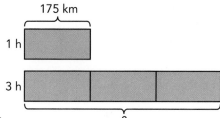

Speed = 175 km/h
Time = 3 h

The racing car can travel 525 kilometers in 3 hours.

Guided Practice

Solve.

5 A high-speed train can travel at a speed of 65 meters per second. How far can the train travel in 2 seconds?

Method 1

1 s ⟶ __?__ m

__?__ s ⟶ __?__ × __?__ = __?__ m

The train can travel __?__ meters in 2 seconds.

Method 2

Distance = Speed × Time
       = __?__ × __?__
       = __?__ m

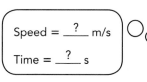

Speed = __?__ m/s
Time = __?__ s

The train can travel __?__ meters in 2 seconds.

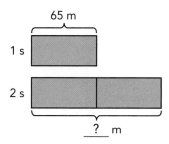

L^{earn} **Find the time given the distance and speed.**

Lucas ran round a field at a speed of 8 meters per second. How long did he take to run a distance of 96 meters?

Method 1

8 m ⟶ 1 s

96 m ⟶ $\frac{96}{8}$ = 12 s

Lucas took 12 seconds to run 96 meters.

Method 2

Time = Distance ÷ Speed

= 96 ÷ 8

= 12 s

Lucas took 12 seconds to run 96 meters.

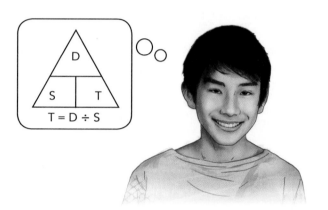

Guided Practice

Solve.

6 The distance between City X and City Y is 216 kilometers. Mr. Thomas rides his motorcycle at a speed of 54 kilometers per hour. How long does he take to travel from City X to City Y?

Method 1

_?_ km ⟶ _?_ h

_?_ km ⟶ $\frac{?}{?}$ = _?_ h

Mr. Thomas takes _?_ hours to travel from City X to City Y.

Method 2

Time = Distance ÷ Speed

= _?_ ÷ _?_

= _?_ h

Mr. Thomas takes _?_ hours to travel from City X to City Y.

Distance = _?_ km

Speed = _?_ km/h

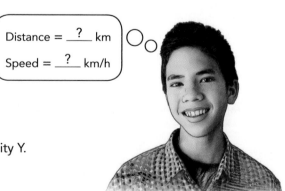

Learn **Find average speed to solve real-world problems.**

The speed that an object is traveling over a distance may not be the same all the time. For example, a bicycle might speed up or slow down as it travels between two points over a given amount of time. You can use an average speed to describe how fast the bicycle is traveling.

Look at the example.

Post A and Post B are 9 meters apart. Post B and Post C are 21 meters apart. A bicycle travels from Post A to Post B in 2 seconds. Then it travels from Post B to Post C in 3 seconds. Find the average speed of the bicycle for the distance from Post A to Post C.

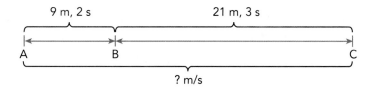

The speed between Post A and Post B is different from the speed between Post B and Post C.

Average speed is the average distance traveled per unit time.

$$\text{Average speed} = \frac{\text{Total distance traveled}}{\text{Total time}}$$

Total distance from Post A to Post C = 9 + 21
                                                                    = 30 m

Total time to travel from Post A to Post C = 2 + 3
                                                                    = 5 s

$$\text{Average speed} = \frac{\text{Total distance traveled}}{\text{Total time}}$$

$$= \frac{30}{5}$$

$$= 6 \text{ m/s}$$

The average speed of the bicycle is 6 meters per second.

Guided Practice

Solve.

7 The distance between Town P and Town Q is 80 miles, and the distance between Town Q and Town R is 320 miles. A van takes $2\frac{1}{2}$ hours to travel from Town P to Town Q. It takes another 5 hours to travel from Town Q to Town R. Find the average speed of the van for the whole journey.

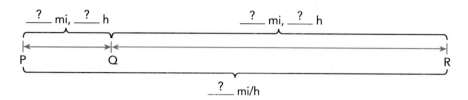

Total distance from Town P to Town R = 80 + ___?___

= ___?___ mi

Total time taken to travel from Town P to Town R = $2\frac{1}{2}$ + ___?___

= ___?___ h

Average speed = $\dfrac{\text{Total distance traveled}}{\text{Total time}}$

= $\dfrac{?}{?}$

= ___?___ ÷ ___?___

= ___?___ mi/h or ___?___ mph

The average speed of the van is ___?___ miles per hour.

8 Celia ran around a 400-meter track two times. It took her 4 minutes to run around the track once, and 6 minutes to run around it again. Find Celia's average speed.

Total distance Celia ran = 2 × ___?___

= ___?___ m

Total time taken to run around the track twice = ___?___ + ___?___

= ___?___ min

Average speed = $\dfrac{\text{Total distance traveled}}{\text{Total time}}$

= $\dfrac{?}{?}$

= ___?___ m/min

Celia's average speed was ___?___ meters per minute.

Practice 5.2

Solve. Show your work.

1 A tennis ball machine can launch 60 tennis balls in 12 minutes. At this rate, how many tennis balls can it launch in 2 hours?

2 Water flows from a faucet at a rate of 5 liters every 25 seconds.

a) At this rate, how much water will flow from the faucet in 45 seconds?

b) At this rate, how long will it take to collect 60 liters of water?

3 There are 1,600 kilocalories in the 5 cups of dog food that Mike gives his adult dog. Mike gives his puppy 2 cups of the same dog food. How many kilocalories are there in this 2-cup serving?

4 The table shows the postal charges for sending letters to Country Y. How much does it cost to send a letter weighing 60 grams to Country Y?

First 20 g	50¢
Per Additional 10 g	30¢

5 A vehicle traveled at a speed of 54 kilometers per hour for 3 hours. Find the distance traveled.

6 A pigeon can fly at a speed of 84 kilometers per hour. How long does it take the pigeon to fly 7 kilometers?

7 Karen walks home from school at a speed of 5 kilometers per hour. She takes 12 minutes to reach home. What is the distance between her school and her home? (Hint: Convert the time from minutes to hours.)

8 Kayla ran from her home to a beach at a speed of 6 meters per second. The distance from her home and the beach was 756 meters.

a) How long did she take to run from her home to the beach?

b) If Kayla wants to take 18 fewer seconds to reach the beach, at what speed must she run?

9 Car A travels 702 miles on 12 gallons of gasoline. Car B travels 873 miles on 15 gallons of gasoline. David wants to buy a car with the lowest fuel consumption. Find out the distance traveled by each car per gallon of gasoline. Then tell which of the two cars, A, or B, David should buy.

10 Post A and Post B are 120 meters apart. Post B and Post C are 300 meters apart. Ben cycled from Post A to Post B in 15 seconds. Then he cycled from Post B to Post C in 55 seconds. Find Ben's average speed for the distance from Post A to Post C.

11 Mr. Alan drove for $2\frac{1}{5}$ hours at a speed of 70 kilometers per hour. He then drove another 224 kilometers. He took 5 hours for the whole journey. What was Mr. Alan's average speed for the whole journey?

12 A family took 2 hours to drive from City A to City B at a speed of 55 miles per hour. On the return trip, due to a snowstorm, the family took 3 hours to travel back to City A.

a) How many miles did the family travel in all?

b) What was the average speed for the entire trip?

Brain @ Work

The distance between Point A and Point B is 3,120 meters. Caroline leaves Point A and Laura leaves Point B at the same time. The two girls cycle toward each other until they meet at Point C. Caroline's speed is 7.2 meters per second, and Laura's speed is 8.4 meters per second.

a) How long does Laura take to reach Point C?

b) What is the distance between Point A and Point C?

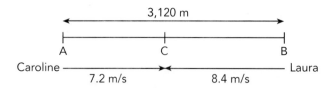

Chapter Wrap Up

Concept Map

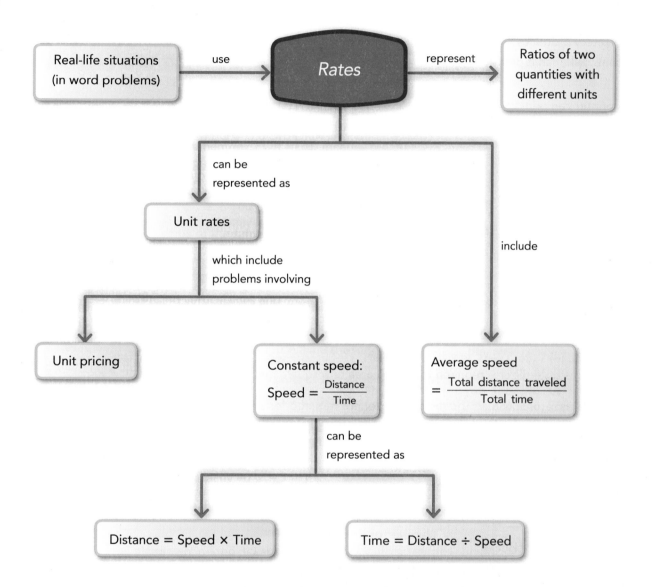

Key Concepts

▶ You can use a rate to compare two quantities with different units.

▶ A unit rate compares a quantity to one unit of another quantity.

▶ Speed is a special rate that expresses distance per unit time.

▶ Distance can be found using the formula: Distance = Speed × Time.

▶ Time can be found using the formula: Time = Distance ÷ Speed.

Chapter Review/Test

Concepts and Skills

Solve.

1 A factory produces 300 video game disks in 15 minutes. How many video game disks can it produce in 1 minute?

2 A printer can print 25 pages per minute. At this rate, how long will it take to print 2,000 pages?

Problem Solving

Solve. Show your work.

3 An empty bathtub is filled with water at a rate of 2.5 liters per minute. How long will it take to fill the bathtub with 30 liters of water?

4 $\frac{2}{3}$ cup of oatmeal is needed to make 10 granola bars. How many such granola bars can be made with 20 cups of oatmeal?

5 150 grams of fertilizer is required for a land area of 6 square meters.

   a) At this rate, how many grams of fertilizer are required for a land area of 13 square meters?

   b) For what land area will 850 grams of fertilizer be sufficient?

6 A machine can stamp 36 bottle caps in 10 seconds. Copy and complete the table.

Number of Seconds	Number of Bottle Caps Stamped
10	36
20	?
30	?
40	?
50	?
60	?

   a) At this rate, how many bottle caps can the machine stamp in 5 minutes?

   b) At this rate, how many minutes will it take to stamp 24,408 bottle caps?

7 The table below shows the charges for using an Internet service.

Plan A	Up to 10 Hours	$6
	Every Subsequent $\frac{1}{2}$ Hour or Part of $\frac{1}{2}$ Hour	$1
Plan B	Up to 12 Hours	$4
	Every Subsequent $\frac{1}{2}$ Hour or Part of $\frac{1}{2}$ Hour	$2

Nicholas used the Internet service for 16 hours and 40 minutes last month.

a) Under which plan would he have to pay less?

b) How much less?

8 Ashley took 3 minutes to run a distance of 540 meters from Point X to Point Y. Grace took 2 minutes to run a distance of 480 meters from Point Z to Point Y.

a) Find the speed of each girl.

b) Which of the two girls ran faster?

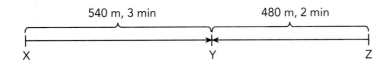

9 The distance between Town A and Town B is 45 kilometers.

a) If a train travels at a speed of 60 kilometers per hour, how long will it take to travel from Town A to Town B?

b) If a train takes 40 minutes to travel from Town A to Town B, what is its speed in kilometers per minute? Round your answer to 1 decimal place.

10 At 7:30 A.M., a bus left Town P for Town Q at a speed of 60 kilometers per hour. 15 minutes later, a car left Town Q and headed for Town P. The car reached Town P at 10:45 A.M. The bus reached Town Q at noon.

a) What is the distance between Town P and Town Q?

b) What was the speed of the car?

11 Brian drove 120 miles at speed of 60 miles per hour. He drove the same distance back home at average speed of 40 miles per hour. Brian adds these speeds and divides by 2 to come up with an average speed of 50 miles per hour. What is wrong with his reasoning? Find his average speed.

Percent

How much is a percent?

Whenever a book is sold, an author receives a percent of the price of each book, which is called a royalty. A cartoonist can also earn royalties based on comic books sales. One common practice to find the royalties amount is to calculate a percent of the net profit. For example, a cartoonist may be paid 5% royalty on the net profit from the sales of his books.

In this chapter, you will find percents being used in real-life examples such as finding the royalties for recording artists, interests on deposits, and sales tax. Percents are also used in population statistics, housing trends, and weather forecasting, to name a few examples.

BIG IDEA

▶ Percent is a concept used to compare quantities expressed per hundred.

Recall Prior Knowledge

Finding equivalent fractions using multiplication

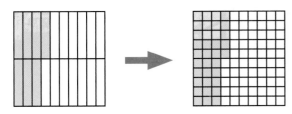 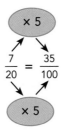

Multiplying the numerator and denominator of the fraction by the same number, 5, is the same as multiplying the fraction by $\frac{5}{5}$, or the number 1. It does not change the value of the fraction.

✔ Quick Check

Find the missing numerators and denominators.

1 $\frac{4}{5} = \frac{8}{?} = \frac{?}{100}$

2 $\frac{9}{25} = \frac{18}{?} = \frac{?}{100}$

Simplifying fractions using division

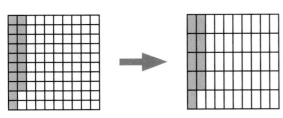 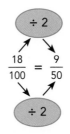

Dividing both the numerator and denominator of the fraction by 2 is the same as dividing the fraction by $\frac{2}{2}$, or 1. It does not change the value of the fraction.

A fraction is in simplest form when the numerator and denominator have no common factor, except 1.

✔ Quick Check

Express each fraction in simplest form.

3 $\frac{48}{100}$

4 $\frac{180}{240}$

Writing fractions with a denominator of 100 as a decimal

$$\frac{35}{100} = 0.35 \qquad\qquad \frac{7}{25} = \frac{28}{100} \qquad\qquad \frac{25}{500} = \frac{5}{100}$$

$$= 0.28 \qquad\qquad\qquad = 0.05$$

✓ Quick Check

Express each fraction as a decimal.

5 $\frac{15}{100}$

6 $\frac{3}{10}$

7 $\frac{2}{5}$

8 $\frac{7}{20}$

9 $\frac{39}{300}$

10 $\frac{25}{125}$

Multiplying fractions by a whole number

$$\frac{5}{6} \times 24 = \frac{5}{1} \times 4 \qquad\qquad \text{Divide by the common factor 6.}$$

$$= \frac{20}{1} \qquad\qquad\qquad \text{Multiply.}$$

$$= 20 \qquad\qquad\qquad\quad \text{Simplify.}$$

$$\frac{3}{8} \times 12 = \frac{3}{2} \times 3 \qquad\qquad \text{Divide by the common factor 4.}$$

$$= \frac{9}{2} \qquad\qquad\qquad\; \text{Multiply.}$$

$$= 4\frac{1}{2} \qquad\qquad\qquad \text{Write as a mixed number.}$$

✓ Quick Check

Find each product.

11 $\frac{3}{7} \times 42$

12 $\frac{3}{22} \times 33$

13 $\frac{5}{6} \times 54$

14 $\frac{6}{25} \times 40$

15 $\frac{7}{9} \times 30$

16 $\frac{9}{24} \times 56$

6.1 Understanding Percent

Lesson Objectives

- Understand percent notation.
- Write equivalent fractions, decimals, and percents.

Vocabulary

percent

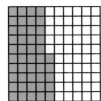 **Meaning of percent**

Percents, like ratios, are used to compare two quantities.
Percents compare one quantity to 100.

> Percent is written as %, which means *out of 100*.

You can express a comparison such as 45 out of 100 as
a fraction, ratio, or percent.

Fraction: $\frac{45}{100}$ Ratio: 45 : 100   Percent: 45%

The large square is divided into 100 parts.
45 out of 100 parts are shaded.
So, 45% of the large square is shaded.

> What percent of the large square is not shaded?

55% of the large square is not shaded.

Express a part of a whole as a fraction and a percent.

a) 72 out of 100 cats are long-haired cats. What percent of the cats are
long-haired cats?

72 out of 100 ⟶ $\frac{72}{100}$ Express the fraction as a percent.

= 72%

72% of the cats are long-haired cats.

Continue on next page

b) A fruit display of 50 apples has 43 green ones.
What percent of the apples are green?

43 out of 50 $\longrightarrow \dfrac{43}{50}$

$$= \dfrac{43 \times 2}{50 \times 2}$$ Multiply the numerator and denominator
by 2 to make the denominator 100.

$$= \dfrac{86}{100}$$ Simplify.

$$= 86\%$$ Express the fraction as a percent.

86% of the apples are green.

c) Of the 2,000 people at a concert, 240 are teachers. The rest are students.
What percent of the people at the concert are students?

240 out of 2,000 $\longrightarrow \dfrac{240}{2,000}$

$$= \dfrac{240 \div 10}{2,000 \div 10}$$ Divide the numerator and denominator
by 10 to make the denominator 200.

$$= \dfrac{24 \div 2}{200 \div 2}$$ Divide the numerator and denominator
by 2 to make the denominator 100.

$$= \dfrac{12}{100}$$ Simplify.

$$= 12\%$$ Express the fraction as a percent.

12% of the people at the concert are teachers.

$$100\% - 12\% = 88\%$$

88% of the people at the concert are students.

Guided Practice

Solve.

1 Out of 25 chairs, 14 are brown. What percent of the chairs are brown?

14 out of 25 $\longrightarrow \dfrac{?}{?}$

$$= \dfrac{? \times 4}{? \times 4}$$

$$= \dfrac{?}{100}$$

$$= \underline{}\%$$

$\underline{}$ % of the chairs are brown.

2 Of the 400 animals in a zoo, 32 were monkeys.

a) What percent of the animals were monkeys?

32 out of 400 $\longrightarrow \dfrac{?}{?}$

$= \dfrac{?}{100}$

$= \underline{?}$ %

$\underline{?}$ % of the animals were monkeys.

b) What percent of the animals were not monkeys?

$\underline{?}$ % $-$ $\underline{?}$ % $=$ $\underline{?}$ %

$\underline{?}$ % of the animals were not monkeys.

Learn **Express percents as fractions or decimals.**

a) Express 24% as a fraction in simplest form.

$24\% = \dfrac{24}{100}$ Express the percent as a fraction.

$= \dfrac{24 \div 4}{100 \div 4}$ Divide both the numerator and denominator by the greatest common factor, 4.

$= \dfrac{6}{25}$

b) Express 78% as a decimal.

$78\% = \dfrac{78}{100}$ Express the percent as a fraction.

$= 0.78$ Express the fraction as a decimal.

Guided Practice

Express each percent as a fraction or a mixed number in simplest form.

3 $48\% = \dfrac{48}{?}$

$= \dfrac{?}{?}$

4 55%

5 108%

Express each percent as a decimal.

6 $13\% = \dfrac{?}{?}$

$= \underline{?}$

7 8%

8 126%

Solve. Show your work.

1 Out of a total of 500 flowers, 65 are roses. What percent of the flowers are roses?

2 Of the 200 packages of bagels sold, 15 of them are sesame seed bagels. What percent of the bagel packages sold are sesame seed bagels?

3 In a survey of music preferences, 81 out of 450 students said that they preferred country music. What percent of the students preferred country music?

4 There are 750 spectators in the stadium, of which 420 are women and the rest are men.

a) What percent of the spectators are women?

b) What percent of the spectators are men?

Express each percent as a fraction or a mixed number in simplest form.

5 65%   **6** 78%   **7** 92%

8 125%   **9** 276%   **10** 580%

Express each percent as a decimal.

11 6%   **12** 43%   **13** 80%

14 367%   **15** 579%   **16** 779%

Solve. Show your work.

17 The music for Nadia's dance routine lasts for exactly 4 minutes. When Nadia dances her routine, she starts with her music and finishes 12 seconds before the music ends. What percent of the time the music is playing is Nadia dancing?

18 *Math Journal* In a game of darts, Annie hits the bull's eye 4 times out of 25 times. Benjamin hits the bull's eye 8 times out of 100 times.

a) Who hits the bull's eye more times?

b) Whose aim is more accurate? Justify your answer.

Fractions, Decimals, and Percents

Lesson Objective

- Write more equivalent fractions, decimals, and percents.

 Hands-On Activity

EXPRESSING FRACTIONS OR MIXED NUMBERS AS PERCENTS

Work in pairs.

Use these fractions and mixed numbers.

$$\frac{7}{9} \quad \frac{3}{5} \quad \frac{1}{2} \quad \frac{7}{10} \quad \frac{3}{4} \quad \frac{7}{8} \quad \frac{5}{6} \quad 1\frac{2}{3} \quad 2\frac{1}{4} \quad 3\frac{2}{5}$$

STEP 1 Find which of the fractions or mixed numbers can be expressed as percents using the method of writing an equivalent fraction. List the fractions that cannot be expressed as percents using this method.

Example

$$\frac{3}{5} = \frac{3 \times 20}{5 \times 20}$$
$$= \frac{60}{100}$$
$$= 60\%$$

First, express $\frac{3}{5}$ as a fraction with a denominator of 100.

Then express the fraction as a percent.

STEP 2 If you want to use the method of writing an equivalent fraction to express a fraction as a percent, what must be true of the fraction or mixed number?

  Math Journal Explain how you would express $1\frac{3}{4}$ as a percent.

Find the percent represented by a fraction by multiplying by 100%.

Not all denominators of fractions are factors or multiples of 100. So, you need another way to find equivalent percents.

$\frac{2}{3} = \frac{2}{3} \times 100\%$ Multiply the fraction by 100%.

$= \frac{200}{3}\%$ Simplify.

$= 66\frac{2}{3}\%$ Write the improper fraction as a mixed number.

$100\% = \frac{100}{100}$
$= 1$
So, $\frac{2}{3} \times 100\%$ has the same value as $\frac{2}{3} \times 1$.

Guided Practice

Express each fraction or mixed number as a percent.

1 $\frac{4}{7} = \frac{4}{7} \times \underline{}\%$

$= \frac{?}{?}\%$

$= \underline{}\%$

2 $1\frac{5}{9} = 1\frac{5}{9} \times \underline{}\%$

$= \frac{?}{9} \times \underline{}\%$

$= \underline{}\%$

3 $\frac{5}{6}$

4 $1\frac{7}{8}$

Express decimals as percents.

Express 0.07 as a percent.

Method 1

$0.07 = \frac{7}{100}$ Express the decimal as a fraction.

$= 7\%$ Express the fraction as a percent.

Method 2

$0.07 = 0.07 \times 100\%$ Multiply the decimal by 100%.

$= 7\%$

$100\% = \frac{100}{100}$
$= 1$
So, $0.07 \times 100\%$ has the same value as 0.07×1.

Guided Practice

Complete.

5 Express 0.82 as a percent.

Method 1	**Method 2**
$0.82 = \dfrac{?}{100}$	$0.82 = \underline{\quad?\quad} \times 100\%$
$= \underline{\quad?\quad}$	$= \underline{\quad?\quad}$

Express each decimal as a percent.

6 0.04

7 0.98

8 0.6

Learn **Express percents as fractions.**

a) Express $33\dfrac{1}{3}\%$ as a fraction in simplest form.

$33\dfrac{1}{3}\% = \dfrac{100}{3}\%$ Express the mixed number as an improper fraction.

$= \dfrac{100}{3} \div 100$ Divide by 100 to express the percent as a fraction.

$= \dfrac{100}{3} \times \dfrac{1}{100}$ Rewrite using the reciprocal of the divisor.

$= \dfrac{100}{300}$ Multiply.

$= \dfrac{1}{3}$ Simplify.

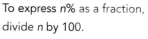

To express $n\%$ as a fraction, divide n by 100.

For example, $19\% = \dfrac{19}{100}$.

b) Express 40.2% as a fraction in simplest form.

$40.2\% = \dfrac{40.2}{100}$ Express the decimal as a fraction.

$= \dfrac{402}{1,000}$ Multiply the numerator and denominator by 10 to make the numerator a whole number.

$= \dfrac{201}{500}$ Simplify.

Guided Practice

Express each percent as a fraction in simplest form.

9 $83\dfrac{1}{3}\%$

10 84.4%

Practice 6.2

Express each fraction or mixed number as a percent.

1 $\frac{3}{5}$

2 $\frac{3}{8}$

3 $\frac{1}{3}$

4 $2\frac{1}{5}$

5 $7\frac{3}{4}$

6 $9\frac{7}{8}$

Express each decimal as a percent.

7 0.46

8 0.7

9 0.06

10 1.52

11 6.03

12 8.9

Express each percent as a fraction in simplest form.

13 5.75%

14 25.5%

15 85.25%

16 $16\frac{2}{3}$ %

17 $42\frac{3}{8}$ %

18 $79\frac{5}{6}$ %

Express each fraction as a percent. Round your answer to the nearest whole number.

19 $\frac{76}{125}$

20 $\frac{98}{230}$

21 $\frac{102}{350}$

Find the missing fractions and decimals.

22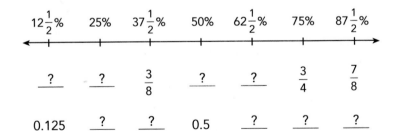

Percent	$12\frac{1}{2}$%	25%	$37\frac{1}{2}$%	50%	$62\frac{1}{2}$%	75%	$87\frac{1}{2}$%
Fraction	?	?	$\frac{3}{8}$	?	?	$\frac{3}{4}$	$\frac{7}{8}$
Decimal	0.125	?	?	0.5	?	?	?

Solve. Show your work.

23 *Math Journal* School A has 450 seniors, and 432 of them plan to go to college. School B has 380 seniors, and 361 of them plan to go to college. In which school does a greater percent of students plan to go to college? Justify your reasoning.

6.3 Percent of a Quantity

Lesson Objective

- Find the percent of a number.

Vocabulary

base

Learn **Find the quantity represented by the percent.**

5% represents 5 units for every 100 units.

5% of a whole quantity refers to the part of the quantity that represents 5%.

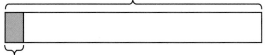

A whole quantity (100%)

How much is the part here? (5%)

The model shows that 100% refers to the whole quantity, or the **base**.

· ·

Find 5% of 160.

Method 1

The model shows that:

$100\% \longrightarrow 160$

$1\% \longrightarrow \dfrac{160}{100} = 1.6$

$5\% \longrightarrow 5 \times 1.6 = 8$

5% of 160 is 8.

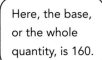

Here, the base, or the whole quantity, is 160.

Method 2

5% of $160 = \dfrac{5}{100} \times 160$

$= \dfrac{1}{20} \times 160$

$= \dfrac{160}{20}$

$= 8$

5% of 160 is 8.

Math Note

"of" means "×".

Guided Practice

Complete. Use the models to help you.

1 What is 40% of 720 centimeters?

Method 1

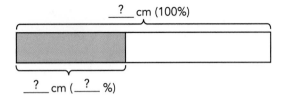

The model shows that:

$100\% \longrightarrow \underline{\quad?\quad}$ cm

$1\% \longrightarrow \dfrac{?}{?} = \underline{\quad?\quad}$ cm

$40\% \longrightarrow \underline{\quad?\quad} \times \underline{\quad?\quad} = \underline{\quad?\quad}$ cm

40% of 720 centimeters is $\underline{\quad?\quad}$ centimeters.

Method 2

$40\% \text{ of } 720 \text{ cm} = \dfrac{?}{100} \times 720$

$= \underline{\quad?\quad}$ cm

40% of 720 centimeters is $\underline{\quad?\quad}$ centimeters.

2 What is 75% of 800 kilograms?

Method 1

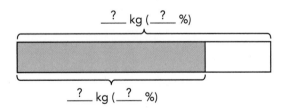

The model shows that:

$100\% \longrightarrow \underline{\quad?\quad}$ kg

$1\% \longrightarrow \dfrac{?}{?} = \underline{\quad?\quad}$ kg

$75\% \longrightarrow \underline{\quad?\quad} \times \underline{\quad?\quad} = \underline{\quad?\quad}$ kg

75% of 800 kilograms is $\underline{\quad?\quad}$ kilograms.

Method 2

$75\% \text{ of } 800 \text{ kg} = \dfrac{?}{?} \times 800$

$= \underline{\quad?\quad}$ kg

75% of 800 kilograms is $\underline{\quad?\quad}$ kilograms.

Find the percent of each whole.

3 30% of 450

4 225% of $60

5 55% of 320

6 110% of $550

Learn **Find the whole given a quantity and its percent.**

Ana has 8% of her CD collection in a box. If there are 96 CDs in the box, how many CDs are in Ana's collection?

The whole collection is 100%. 8% of the collection is 96 CDs.

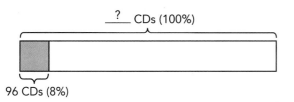

___?___ CDs (100%)

96 CDs (8%)

The model shows that:

8% ⟶ 96

1% ⟶ $\frac{96}{8}$ = 12

100% ⟶ 100 × 12 = 1,200

Ana's collection is 1,200 CDs.

Guided Practice

Solve. Use the model to help you.

7 27% of the students in a school are in grade 6. This is 540 students. How many students are there in the school?

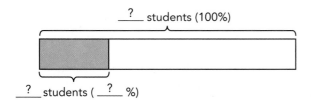

___?___ students (100%)

___?___ students (___?___ %)

The model shows that:

___?___ % ⟶ ___?___ students

1% ⟶ $\frac{?}{?}$ = ___?___ students

100% ⟶ 100 × ___?___ = ___?___ students

There are ___?___ students in the school.

Solve. You may draw a model to help you.

8 At an amusement park, 60% of the people were adults, and the rest were children. There were 720 adults. How many people were at the amusement park in all?

___?___ % ⟶ ___?___ people

1% ⟶ $\frac{?}{?}$ = ___?___ people

100% ⟶ ___?___ × ___?___ = ___?___ people

There were ___?___ people at the amusement park in all.

Find the missing value.

9 20% of ___?___ is 163.

10 45% of ___?___ is 150.

Practice 6.3

Solve. Use the models to help you.

1 What is 15% of 12 meters?

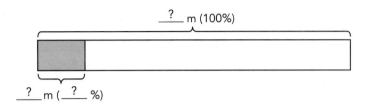

2 A park ranger finds that 35% of the park's visitors stay at the campground. If 105 visitors stayed at the campground one day, how many visitors did the park have that day?

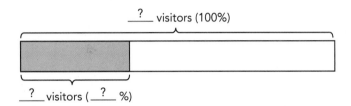

Find the quantity represented by each percent.

3 45% of $360

4 66% of 740 kilometers

Solve. Show your work.

5 There are 1,500 students in a school. 65% of them are girls. How many girls are there in the school?

6 A school raises $4,000 for its new library. 36% of the money is used to buy reference books. How much money is used to buy reference books?

7 Ms. Galan spent 55% of her savings on a television that cost $550. How much money did she have in her savings before she bought the television?

8 75% of a number is 354. Find the number.

9 Ahyoka has 250 CDs. 10% are country, 70% are pop, and the rest are hip-hop. How many CDs are hip-hop?

10 There are 820 people at a stadium. 65% of them are adults, 20% of them are boys, and the rest are girls. How many girls are there at the stadium?

11 Ms. Stapleton had 2,600 hens, ducks, and goats on her farm. 35% of them were hens, and 25% of them were goats. How many ducks did she have on her farm?

12 There are 1,505 fruits for sale at a farmer's market. 39% of them are apples, 28% are oranges, 13% are honeydew melons, and the rest are watermelons. How many watermelons are there?

13 120% of a number is 45. Find the number.

14 250% of a number is 60. Find the number.

15 400% of a number is 45. Find the number.

16 Last month, Alex spent 40% of his salary on a laptop. He then spent 30% of it on his bills and saved the remaining $1,200. What was his salary?

17 20% of the spectators at a tennis match are women. 10% of them are girls, 30% are boys, and the remaining 3,600 spectators are men. Find the total number of spectators at the match.

18 Jovita made 300 greeting cards. She sold 40% of the cards, gave 85% of the remaining cards to her friends, and kept the rest of the cards for herself. How many greeting cards did she keep for herself?

19 Patrick saved $500. He received 25% of the money for his birthday, saved 30% of the remainder from his allowance, and earned the rest of it by mowing lawns. How much of his savings did he earn by mowing lawns?

20 *Math Journal* Michelle and Michael checked some books out of the library. 20% of the books Michelle checked out were fiction books, and 40% of the books Michael checked out were fiction books. Your friend thinks that Michael checked out more fiction books than Michelle. Explain the error in your friend's thinking. Use an example to support your reasoning.

6.4 Real-World Problems: Percent

Lesson Objective

• Solve problems involving percent.

Vocabulary

sales tax	commission
interest	interest rate

Learn **Find the percent represented by a quantity.**

In her last basketball game, Julie scored 18 of her team's 48 points.

a) What percent of her team's points did Julie score?

Method 1

$$\text{Fraction of her team's points Julie scored} = \frac{\text{Julie's points}}{\text{Team's points}}$$

$$= \frac{18}{48}$$

$$= \frac{3}{8}$$

$$\frac{3}{8} \times 100\% = \frac{300}{8}\%$$

$$= 37\frac{1}{2}\%$$

Julie scored $37\frac{1}{2}$ % of her team's points.

Method 2

48 points ⟶ 100%

1 point ⟶ $\frac{100}{48}$ %

18 points ⟶ $18 \times \frac{100}{48}\% = 37\frac{1}{2}\%$

Julie scored $37\frac{1}{2}$ % of her team's points.

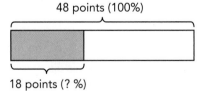

48 points (100%)

18 points (? %)

b) What percent of her team's points did the rest of Julie's team score?

$$100\% - 37\frac{1}{2}\% = 62\frac{1}{2}\%$$

The rest of Julie's team scored $62\frac{1}{2}$ % of her team's points.

Guided Practice

Solve.

1 Mr. Jefferson is making 80 cups of fruit punch for the grand opening of his bakery. He uses 52 cups of fruit juice and the rest is sparkling water.

a) What percent of the punch is fruit juice?

Method 1

Fraction of fruit juice in punch $= \dfrac{?}{?}$

Percent of fruit juice in punch $= \dfrac{?}{?} \times \underline{\ ?\ } \%$

$ = \underline{\ ?\ } \%$

$\underline{\ ?\ } \%$ of the punch is fruit juice.

Method 2

$\underline{\ ?\ }$ cups $\longrightarrow 100\%$

1 cup $\longrightarrow \dfrac{100}{?} \%$

$\underline{\ ?\ }$ cups $\longrightarrow ? \times \dfrac{100}{?} \% = \underline{\ ?\ } \%$

$\underline{\ ?\ } \%$ of the punch is fruit juice.

b) What percent of the punch is sparkling water?

$100\% - \underline{\ ?\ } \% = \underline{\ ?\ } \%$

$\underline{\ ?\ } \%$ of the punch is sparkling water.

Learn Solve word problems involving taxes.

a) Steven and his family had dinner in a restaurant. The total cost of the food was $68.50, and an 8% **sales tax** was added to the bill. What was the total bill?

Method 1

Sales tax $= 8\%$ of $68.50

$ = \dfrac{8}{100} \times \$68.50$

$ = \$5.48$

$\$68.50 + \$5.48 = \$73.98$

The total bill was $73.98.

Method 2

Sales tax:

$100\% \longrightarrow \$68.50$

$1\% \longrightarrow \$\dfrac{68.50}{100}$

$8\% \longrightarrow 8 \times \$\dfrac{68.50}{100} = \$5.48$

$\$68.50 + \$5.48 = \$73.98$

The total bill was $73.98.

Check for reasonableness: Estimate the value of 8% of $68.50. 8% is close to 10% and $68.50 is close to $70, so the answer should be close to 10% of $70, or $7.

The estimate shows a total bill of $70 + $7 = $77 is reasonable.

Continue on next page

b) Jackie bought a pair of shoes. The following shows the cost of the shoes and the sales tax.

Shoes	$52.00
Sales tax	$2.60

The sales tax was calculated based on the cost of the shoes. What was the sales tax rate?

What is another way to do this problem?

The cost of the shoes is 100%.

$52.00 ⟶ 100%

$1.00 ⟶ $\frac{100}{52.00}$ %

$2.60 ⟶ $2.60 \times \frac{100}{52.00}$ %

$= 5\%$

The sales tax rate was 5%.

Check for reasonableness: Estimate the value of 5% of $52. $52 is close to $50, so the answer should be close to 5% of $50. 5% of $50 is half of $5, or $2.50, which is close to $2.60.

The answer is reasonable.

Guided Practice

Solve. Check for reasonableness.

2 A laptop computer displayed at a shop costs $720. A sales tax of 7% will be added to the price. What is the total cost of the laptop computer?

Method 1

Sales tax = __?__ % of $720

$= \frac{?}{?} \times \$720$

$= \$\underline{\ ?\ }$

$\$720 + \$\underline{\ ?\ } = \$\underline{\ ?\ }$

The total cost of the laptop computer is $\underline{\ ?\ }$.

Method 2

Sales tax:

$100\% \longrightarrow \$\underline{\ ?\ }$

$1\% \longrightarrow \$\frac{?}{?}$

$\underline{\ ?\ }\% \longrightarrow \underline{\ ?\ } \times \$\frac{?}{?} = \$\underline{\ ?\ }$

$\$720 + \$\underline{\ ?\ } = \$\underline{\ ?\ }$

The total cost of the laptop computer is $\underline{\ ?\ }$.

3 Dave went to lunch with his friends. The food cost $78.50, and a sales tax of $4.71 was added to the cost of the meal. What was the sales tax rate?

The cost of the food is __?__ %.

$ __?__ ⟶ __?__ %

$1 ⟶ $\frac{?}{?}$ %

$ __?__ ⟶ __?__ × $\frac{?}{?}$ % = __?__ %

The sales tax rate was __?__ %.

Learn **Solve word problems by finding the whole given a quantity and its percent.**

The sixth grade class sells magazines to raise funds for a charity. 8% of the magazines sales will be donated to the charity. If the class raises $400 for the charity, what is the dollar amount of the magazine sales?

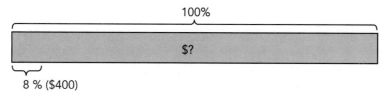

100%

$?

8 % ($400)

8% ⟶ $400
1% ⟶ $400 ÷ 8 = $50
100% ⟶ 100 × $50 = $5,000

The dollar amount of the magazine sales is $5,000.

Check for reasonableness: Estimate the value of 8% of $5,000. 8% is close to 10%, so the amount raised for charity, $400, should be close to 10% of $5,000, or $500.

The answer is reasonable.

Guided Practice
Solve. Check for reasonableness.

4 Mr. Diaz earns a 3% commission on all the furniture he sells. If he receives $2,880 in commission, what is the dollar amount of his sales?

__?__ % ⟶ $ __?__

1% ⟶ $ $\frac{?}{?}$ = $ __?__

100% ⟶ 100 × $ __?__ = $ __?__

The dollar amount of his sales is $ __?__ .

A **commission** is a percent of total sales earned by a salesperson.

Solve word problems involving interest.

When you deposit money in a savings account, the bank pays you interest on the money. The **interest rate** is the rate at which your money earns interest in a given amount of time.

a) Marina deposits $1,500 in a savings account. The bank will pay her 5% interest at the end of a year. How much interest will Marina receive?

$$\text{Interest} = 5\% \text{ of } \$1,500 \text{ for } 1 \text{ year}$$
$$= \frac{5}{100} \times \$1,500 \times 1$$
$$= \$75$$

Marina will receive $75 in interest.

b) The Astronomy Society has $24,000 in an account that has an interest rate of 3% per year. How much interest will it earn at the end of $\frac{1}{2}$ year?

$$\text{Interest} = \frac{3}{100} \times \$24,000 \times \frac{1}{2}$$
$$= \$360$$

The Astronomy Society will earn $360 in interest at the end of $\frac{1}{2}$ year.

Guided Practice

Solve.

5 A firm has $30,000 in a bank account at the beginning of the year. Interest will be paid at a rate of 2% at the end of the year. How much interest will the firm receive for the year?

$$\text{Interest} = \underline{\;?\;} \% \text{ of } \$\underline{\;?\;} \text{ for } 1 \text{ year}$$
$$= \frac{?}{?} \times \$\underline{\;?\;} \times 1$$
$$= \$\underline{\;?\;}$$

The firm will receive $\underline{\;?\;}$ in interest for the year.

6 A company has $500,000 in a savings account. The interest is 4% per year. How much interest will it earn at the end of $\frac{1}{2}$ year?

$$\text{Interest} = \frac{?}{100} \times \$\underline{\;?\;} \times \frac{?}{?}$$
$$= \$\underline{\;?\;}$$

The company will earn $\underline{\;?\;}$ in interest at the end of $\frac{1}{2}$ year.

Practice 6.4

Solve. Show your work. Check that your answers are reasonable.

1. Ellen had 25 hair clips. 7 of them were blue and the rest were purple.

    a) What percent of the hair clips were blue?

    b) What percent of the hair clips were purple?

2. Gabriel had $60. He spent $36 on a pair of shoes and the rest on a shirt.

    a) What percent of the money did he spend on the pair of shoes?

    b) What percent of the money did he spend on the shirt?

3. Ms. Pierce bought a camera that cost $450. In addition, she had to pay 4% sales tax. How much did Ms. Pierce pay for the camera?

4. Mr. Osmond bought a computer that cost $2,500. How much did he pay for the computer if the sales tax rate was 7%?

5. There were 320 girls and 180 boys at a playground. What percent of children were girls?

6. Sally spent $36 and had $12 left. What percent of her money did she spend?

7. An artist receives 20% royalty on the retail price of his recordings. If he receives $36,000 in royalties, what is the dollar amount of the retail price of his recordings?

8. A club deposited $50,000 in a savings account at the beginning of the year. Interest will be paid at a rate of 3% at the end of the year. How much interest will the club receive for the year?

9. Company X has $128,000 in a savings account that pays 6% interest per year. How much interest will it earn at the end of $\frac{1}{2}$ year?

6.5 Percent of Change

Lesson Objective

- Solve problems involving percent increase and decrease.

Vocabulary

markup   discount

 Solve word problems involving percent increase and decrease.

Mr. Sato sells fish at a 60% **markup**. He pays $3.75 per pound for haddock one week. At what price per pound will he sell it?

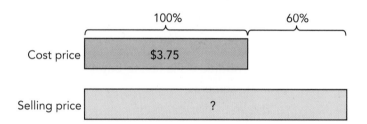

Method 1

$60\% \text{ of } \$3.75 = \dfrac{60}{100} \times \$3.75$

$= \$2.25$

The price is marked up by $2.25.

$3.75 + $2.25 = $6.00

Mr. Sato will sell the haddock at $6.00 per pound.

The markup is the rate at which the price of merchandise increases over its cost. This increase pays the merchant's costs.

Method 2

$100\% \longrightarrow \$3.75$

$1\% \longrightarrow \$3.75 \div 100 = \$\dfrac{3.75}{100}$

$60\% \longrightarrow 60 \times \$\dfrac{3.75}{100} = \$2.25$

The price is marked up by $2.25.

$3.75 + $2.25 = $6.00

Mr. Sato will sell the haddock at $6.00 per pound.

Guided Practice

Solve.

1 At a post office, the weight of the mail at 10:00 A.M. was 80 pounds. Two hours later, the weight of the mail had increased by 30%. Find the weight of the mail at noon.

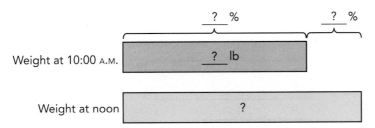

Method 1

30% of $80 = \dfrac{?}{?} \times \underline{\quad?\quad}$

$\quad\quad\quad = \underline{\quad?\quad}$

The weight of the mail had increased by $\underline{\quad?\quad}$ pounds.

$80 + \underline{\quad?\quad} = \underline{\quad?\quad}$

The weight of the mail at noon was $\underline{\quad?\quad}$ pounds.

Method 2

$100\% \longrightarrow 80$ lb

$1\% \longrightarrow 80 \div 100 = \underline{\quad?\quad}$ lb

$\underline{\quad?\quad}\% \longrightarrow \underline{\quad?\quad} \times \underline{\quad?\quad} = \underline{\quad?\quad}$ lb

The weight of the mail had increased by $\underline{\quad?\quad}$ pounds.

$80 + \underline{\quad?\quad} = \underline{\quad?\quad}$

The weight of the mail at noon was $\underline{\quad?\quad}$ pounds.

 2 The price of a new car was $22,800 in April. However, the price of the car was reduced by 5% in May. Find the price in May.

In May, the price of the car was $\underline{\quad?\quad}$ % as compared to the price of the car in April.

$100\% \longrightarrow \$\underline{\quad?\quad}$

$1\% \longrightarrow \$\underline{\quad?\quad} \div 100 = \$\underline{\quad?\quad}$

$\underline{\quad?\quad}\% \longrightarrow \underline{\quad?\quad} \times \$\underline{\quad?\quad} = \$\underline{\quad?\quad}$

The price of the car in May was $\$\underline{\quad?\quad}$.

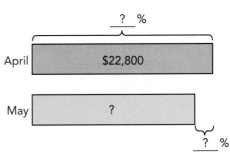

Learn **Solve word problems by finding a quantity represented by a percent.**

William had a length of brass chain. He used 30% of the chain to make some necklaces. The remaining length of the brass chain was 385 centimeters long. He then used 25% of the remaining chain to make some key chains.

a) What was the original length of the brass chain?

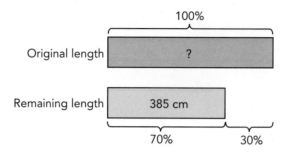

100% − 30% = 70%

70% ⟶ 385 cm

1% ⟶ 385 ÷ 70 = 5.5 cm

100% ⟶ 100 × 5.5 = 550 cm

The original length of the brass chain was 550 centimeters.

b) What was the remaining length of the brass chain after making the key chains?

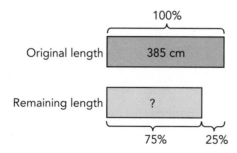

100% − 25% = 75%

$75\% \times 385 = \dfrac{75}{100} \times 385$

$= 288.75$

The remaining length of the brass chain after making the key chains was 288.75 centimeters.

You need to find 75% of the remaining chain.

So, take the length of the remaining chain as 100%.

Guided Practice

Solve.

3 One Friday, a restaurant received enough orange juice for a week. After the
weekend, the restaurant's orange juice supply had decreased by 24% to
76 quarts. After Monday, the supply had further decreased by 20%.

a) What was the original amount of orange juice received?

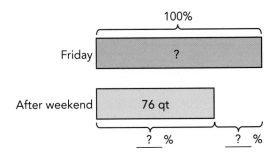

$100\% - \underline{\ ?\ }\% = \underline{\ ?\ }\%$

$\underline{\ ?\ }\% \longrightarrow \underline{\ ?\ }$ qt

$1\% \longrightarrow \underline{\ ?\ } \div \underline{\ ?\ } = \underline{\ ?\ }$ qt

$100\% \longrightarrow 100 \times \underline{\ ?\ } = \underline{\ ?\ }$ qt

The original amount of orange juice received was $\underline{\ ?\ }$ quarts.

b) How much orange juice was left after Monday?

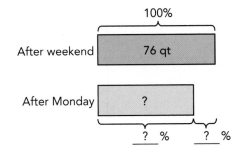

$100\% - \underline{\ ?\ }\% = \underline{\ ?\ }\%$

$\underline{\ ?\ }\% \times 76 = \dfrac{?}{?} \times \underline{\ ?\ }$

$= \underline{\ ?\ }$

$\underline{\ ?\ }$ quarts of orange juice was left after Monday.

Find percent increase or decrease to solve word problems.

The regular price of a Statue of Liberty souvenir was $32. During a sale, its price was reduced to $24. Find the percent **discount**.

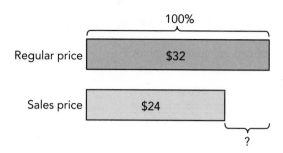

$32 − $24 = $8

The discount was $8.

$32 ⟶ 100%

$1 ⟶ $\frac{100}{32}$ %

$8 ⟶ 8 × $\frac{100}{32}$ % = 25%

The percent discount was 25%.

Guided Practice

Solve.

4 Dennis bought an antique model train for $64. Two years later, he sold it for $72. What was the percent increase in the price of the model train?

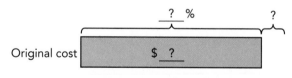

You need to compare the selling price with the original cost.

So, take the original cost as __?__ %.

$\underline{}^{?} − \$\underline{}^{?} = \$\underline{}^{?}$

The increase in price was $__?__.

$\underline{}^{?} ⟶ 100%$

$1 ⟶ $\frac{?}{?}$ %

$\underline{}^{?} ⟶ 8 × \frac{?}{?} \% = \underline{}^{?} \%$

The percent increase in the price of the model train was __?__ %.

5 The original length of a spring was 28 millimeters. It was stretched to a length of 35 millimeters. Find the percent increase in its length.

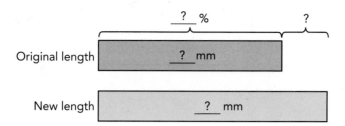

__?__ mm − __?__ mm = __?__ mm

The increase in length was __?__ millimeters.

$\dfrac{?}{?}$ × 100% = __?__ %

The percent increase in its length was __?__ %.

Learn Find percent increase or decrease to solve multi-step problems.

The original price of a book in 2003 was $12. In 2005, the price of the same book increased to $15. In 2007, the price of the book was $3 more than the price of the book in 2005.

a) Find the percent increase in the price of the book from 2003 to 2005.

b) Find the percent increase in the price of the book from 2005 to 2007.

a)

| 2003 | $12 |
| 2005 | $15 | ?
| 2007 | | ?
                   $3

Increase in price of book from 2003 to 2005 = $15 − $12
$$= \$3$$

Percent increase $= \dfrac{3}{12} \times 100\%$

$$= 25\%$$

The percent increase in the price of the book from 2003 to 2005 was 25%.

Continue on next page

b) Percent increase in price $= \dfrac{3}{15} \times 100\%$

$$= 20\%$$

The percent increase in the price of the book from 2005 to 2007 was 20%.

> You are comparing the price of the book in 2005 with the price of the book in 2007. So, take the price of the book in 2005 as 100%.

Guided Practice

Solve.

6 The amount of the water in a dispenser was 50 liters at first. After 10 minutes, it decreased to 45 liters. Another 15 minutes later, the amount of water had decreased to 40 liters.

a) Find the percent decrease in the amount of water after the first 10 minutes.

At first	50 L

After 10 min | 45 L | ?

After 25 min | 40 L | ?

Decrease in amount of water = 50 L − 45 L

$$= \underline{\ ?\ }\ L$$

$\dfrac{?}{?} \times 100\% = \underline{\ ?\ }\%$

The percent decrease in the amount of water after the first 10 minutes was $\underline{\ ?\ }$ %.

b) What was the percent decrease in the amount of water from 45 liters to 40 liters?

Decrease in amount of water = 45 L − 40 L

$$= \underline{\ ?\ }\ L$$

$\dfrac{?}{?} \times 100\% = \underline{\ ?\ }\%$

The percent decrease in the amount of water from 45 liters to 40 liters was $\underline{\ ?\ }$ %.

Learn Solve word problems involving fractions and percents.

One year, Keith's savings was $200. Andrew's savings was $\frac{4}{5}$ of Keith's savings.

The next year, Andrew increased his savings by 20%. Find the increase in Andrew's savings.

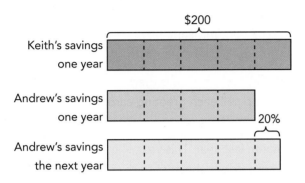

$200

Keith's savings
one year

Andrew's savings
one year   20%

Andrew's savings
the next year

Andrew's savings one year $= \frac{4}{5} \times \$200$

$= \$160$

100% ⟶ $160
1% ⟶ $160 ÷ 100 = $1.60
20% ⟶ 20 × $1.60 = $32

You are comparing Andrew's savings one year with his savings the next year.

So, take his savings one year as 100%.

The increase in Andrew's savings was $32.

Guided Practice

Solve.

7 On Monday, Camille scored 120 points in a video game and Emily scored

$\frac{5}{4}$ as many points as Camille. On Tuesday, Emily scored 30% more points

than what she scored on Monday. Find the increase in the number of points
Emily scored on Tuesday.

Emily's score on Monday $= \frac{5}{4} \times 120$

$= \underline{}^{?}$ points

100% ⟶ $\underline{}^{?}$ points

1% ⟶ $\frac{?}{100}$ points

30% ⟶ $30 \times \frac{?}{100} = \underline{}^{?}$ points

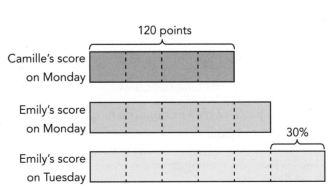

120 points

Camille's score
on Monday

Emily's score
on Monday   30%

Emily's score
on Tuesday

The increase in the number of points Emily
scored on Tuesday was $\underline{}^{?}$.

Practice 6.5

Solve. Show your work.

1 Tom earned $600 last summer delivering newspapers. This summer, he earned 20% more. How much did he earn this summer?

2 A gift shop buys greeting cards at $3.50 each, and sells them at an 80% markup. At what price does the gift shop sell each greeting card?

3 Ms. Kendrick earned $3,600 each month last year. This year, she is given a pay raise of 15%. How much more money does she earn each month this year than she earned each month last year?

4 The original price of a computer was $1,250. At a year-end sale, the selling price of the computer was $900. Find the percent discount.

5 Last year, Alex earned a monthly salary of $250, and Ben earned a monthly salary of $180. This year, each of them received a pay increase of 25%. This year, how much more did Alex earn in one month than Ben?

6 Alan deposited $300 into a savings account. At the end of the first year, the amount of money in the account had increased to $336. At the end of the second year, he had $420.

   a) Find the percent increase in the amount of money in his savings account at the end of the first year.

   b) Find the percent increase in the amount of money in his savings account from the end of the first year to the end of the second year.

7 Linda had an orange ribbon and a blue ribbon. The orange ribbon was 2 meters long. The blue ribbon was $\frac{4}{5}$ as long as the orange ribbon. Linda cut off a piece of blue ribbon. The length of the piece was 25% of the length of the blue ribbon.

   a) What was the length of the blue ribbon before it was cut?

   b) Find the length of the piece of blue ribbon that Linda cut off.

8 One year, the number of subscribers for Newspaper A was 7,600, and the number of subscribers for Newspaper B was $\frac{3}{4}$ of the number of subscribers for Newspaper A. The next year, the number of subscribers for Newspaper B increased by 25%. Find the total number of subscribers for Newspaper B the next year.

9 Ryan had 240 CDs. Sharon had $\frac{9}{2}$ of the number of CDs Ryan had. Sharon gave 75 CDs to her friends. Find the percent decrease in the number of CDs Sharon had. Round your answer to 2 decimal places.

10 Shaun collected $925 on the first day of a charity fundraiser. On the second day, he collected $728. By the third day, he had collected a total of $2,538.

a) What was the percent decrease in the amount of money collected from the first day to the second day? Round your answer to 1 decimal place.

b) Find the percent increase or decrease in the amount collected from the second day to the third day. Round your answer to 1 decimal place.

11 *Math Journal* Jason and Robert each solved the following problem:

In a science experiment, Mark had to record the change in the height of a candle when it is lighted. The height of the candle was 25 centimeters at first. After burning for 10 minutes, the height of the candle decreased to 20 centimeters. Another 20 minutes later, the height of the candle decreased to 15 centimeters. Find the percent decrease in its height from 20 centimeters to 15 centimeters.

Jason's answer:

20 cm − 15 cm = 5 cm

$\frac{5}{25} \times 100\% = 20\%$

The percent decrease in its height was 20%.

Robert's answer:

20 cm − 15 cm = 5 cm

$\frac{5}{20} \times 100\% = 25\%$

The percent decrease in its height was 25%.

Whose answer is incorrect? Explain why.

Brain @ Work

1. A shopping club is having a sale. Members and nonmembers of the club receive different discounts, as shown below.

For Members: 25% off the selling price and a further $20 off with a minimum purchase of $500	For Nonmembers: 10% off the selling price and a further $20 off with a minimum purchase of $500

a) Sally is not a member of the shopping club. She wants to purchase a camcorder that is selling at $580. How much does Sally have to pay for the camcorder?

b) Tabitha is a member of the shopping club. She wants to purchase a computer laptop that is selling at $990. How much does Tabitha have to pay for the computer laptop?

2. In the figure, the area of the shaded part is 40% of the area of Square P. It is also 20% of the area of Square Q. What percent of the figure is shaded? Round your answer to 2 decimal places. (Hint: Find the ratio of the area of the shaded part to the unshaded part.)

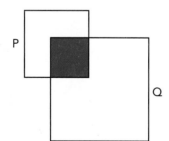

Chapter Wrap Up

Concept Map

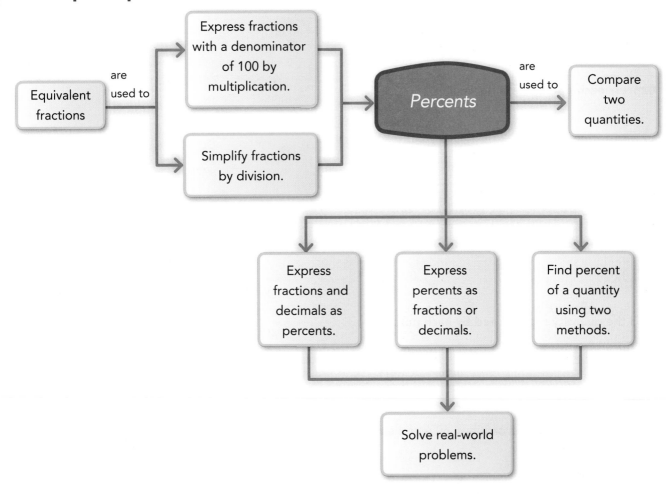

| Equivalent fractions | are used to | Express fractions with a denominator of 100 by multiplication. | | Percents | are used to | Compare two quantities. |

Equivalent fractions — are used to → Express fractions with a denominator of 100 by multiplication. / Simplify fractions by division. → **Percents** — are used to → Compare two quantities.

Percents:
- Express fractions and decimals as percents.
- Express percents as fractions or decimals.
- Find percent of a quantity using two methods.

→ Solve real-world problems.

Key Concepts

▶ A percent is a part-whole comparison in which the whole is divided into 100 equal parts.

▶ A percent can be expressed as a fraction with a denominator of 100 or as a decimal.

▶ 100% has the same value as 1. It is used to find a percent when the denominator of a fraction is not a factor or a multiple of 100.

▶ You can use models to find a percent of a quantity or a percent change.

Chapter Review/Test

Concepts and Skills

Express each percent as a fraction in simplest form.

1 46%

2 $16\frac{2}{3}$ %

3 8.8%

Express each percent as a decimal.

4 34%

5 60%

6 9%

Express each fraction as a percent.

7 $\frac{17}{20}$

8 $\frac{21}{25}$

9 $\frac{270}{300}$

Express each decimal as a percent.

10 0.02

11 0.63

12 0.9

Find the quantity represented by each percent.

13 35% of 500 kilograms

14 68% of $2,800

Solve. Show your work.

15 There were 45 adults on a bus. 60% of them were women. How many women were on the bus?

16 Iris had $900. She spent 22% of this amount on a mobile phone. How much did she pay for the mobile phone?

17 22% of a number is 44. Find the number.

18 125% of a number is 65. Find the number.

Problem Solving

Solve. Show your work.

19 Harold had 1,400 stamps. He gave 350 of them to his brother and the rest to his sister.

   a) What percent of the stamps did he give to his brother?

   b) What percent of the stamps did he give to his sister?

20 There were 15 girls and 25 boys in the Science club. What percent of the members were girls?

21 Tyrone paid $2,800 plus 7% sales tax on mountain bikes for a bike club. How much did Tyrone pay in total for the mountain bikes?

22 Howard opens a savings account with a deposit of $800. The bank will pay him 3% interest per year.

   a) How much interest will Howard receive at the end of $\frac{1}{2}$ year?

   b) How much interest will he receive at the end of 1 year?

23 A grocery shop sells walnuts at a 40% markup. The shop pays $4.50 per pound for the walnuts. At what price per pound will the shop sell the walnuts?

24 Inez earns $160 per month by babysitting. She saves 25% of her monthly salary. If her salary increases by 10%, how much will she now save each month?

25 Last year, Manuel saved $50 per month. This year, he increases his monthly savings by 25%. He plans to buy a smart phone for $375. At this rate, how long will it take him to save enough money to buy the smart phone if he starts saving for it this year?

26 The original price of a watch was $550. During a mid-year sale, the selling price of the watch was $440. Find the percent discount.

27 In January, the price of a kilogram of Brand X rice was $7.60. In May, the price of a kilogram of Brand X rice became $8.80. Find the percent increase in price. Round your answer to 2 decimal places.

28 A tank contained 35 gallons of water at first. Due to a leak at the bottom of the tank, the amount of water in the tank decreased to 32 gallons after 1 hour. After another hour, the amount of water in the tank was 26 gallons.

   a) Find the percent decrease in the amount of water from 35 gallons to 32 gallons. Round your answer to 1 decimal place.

   b) Find the percent decrease in the amount of water from 32 gallons to 26 gallons. Round your answer to 1 decimal place.

Algebraic Expressions

How safe is it?

Imagine this: You are standing on a bridge, about to experience the thrill of bungee jumping. A fast-flowing river rushes by beneath you, and a bungee cord is strapped around your ankles. How safe is it for you to make the jump? Is the bungee cord the right length?

To answer this question, you can use an algebraic expression to calculate how much the bungee cord will stretch when you jump. For example, the amount the cord stretches is 80.9 feet for a 100-pound person, and 111.5 feet for a 150-pound person.

In this chapter, you will learn how variables and algebraic expressions can be used in daily life. For example, the manufacturer of the bungee cords uses an algebraic expression to find the weights that are safe for jumping.

BIG IDEA

▶ Algebraic expressions can be used to describe situations and solve real-world problems.

Recall Prior Knowledge

Using bar models to show the four operations

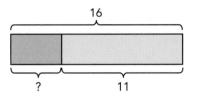

$? = 14 + 9$
$= 23$

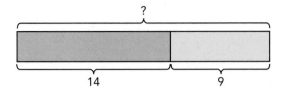

$? = 16 - 11$
$= 5$

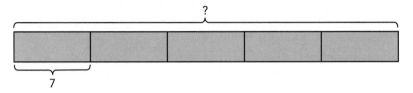

$? = 5 \times 7$
$= 35$

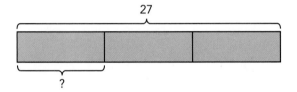

$? = 27 \div 3$
$= 9$

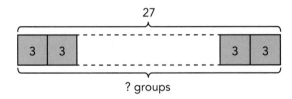

$? = 27 \div 3$
$= 9$

✓ Quick Check

Draw a bar model to show each operation.

1. $15 + 4$

2. $17 - 9$

3. 6×5

4. $28 \div 4$

Finding common factors and greatest common factor of two whole numbers

List the common factors of 6 and 14. Then find their greatest common factor.

$6 = 1 \times 6$ $14 = 1 \times 14$
$6 = 2 \times 3$ $14 = 2 \times 7$

Factors of 6: 1, 2, 3, 6
Factors of 14: 1, 2, 7, 14

The common factors of 6 and 14 are 1 and 2.
The greatest common factor of 6 and 14 is 2.

✔ Quick Check

Find the common factors and greatest common factor of each pair of numbers.

5 6 and 9

6 4 and 12

7 5 and 15

8 8 and 28

Meaning of mathematical terms

The sum of 3 and 4 is $3 + 4$.
The difference "3 less than 4" is $4 - 3$.
The product of 3 and 4 is 3×4.

The quotient of 3 and 4 is $3 \div 4$ or $\dfrac{3}{4}$. 3 is the dividend and 4 is the divisor.

✔ Quick Check

Complete with quotient, sum, difference, product, dividend, or divisor.

9 The __?__ "5 less than 7" is $7 - 5$.

10 The __?__ of 5 and 7 is $\dfrac{5}{7}$. 7 is the __?__ and 5 is the __?__.

11 The __?__ of 5 and 7 is 7×5.

12 The __?__ of 5 and 7 is $5 + 7$.

7.1 Writing Algebraic Expressions

Lesson Objective

• Use variables to write algebraic expressions.

Vocabulary

variable

algebraic expression

terms

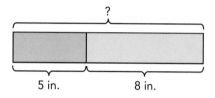

Use variables to represent unknown numbers and write addition expressions.

a) A 5-inch ribbon is taped to an 8-inch ribbon. What is the total length of the two ribbons?

?

5 in.   8 in.

5 + 8 = 13
The total length of the two ribbons is 13 inches.

b) A ribbon of unknown length is taped to a 9-inch ribbon. What is the total length of the two ribbons?

> You can use a letter, called a variable, to represent the unknown length.

> A variable can be replaced by different values. x is a variable, so it can represent different values.
> If the length of the first ribbon is 12 inches, then x is 12.

Let x represent the length, in inches, of the first ribbon.

?

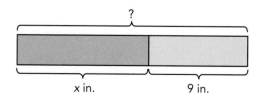

x in.   9 in.

Continue on next page

Lesson 7.1 Writing Algebraic Expressions   **221**

The total length of the two ribbons is (x + 9) inches.

$x + 9$ is an **algebraic expression** in terms of x.
x and 9 are the **terms** of this expression.

You can say that
$x + 9$ is the sum
of x and 9.

earn **Use variables to write subtraction expressions.**

a) A straw of length 10 centimeters is cut from a straw of length 24 centimeters.
What is the length of the remaining straw?

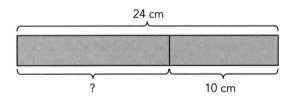

24 cm

?   10 cm

$24 - 10 = 14$
The length of the remaining straw is 14 centimeters.

b) A straw of length 6 centimeters is cut from a straw of length y centimeters. What
is the length of the remaining straw?

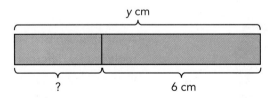

y cm

?   6 cm

y and 6 are the terms of the
expression $y - 6$.

You can say that $y - 6$ means
"6 less than y".

The length of the remaining straw is $(y - 6)$ centimeters.
$y - 6$ is an algebraic expression in terms of y.

Guided Practice

Write an algebraic expression for each of the following.

1 The sum of x and 10

2 The difference "7 less than y"

3 Jim is now z years old.

    a) His brother is 4 years older than Jim. Find his brother's age in terms of z.

    b) His sister is 3 years younger than Jim. Find his sister's age in terms of z.

Learn **Use variables to write multiplication expressions.**

    a) There are 12 crackers in each box. How many crackers are there in 2 boxes?

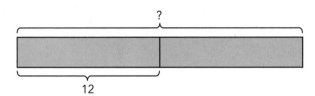

$2 \cdot 12 = 24$
There are 24 crackers in 2 boxes.

....

    b) There are z crackers in each box. How many crackers are there in 4 boxes?

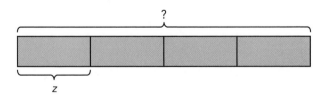

4z is the only term of the expression 4z.

You can say that 4z is the product of z and 4.

$4 \cdot z = 4z$
There are 4z crackers in 4 boxes.
4z is an algebraic expression in terms of z.

Use variables to write division expressions.

a) A 12-inch rod is divided into 3 parts of equal length. What is the length of each part?

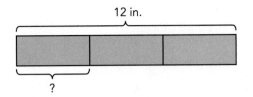

12 ÷ 3 = 4
The length of each part is 4 inches.

b) A rod of length *w* inches is divided into 7 parts of equal length. What is the length of each part?

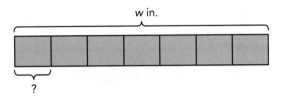

Math Note

$\frac{w}{7}$ can also be written as $\frac{1}{7}w$.

The length of each part is (*w* ÷ 7) inches or $\frac{w}{7}$ inches.

$\frac{w}{7}$ is an algebraic expression in terms of *w*.

$\frac{w}{7}$ is the only term of the expression $\frac{w}{7}$.

You can say that $\frac{w}{7}$ is the quotient of *w* and 7. *w* is the dividend and 7 is the divisor.

Guided Practice

Write an algebraic expression for each of the following.

4 The product of *z* and 6

5 The quotient of *w* and 8

6 Mia bought a pair of shoes for *p* dollars. She also bought a dress that cost 5 times as much as the shoes, and a belt that cost $\frac{1}{4}$ of the price of the shoes.

a) Find the cost of the dress in terms of *p*.

b) Find the cost of the belt in terms of *p*.

Practice 7.1

Write an algebraic expression for each of the following.

1 The sum of 4 and p

2 The difference "8 less than q"

3 The product of 3 and r

4 The quotient of s and 5

5 Cheryl is now x years old.

    a) Her father is 24 years older than Cheryl. Find her father's age in terms of x.

    b) Her brother is 2 years younger than Cheryl. Find her brother's age in terms of x.

    c) Her sister is twice as old as Cheryl. Find her sister's age in terms of x.

    d) Her cousin is $\frac{1}{3}$ Cheryl's age. Find her cousin's age in terms of x.

6 Multiply k by 5, and then add 3 to the product.

7 Divide m by 7, and then subtract 4 from the quotient.

8 Divide j by 9, and then multiply the quotient by 2.

9 The sum of $\frac{1}{3}$ of z and $\frac{1}{5}$ of z

Solve.

10 Jeremy bought 5 pencils for w dollars. Each pen costs 35¢ more than a pencil. Write an algebraic expression for each of the following in terms of w.

    a) The cost, in dollars, of a pen

    b) The number of pencils that Jeremy can buy with $20

11 The figure shown is formed by a rectangle and a square. Express the area of the figure in terms of x.

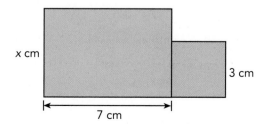

Evaluating Algebraic Expressions

Lesson Objective

• Evaluate algebraic expressions for given values of the variable.

Vocabulary

evaluate

substitute

Learn — **Algebraic expressions can be evaluated for given values of the variable.**

a) Simon has x marbles and Cynthia has 3 marbles. How many more marbles does Simon have than Cynthia?

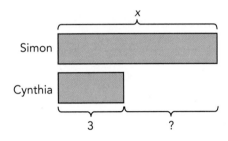

From the model, Simon has (x − 3) more marbles than Cynthia.

To know exactly how many more marbles Simon has than Cynthia, you need to know the value of x.

When x = 5, $x - 3 = 5 - 3$
               $= 2$

When x = 5, Simon has 2 more marbles than Cynthia.

When x = 9, $x - 3 = 9 - 3$
               $= 6$

When x = 9, Simon has 6 more marbles than Cynthia.

When x = 17, $x - 3 = 17 - 3$
               $= 14$

When x = 17, Simon has 14 more marbles than Cynthia.

b) Evaluate $x + 12$ when $x = 5$.

When $x = 5$,
$$x + 12 = 5 + 12$$
$$= 17$$

c) Evaluate $16 - y$ when $y = 9$.

When $y = 9$,
$$16 - y = 16 - 9$$
$$= 7$$

d) Evaluate $3z + 6$ when $z = 4$.

When $z = 4$,
$$3z + 6 = (3 \cdot 4) + 6$$
$$= 12 + 6$$
$$= 18$$

To evaluate an expression for a given value of the variable, **substitute** the given value of the variable into the expression. Then find the value of the expression.

e) Evaluate $\frac{w}{4} - 4$ when $w = 20$.

When $w = 20$,
$$\frac{w}{4} - 4 = \frac{20}{4} - 4$$
$$= 5 - 4$$
$$= 1$$

Guided Practice

Evaluate each algebraic expression for the given value of x.

 1

Expression	Value of x	Value of expression
$11 + x$	12	$11 + 12 = 23$
$x - 15$	22	___?___
$2x + 10$	7	$2(7) + 10 =$ ___?___
$3x - 13$	6	___?___
$20 - 3x$	5	___?___
$\frac{4x}{3}$	9	___?___
$22 - \frac{x}{5}$	20	___?___
$\frac{22 - x}{5}$	20	___?___

Practice 7.2

Evaluate each expression for the given value of the variable.

1 $x + x + 5$ when $x = 7$

2 $3x + 5$ when $x = 5$

3 $5y - 8$ when $y = 3$

4 $40 - 9y$ when $y = 2$

5 $33 - 7w + 6$ when $w = 4$

6 $\dfrac{7w}{6}$ when $w = 18$

7 $4 + \dfrac{5z}{6}$ when $z = 12$

8 $\dfrac{4 + 5z}{6}$ when $z = 12$

9 $20 - \dfrac{4r}{5}$ when $r = 10$

10 $\dfrac{8r}{9} - 15$ when $r = 27$

11 $16 - \dfrac{2z - 4}{3}$ when $z = 18$

12 $16 - \dfrac{2z}{3} - 4$ when $z = 18$

Evaluate each expression when $x = 3$.

13 $\dfrac{x + 1}{2} + \dfrac{5x - 3}{10}$

14 $\dfrac{11 + x}{2} - \dfrac{9x - 3}{4}$

15 $\dfrac{7x - 6}{3} + 4(8 + 2x)$

16 $13(11 - 3x) - \dfrac{5(16 - 4x)}{2}$

17 $5(x + 2) + 2(6 - x) + \dfrac{2x + 3}{3}$

18 $\dfrac{5x - 3}{4} + \dfrac{5(x + 5)}{8} + 3(13 - 2x)$

19 $\dfrac{2x + 4}{5} - \dfrac{x + 1}{4} + \dfrac{x}{6}$

20 $7x - \dfrac{x}{5} + \dfrac{7 - x}{9}$

Evaluate each of the following when $y = 7$.

21 $(5y + 2)$ minus $(2y + 5)$.

22 The sum of $\dfrac{y}{3}$ and $\dfrac{4y}{9}$

23 The product of $(y + 1)$ and $(y - 1)$

24 $8(2y - 1)$ minus $\dfrac{14y + 37}{5}$.

25 The quotient of $9(7y - 15)$ and $\dfrac{110 - 6y}{4}$

26 The sum of $\dfrac{5y}{6}$ and $4\left(\dfrac{3y}{7} + 2y\right)$

27 The quotient of $\left(\dfrac{y}{2} + \dfrac{2y}{3}\right)$ and $\left(\dfrac{5y}{6} - \dfrac{y}{3}\right)$

7.3 Simplifying Algebraic Expressions

Lesson Objectives

- Simplify algebraic expressions in one variable.
- Recognize that the expression obtained after simplifying is equivalent to the original expression.

earn Algebraic expressions can be **simplified**.

a) A straw of length y inches is joined to another straw of the same length. What is the total length of the two straws?

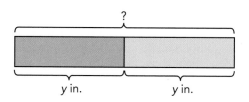

?

y in. y in.

| 4 | 4 |

$4 + 4 = 2 \cdot 4$

| 5 | 5 |

$5 + 5 = 2 \cdot 5$

| y | y |

$y + y = 2 \cdot y$

$2 \cdot y$ is the same as $2y$.

The total length of the two straws is $(y + y)$ inches.

$$y + y = 2 \cdot y$$
$$= 2y$$

$y + y$ has been simplified to $2y$.

In the term $2y$, 2 is called the **coefficient** of y.

b) Each side of the triangle below has length p centimeters.

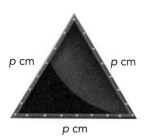

p cm p cm

p cm

Find the perimeter of the triangle in terms of p. Then state the coefficient of the variable.

Continue on next page

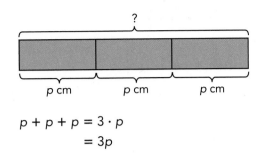

$$p + p + p = 3 \cdot p$$
$$= 3p$$

The perimeter of the triangle is 3p centimeters.
In the term 3p, the coefficient of p is 3.

c) The figure shows six rods and their lengths. Find the total length of the six rods in terms of z. Then state the coefficient of the variable in the expression.

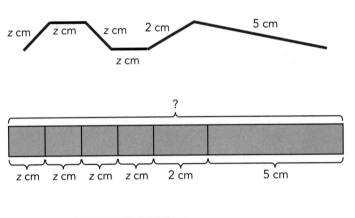

Add the variables together. Then add the numbers.

$$z + z + z + z + 2 + 5 = (4 \cdot z) + 2 + 5$$
$$= 4z + 7$$

The total length of the six rods is (4z + 7) centimeters.
In the term 4z, the coefficient of z is 4.

Guided Practice

Simplify each expression. Then state the coefficient of the variable in the expression.

1 $x + x + x + x + x$

2 $y + y + 6$

3 $m + m + m + 5 + 4$

4 $n + n + n + n + n + n + 12 - 8$

Solve.

5 A square has sides of length x centimeters. Find the perimeter of the square in terms of x.

x cm

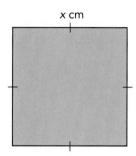

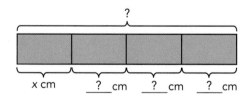

x cm $\underline{\ ?\ }$ cm $\underline{\ ?\ }$ cm $\underline{\ ?\ }$ cm

$x + \underline{\ ?\ } + \underline{\ ?\ } + \underline{\ ?\ } = \underline{\ ?\ }$

The perimeter of the square is $\underline{\ ?\ }$ centimeters.

6 The figure shows a trapezoid. The length of each side is given as shown. Find the perimeter of the trapezoid in terms of w.

10 cm

w cm w cm

w cm

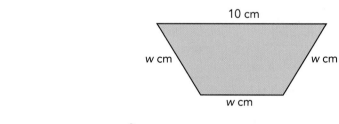

w cm $\underline{\ ?\ }$ cm $\underline{\ ?\ }$ cm $\underline{\ ?\ }$ cm

$w + \underline{\ ?\ } + \underline{\ ?\ } + \underline{\ ?\ } = \underline{\ ?\ }$

The perimeter of the trapezoid is $\underline{\ ?\ }$ centimeters.

Hands-On Activity

RECOGNIZE THAT SIMPLIFIED EXPRESSIONS ARE EQUIVALENT

Work in pairs.

 1 Make the following set of paper strips.

Let the length of the shortest strip be m units. Make and label 5 such strips.

| m | m | m | m | m |

Make and label 4 more strips of lengths $2m$ units, $3m$ units, $4m$ units, and $5m$ units.

| $2m$ | $3m$ |

| $4m$ | $5m$ |

 2 Take one of the longer strips and place it horizontally.

Example

| $3m$ |

 3 Ask your partner to use the pieces of the shortest strips to match the length of the chosen strip in **2**.

Example

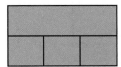

4 Write an algebraic expression to describe the number of short strips used, and simplify it. For example in **3**, write $m + m + m = 3m$.

5 Repeat the activity with other lengths of strips.

 Math Journal How do the lengths of the strips show that the expressions are equivalent?

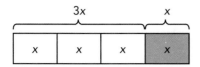

Like terms can be added.

a) Simplify $3x + x$.

$$3x + x = x + x + x + x$$
$$= 4x$$

> 3x and x are the terms of the expression 3x + x.
> 3x and x are called like terms.
> In the expression 2y + 4y + 6 + 3, 2y and 4y are like terms. So are 6 and 3.

> 3x + x and 4x are **equivalent expressions** because they are equal for all values of x.
> If x = 1, 3x + x = 4 and 4x = 4.
> If x = 2, 3x + x = 8 and 4x = 8.

b) Simplify $4z + 2z$.

$$4z + 2z = z + z + z + z + z + z$$
$$= 6z$$

Guided Practice

Complete.

7 Simplify $x + 8x$.

$x + 8x =$ ___?___

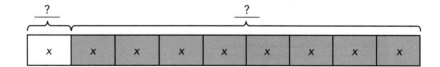

Simplify each expression.

8 $3r + 2r$

9 $5y + 6y$

State whether each pair of expressions are equivalent.

10 $3a$ and $a + a + a$

11 $2h + 2h$ and $4h$

12 $2k + 5$ and $(k + k) \cdot 5$

13 $6z + 4z$ and $10 + 2z$

14 $1p + 3p$ and $13p$

15 $3n + 2 + 4n$ and $2 + 7n$

Like terms can be subtracted.

a) Simplify $2v - v$.

$2v - v = v$

$2v - v$ and v are equivalent expressions because they are equal for all values of v.

If $v = 2$, $2v - v = 2$ and $v = 2$.
If $v = 3$, $2v - v = 3$ and $v = 3$.

b) Simplify $5w - 3w$.

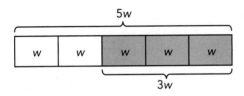

$5w - 3w = 2w$

c) Simplify $y - y$.

$y - y = 0$

Math Note

Any term that is subtracted from itself is equal to zero.

Guided Practice

Complete.

16 Simplify $4s - s$.

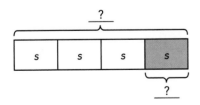

$4s - s = \underline{\quad?\quad}$

Simplify each expression.

17 $12z - 7z$

18 $3p - 3p$

State whether each pair of expressions are equivalent.

19 $f - 6$ and $6 - f$

20 $5c - 5c$ and $a - a$

Use order of operations to simplify algebraic expressions.

a) Simplify $x + 6x + 2x$.

$x + 6x + 2x = 7x + 2x$ Work from left to right.
$ = 9x$ Add.

b) Simplify $7x - 5x - x$.

$7x - 5x - x = 2x - x$ Work from left to right.
$ = x$ Subtract.

c) Simplify $9x - 3x + 2x$.

$9x - 3x + 2x = 6x + 2x$ Work from left to right.
$ = 8x$ Add.

> **Caution** ////////
> When adding and subtracting algebraic terms with no parentheses, always work from left to right.
> For example:
> $7x - 5x - x \neq 7x - 4x$
> $9x - 3x + 2x \neq 9x - 5x$

Guided Practice

Simplify each expression.

21 $(j + 3j) + 2j = \underline{\quad?\quad} + 2j$
$ = \underline{\quad?\quad}$

22 $4j + 5j + 2j$

23 $9t - 3t - 4t$

24 $5t - t - 4t$

25 $8w - 6w + 3w$

26 $7w + 2w - 6w$

Collect like terms to simplify algebraic expressions.

a) The figure shows a parallelogram. Find the perimeter of the parallelogram.

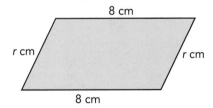

8 cm

r cm r cm

8 cm

$r + 8 + r + 8$ Identify like terms.
$= r + r + 8 + 8$ Change the order of terms to collect like terms.
$= 2r + 16$ Simplify.

> **Math Note** 🎵🎵🎵🎵🎵🎵
> Commutative Property of Addition:
> Two numbers can be added in any order.
>
> So, $4 + a = a + 4$.

The perimeter of the parallelogram is $(2r + 16)$ centimeters.

Continue on next page

b) Simplify $5x - 2 + 3x$.

$$5x - 2 + 3x$$ Identify like terms.

$$= 5x + 3x - 2$$ Change the order of terms to collect like terms.

$$= \quad 8x \quad - 2$$ Simplify.

$5x - 2 + 3x$ and $8x - 2$ are equivalent expressions because they are equal for all values of x.

If $x = 2$, $5x - 2 + 3x = 14$ and $8x - 2 = 14$.
If $x = 3$, $5x - 2 + 3x = 22$ and $8x - 2 = 22$.

Caution ▨▨▨▨▨▨▨

$8x - 2 \neq 6x$ because $8x$ and 2 are not like terms. $8x - 2$ cannot be simplified further.

Guided Practice

Complete.

27 The figure shows a quadrilateral. Find the perimeter of the quadrilateral.

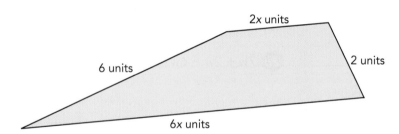

2x units

6 units

2 units

6x units

$$6x + 6 + 2x + 2 = 6x + 2x + 6 + 2$$
$$= \underline{\quad?\quad} + \underline{\quad?\quad}$$

The perimeter of the quadrilateral is $\underline{\quad?\quad}$ units.

Simplify each expression.

28 $4x - 3 + 3x$

29 $5y + 4 - 2y$

30 $8y - 7 - 4y$

31 $7z + 9 - 2z - 2$

32 $5 + 11z - 4 + 6z$

33 $8g + 10 - 3g + 7$

34 $12 + 6g - 5 - 4g$

35 $27 + 3r - 9 + 15r$

Practice 7.3

Simplify each expression. Then state the coefficient of the variable in each expression.

1 $u + u + u + u$

2 $v + v + 5 - 2$

3 $w + w + w + w + w + w + 15 - 7$

Simplify each expression.

4 $3p + p$

5 $4p + 5p$

6 $7p - 2p$

7 $3p - 2p + 5p$

8 $2p + 3p + 4p + 5p - 6p - 7p$

State whether each pair of expressions are equivalent.

9 $5x$ and $x + x + 3x$

10 $4y + 2y + y$ and $5y + y$

11 $2z + 5$ and $z + 8 + z - 3$

12 $2w - 5$ and $5 - 2w$

13 $11u - 4u$ and $11 - 4 + u$

14 $3v + v$ and $\dfrac{12v}{3}$

Simplify each expression.

15 $3x + 5 + 4x + 6$

16 $3x + 2x + 3x + 2$

17 $17 + 4w - 12 - w$

18 $9 + 5u + 6u - 7 - 8u + 4$

Solve.

19 A book has a length of $(b + 2)$ inches and a width of b inches. Write a simplified expression for the perimeter of the book.

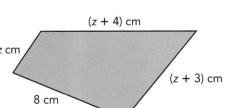
$(b + 2)$ in.

b in.

20 The figure shows a quadrilateral. The length of each side is given as shown. Find the perimeter of the quadrilateral in terms of z.

$(z + 4)$ cm

z cm

$(z + 3)$ cm

8 cm

21 Anne is currently *h* years old. Bill is currently *2h* years old and Charles is currently 8 years old. Find an expression for each person's age after *h* years. Then find an expression for the sum of their ages after *h* years.

22 There are 18 boys in a class. There are *w* fewer boys than girls. How many students are there in the class?

23 A rectangular garden has a length of (y + 2) yards and a width of ($4y$ − 1) yards. Find the perimeter of the garden in terms of *y*.

24 Kayla had $64b$ dollars. She gave $\frac{1}{8}$ of it to Luke and spent $45. How much money did Kayla have left? Express your answer in terms of *b*.

25 A rectangle has a length of ($2m$ + 1) units and a width of (10 − *m*) units. A square has sides of length $\frac{2m + 1}{2}$ units.

a) Find the perimeter of the rectangle.

b) Find the perimeter of the square.

c) Find the sum of the perimeters of the two figures if *m* = 6.

d) If *m* = 6, the perimeter of the rectangle is greater than the perimeter of the square. Find how many units greater the rectangle's perimeter is than the square's perimeter.

 26 *Math Journal* Rita simplified the expression $10w - 5w + 2w$ in this way:

$$10w - 5w + 2w = 10w - 7w$$
$$= 3w$$

Is Rita's answer correct? If not, explain why it is incorrect.

7.4 Expanding and Factoring Algebraic Expressions

Lesson Objectives

- Expand simple algebraic expressions.
- Factor simple algebraic expressions.

Vocabulary

expand   factor

Learn **Use the distributive property to expand algebraic expressions.**

a) Expand $2(r + 8)$.

$2(r + 8)$ means 2 groups of $r + 8$:

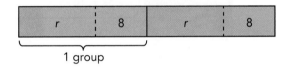

1 group

Rearrange the terms to collect the like terms:

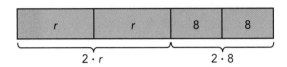

$2 \cdot r$ $2 \cdot 8$

From the models,

$2(r + 8) = 2 \cdot (r + 8)$
$= 2 \cdot r + 2 \cdot 8$
$= 2r + 16$

$2 \cdot (r + 8)$
$= (r + 8) + (r + 8)$
$= r + r + 8 + 8$
$= 2r + 16$

$2r + 16$ is the expanded form of $2(r + 8)$.

$2(r + 8)$ and $2r + 16$ are equivalent expressions because they are equal for all values of r.
If $r = 2$, $2(r + 8) = 20$ and $2r + 16 = 20$.
If $r = 6$, $2(r + 8) = 28$ and $2r + 16 = 28$.

Continue on next page

b) Expand $3(k + 6)$.

$3(k + 6)$ means 3 groups of $k + 6$:

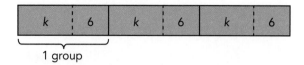

1 group

Rearrange the terms to collect the like terms:

$3 \cdot k$ $3 \cdot 6$

From the models,

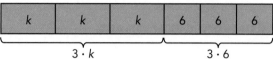

$3(k + 6) = 3 \cdot (k + 6)$
$= 3 \cdot k + 3 \cdot 6$
$= 3k + 18$

$3k + 18$ is the expanded form of $3(k + 6)$.

$3 \cdot (k + 6)$
$= (k + 6) + (k + 6) + (k + 6)$
$= k + k + k + 6 + 6 + 6$
$= 3k + 18$

$3(k + 6)$ and $3k + 18$ are equivalent expressions because they are equal for all values of k.

Guided Practice

Expand each expression.

1 $3(x + 4)$

2 $6(2x + 3)$

3 $2(7 + 6x)$

4 $5(y - 3)$

5 $4(4y - 1)$

6 $9(5x - 2)$

State whether each pair of expressions are equivalent.

7 $6(x + 5)$ and $6x + 30$

8 $7(x + 3)$ and $21 + 7x$

9 $4(y - 4)$ and $4y - 4$

10 $3(y - 6)$ and $18 - 3y$

Hands-On Activity

RECOGNIZE THAT EXPANDED EXPRESSIONS ARE EQUIVALENT

STEP 1 Draw a rectangle that is 8 centimeters wide and more than 3 centimeters long on a piece of paper. Then cut out the rectangle.

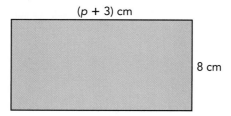

$(p + 3)$ cm

8 cm

STEP 2 Find the area of the rectangle in terms of p.

STEP 3 Then cut the rectangle into two rectangles A and B as shown.

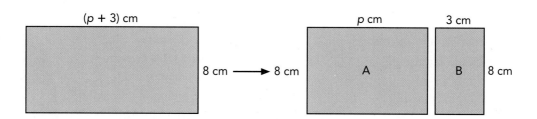

$(p + 3)$ cm

8 cm ⟶ 8 cm

p cm   3 cm

A   B   8 cm

STEP 4 Find the areas of rectangle A and rectangle B.

STEP 5 Using your answers found in **STEP 2** and **STEP 4**, state how the three areas are related.

STEP 6 You may repeat the activity using rectangles of other sizes.

Learn **Algebraic expressions can be factored by taking out a common factor.**

You can expand the expression $3(4z + 1)$ by writing it as $12z + 3$.
You can also start with the expression $12z + 3$ and write it as $3(4z + 1)$.
When you write $12z + 3$ as $3(4z + 1)$, you have factored $12z + 3$.

a) Factor $2y + 10$.

List the factors of each term in the expression.

$10 = 1 \cdot 10$ $2y = 1 \cdot 2y$
$10 = 2 \cdot 5$ $2y = 2 \cdot y$

To factor an expression, look for common factors in the terms of the expression.

The factors of 10 are 1, 2, 5, and 10.
The factors of $2y$ are 1, 2, y, and $2y$.
Excluding 1, the common factor of 10 and $2y$ is 2.

$2y + 10 = \mathbf{2} \cdot y + \mathbf{2} \cdot 5$
$\qquad = \mathbf{2} \cdot (y + 5)$ Take out the common factor 2.
$\qquad = 2(y + 5)$

$2(y + 5)$ is the factored form of $2y + 10$.

Check: Expand the expression $2(y + 5)$ to check the factoring.

$2(y + 5) = 2 \cdot y + 2 \cdot 5$
$\qquad = 2y + 10$

$2y + 10$ is factored correctly.

Factoring is the inverse of expanding. You can use expanding to check if you have factored an expression correctly.

Since they are equal for all values of y, $2y + 10$ and $2(y + 5)$ are equivalent expressions.

b) Factor $6z - 9$.

List the factors of each term in the expression.

$9 = 1 \cdot 9$ $6z = 1 \cdot 6z$

$9 = 3 \cdot 3$ $6z = 2 \cdot 3z$

$6z = 3 \cdot 2z$

$6z = 6 \cdot z$

The factors of 9 are 1, 3, and 9.
The factors of $6z$ are 1, 2, 3, 6, z, $2z$, $3z$, and $6z$.
Excluding 1, the common factor of 9 and $6z$ is 3.

$6z - 9 = 3 \cdot 2z - 3 \cdot 3$

$\quad\quad\quad = 3 \cdot (2z - 3)$ Take out the common factor 3.

$\quad\quad\quad = 3(2z - 3)$

$3(2z - 3)$ is the factored form of $6z - 9$.

Guided Practice

Factor each expression.

11 $3x + 3$

12 $4x + 6$

13 $8 + 6y$

14 $5y - 10$

15 $4 - 10z$

16 $12 - 8x$

17 $8f + 6$

18 $12t - 8$

19 $15 + 5q$

20 $32m - 40$

State whether each pair of expressions are equivalent.

21 $8x + 6$ and $2(4x + 3)$

22 $3(y + 6)$ and $18 + 3y$

23 $5x - 10$ and $5(x - 5)$

24 $4(y - 4)$ and $16 - 4y$

25 $3(x + 5)$ and $15 + 3x$

26 $12 - 8y$ and $4(2y - 3)$

Expand each expression.

1 $5(x + 2)$

2 $7(2x - 3)$

3 $4(y - 3)$

4 $8(3y - 4)$

5 $3(x + 11)$

6 $9(4x - 7)$

Factor each expression.

7 $6p + 6$

8 $3p + 18$

9 $12 + 3q$

10 $4w - 16$

11 $14r - 8$

12 $12r - 12$

State whether each pair of expressions are equivalent.

13 $4x + 12$ and $4(x + 3)$

14 $5(x - 1)$ and $5x - 1$

15 $7(5 + y)$ and $7y + 35$

16 $9(y - 2)$ and $18 - 9y$

Expand and simplify each expression.

17 $3(m + 2) + 4(6 + m)$

18 $5(2p + 5) + 4(2p - 3)$

19 $4(6k + 7) + 9 - 14k$

Simplify each expression. Then factor the expression.

20 $14x + 13 - 8x - 1$

21 $8(y + 3) + 6 - 3y$

22 $4(3z + 7) + 5(8 + 6z)$

Solve.

23 Expand and simplify the expression $3(x - 2) + 9(x + 1) + 5(1 + 2x) + 2(3x - 4)$.

24 Are the two expressions equivalent? Justify your reasoning.
$15(y + 6) + 10(y - 5) + 20(2y + 3)$ and $5(20 + 13y)$

25 A yard of lace costs w cents and a yard of fabric costs 40¢ more than the lace. Kimberly wants to buy one yard of lace and 2 yards of fabric. How much money will she need? Express your answer in terms of w.

26 The average weight of 6 packages is $(9m + 8)$ pounds. 2 more packages, with weights of $(12m + 12)$ pounds and $(14m + 12)$ pounds, are added to the original 6 packages. Find the average weight of the 8 packages.

27 The figure shows two rectangles joined to form rectangle $ABCD$.

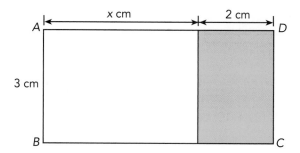

a) Write the length of $\overline{BC}$ in terms of x. Then write an expression for the area of the rectangle $ABCD$ in terms of x.

b) Write an expression for the area of each of the two smaller rectangles.

c) *Math Journal* Explain how you can use your answers in **a)** and **b)** to show that the following expressions are equivalent.

$$3x + 6 \text{ and } 3(x + 2)$$

7.5 Real-World Problems: Algebraic Expressions

Lesson Objective

- Solve real-world problems involving algebraic expressions.

Learn **Write an addition or subtraction algebraic expression for a real-world problem and evaluate it.**

The figure shows a triangle ABC.

a) What is the perimeter of the triangle ABC in terms of s?

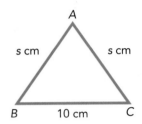

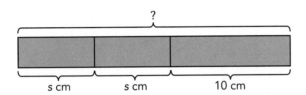

$$s + s + 10 = 2s + 10$$

The perimeter of the triangle ABC is $(2s + 10)$ centimeters.

b) The perimeter of a trapezoid is 7 cm shorter than the perimeter of triangle ABC. Find the perimeter of the trapezoid.

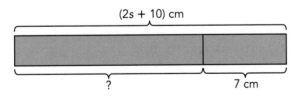

$$2s + 10 - 7 = 2s + 3$$

The perimeter of the trapezoid is $(2s + 3)$ centimeters.

c) If $s = 7$, find the perimeter of the triangle ABC.

When $s = 7$,
$$\begin{aligned} 2s + 10 &= (2 \cdot 7) + 10 \\ &= 14 + 10 \\ &= 24 \end{aligned}$$

$AC = s$ cm. Since $s = 7$, $AC = 7$ cm.

The perimeter of the triangle ABC is 24 centimeters.

Guided Practice

Complete.

1 Raoul is *y* years old. Kayla is 6 years older than Raoul and Isaac is 4 years younger than Raoul.

a) Find Kayla's age.

Kayla is __?__ years old.

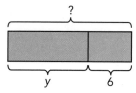

b) Find Isaac's age.

Isaac is __?__ years old.

c) If *y* = 12, find the sum of Raoul's age and Isaac's age.

When *y* = 12,

Isaac's age:

$$\underline{\quad?\quad} - \underline{\quad?\quad} = \underline{\quad?\quad} - \underline{\quad?\quad}$$

$$= \underline{\quad?\quad} \text{ years old}$$

Sum of Raoul's age and Isaac's age:

$$\underline{\quad?\quad} + \underline{\quad?\quad} = \underline{\quad?\quad}$$

The sum of Raoul's age and Isaac's age is __?__ years.

Learn **Write a multiplication or division algebraic expression for a real-world problem and evaluate it.**

A car uses 1 gallon of gas for every 25 miles traveled.

a) How far can the car travel on *w* gallons of gas?

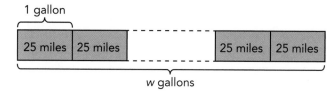

1 gallon ⟶ 25 miles

w gallons ⟶ *w* · 25 = 25*w* miles

The car can travel 25*w* miles on *w* gallons of gas.

Continue on next page

b) How much gas is used if the car travels 5w miles? Evaluate this expression when w = 72.

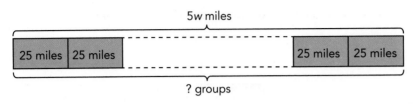

5w miles

25 miles | 25 miles | | 25 miles | 25 miles

? groups

25 miles ⟶ 1 gallon

5w miles ⟶ $5w \div 25 = \dfrac{5w}{25}$

$\qquad\qquad\qquad = \dfrac{w}{5}$ gallons

$\dfrac{w}{5}$ gallons of gas is used.

When w = 72,

$\dfrac{w}{5} = \dfrac{72}{25}$

$\qquad = 14.4$

Guided Practice

Complete.

2 A pickup truck uses 1 gallon of gas for every 14 miles traveled.

a) How far can it travel on 3p gallons of gas?

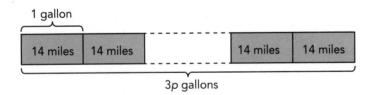

1 gallon

14 miles | 14 miles | | 14 miles | 14 miles

3p gallons

1 gallon ⟶ __?__ miles

3p gallons ⟶ __?__ · __?__ = __?__ miles

It can travel ___?___ miles on 3p gallons of gas.

b) How many gallons of gas have been used after the pickup truck has traveled *v* miles? Evaluate this expression when *v* = 56.

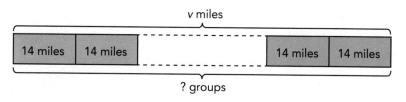

v miles

| 14 miles | 14 miles | | 14 miles | 14 miles |

? groups

14 miles → ____?____ gallon

v miles → ___?___ ÷ ___?___ = ___?___ gallons

___?___ gallons have been used.

When *v* = 56,

$$\frac{?}{} = \frac{?}{}$$

$$= \underline{\ ?\ }$$

Learn Write an algebraic expression using several operations and evaluate it.

Gillian thinks of a number *y*. She multiplies it by 3 and then subtracts 9 from the product. What is her answer? Evaluate this expression when *y* = 12.

y multiplied by 3:

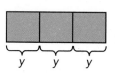

y   *y*   *y*

$y \cdot 3 = 3y$

Subtract 9 from the product:

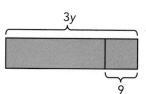

3y

9

$3y - 9$

Gillian's answer is $3y - 9$.

When *y* = 12,
$3y - 9 = (3 \cdot 12) - 9$
$= 36 - 9$
$= 27$

Guided Practice

Complete.

3 There were three questions in a mathematics test. Salma earned m points for the first question and twice the number of points for the second question.

    a) How many points did she earn for the first two questions?

First question: _?_ points

Second question: _?_ points

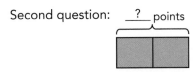

_?_ + _?_ = _?_

She earned _?_ points for the first two questions.

    b) If she received a total of 25 points on the test, how many points did she earn for the third question?

25 points

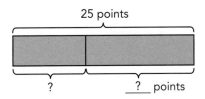

?   _?_ points

She earned _?_ points for the third question.

    c) If $m = 5$, find the points she earned for each question.

First question: $m = 5$

Second question: $2m = 2 \cdot$ _?_

$$= \underline{\quad?\quad}$$

Third question: $25 - 3m = 25 - (3 \cdot \underline{\;?\;})$

$$= 25 - \underline{\;?\;}$$

$$= \underline{\;?\;}$$

She earned _?_ points for the first question, _?_ points for the second question and _?_ points for the third question.

Practice 7.5

1 Jenny is x years old. Thomas is 3 times as old as she is. Jenny is 5 years older than Alexis.

   a) Find Alexis's age in terms of x.

   b) Find Thomas's age in terms of x.

   c) If $x = 12$, how much older is Thomas than Jenny?

2 A van travels from Town A to Town B. It uses 1 gallon of gas for every 24 miles traveled.

   a) How many gallons of gas does the van use if it travels $3x$ miles?

   b) The van uses $2y$ gallons of gas for its journey from Town A to Town B. Find the distance between Town A and Town B.

3 Brian bought x apples and some oranges. Brian bought 3 more oranges than apples.

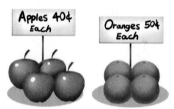

   a) Find the total number of fruit Brian bought in terms of x.

   b) Find the total amount of money, in cents, that Brian spent on the fruit. Give your answer in terms of x.

   c) If Brian could have bought exactly 12 pears with the amount of money that was spent on the apples and oranges, find the cost of each pear, in cents, in terms of x.

4 A rectangle has a width of x centimeters and a perimeter of $8x$ centimeters. A square has sides of length $\frac{1}{4}$ that of the length of the rectangle.

   a) Find the length of the rectangle.

   b) Find the perimeter of the square.

   c) Find how many centimeters greater the rectangle's perimeter is than the square's perimeter if $x = 4$.

   d) Find how many square centimeters greater the rectangle's area is than the square's area if $x = 4$.

5 José bought 4 comic books and 2 nonfiction books. The 4 comic books cost him 8y dollars. If the cost of one nonfiction book is (3 + 7y) dollars more expensive than the cost of one comic book, find

a) the cost of the 2 nonfiction books in terms of y.

b) the total amount that José spent on the books if y = 4.

6 Wyatt has (2x − 1) one-dollar bills and (4x + 2) five-dollar bills. Susan has 3x dollars more than Wyatt.

a) Find the total amount of money that Wyatt has in terms of x.

b) Find the number of pens that Wyatt can buy if each pen costs 50 cents.

c) If x = 21, find how much money Susan will have now if Wyatt gives her half the number of five-dollar bills that he has.

Brain @ Work

Find the perimeter of the figure in terms of x, given that all the angles in the figure are right angles. If x = 5.5, evaluate this expression.

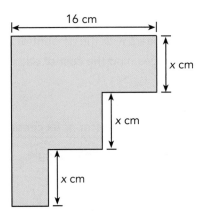

Chapter Wrap Up

Concept Map

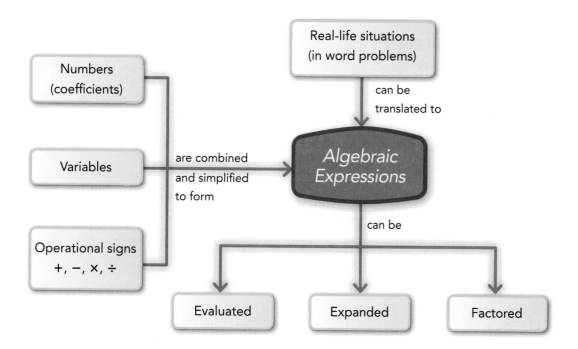

Key Concepts

▶ A letter or variable in an algebraic expression represents an unknown specific number or any number.

▶ The expression $x + x + x + x + x + x + x$ is equivalent to $7x$.

▶ Expanding and factoring are inverse operations.

Chapter Review/Test

Concepts and Skills

Write an algebraic expression for each of the following.

1. A number that is 5 more than twice x

2. The total cost, in dollars, of 4 pencils and 5 pens if each pencil costs w cents and each pen costs $2w$ cents

3. The length of a side of a square whose perimeter is r units

4. The perimeter of a rectangle whose sides are of lengths $(3z + 2)$ units and $(2z + 3)$ units

Evaluate each expression for the given value of the variable.

5. $3(x + 4) - \frac{x}{2}$ when $x = 2$

6. $\frac{5p + 9}{2} + \frac{2p + 5}{3}$ when $p = 5$

Simplify each expression.

7. $24k + 11 - 5k - 4$

8. $10 + 13h - 6 - 4h + 9 + 12h$

Expand each expression.

9. $5(m + 3) + 2(m + 8)$

10. $9(x + 2) + 4(5 + x)$

Factor each expression.

11. $5a - 25$

12. $28 - 7x$

13. $12z + 28 - 7z - 3$

State whether each pair of expressions are equivalent.

14. $3(x + 5)$ and $5(x + 3)$

15. $6y - 26$ and $2(3y - 13)$

16. $18 - 12p$ and $3(5 + 6p) + 3(2p + 1)$

17. $15 - 5q$ and $5(q - 3)$

Problem Solving

Solve. Show your work.

18. Juan is g years old and Eva is 2 years younger than Juan.

    a) Find the sum of their ages in terms of g.

    b) Find the sum of their ages in g years' time, in terms of g.

19 Parker bought 4 times as many marbles as Molly. Cole bought 5 fewer marbles than Parker. If Molly bought p marbles, how many marbles did Cole buy?

20 Andrea baked h muffins. Violet baked 8 fewer muffins than Andrea. Find the average number of muffins baked by both girls, in terms of h.

21 A square garden has a side length that is 3 meters shorter than the length of a rectangular garden. Find the perimeter of the rectangular garden in terms of y.

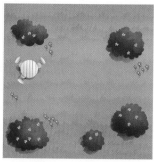

Perimeter = 8y meters

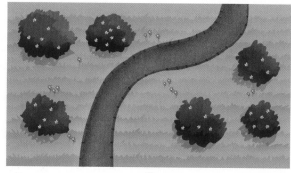

(2y + 1) meters

?

22 Mrs. Roberts sewed m shirts using 2 yards of cloth for each shirt. She also sewed $(m + 2)$ dresses, using 5 yards of cloth for each dress.

   a) How much cloth did she use altogether? Give your answer in terms of m.

   b) If $m = 7$, find how much more cloth she used to sew the dresses than the shirts.

23 A glass jug can hold $(6p + 8)$ quarts more water than a plastic container. 2 glass jugs and 2 plastic containers contain $56p$ quarts of water in all.

   a) How much water can the plastic container hold? Give your answer in terms of p.

   b) If $p = 3$, find how much water can 1 glass jug and 1 plastic container hold in all.

24 Mr. Lee can paint 20 chairs in t hours. He uses 3 liters of paint for every 12 chairs that he painted.

   a) Find, in terms of t, the number of chairs that he can paint in 3 hours.

   b) Find, in terms of t, the time taken by Mr. Lee to paint 7 chairs.

   c) If $t = 4$, find the amount of paint Mr. Lee has used after painting for 4 hours.

Cumulative Review Chapters 4–7

Concepts and Skills

Write each ratio in simplest form. (Lesson 4.2)

1 12 : 28

2 32 : 18

3 36 : 81

4 64 : 40

Find the missing term in each pair of equivalent ratios. (Lesson 4.2)

5 35 : 25 = __?__ : 5

6 48 : 33 = 16 : __?__

7 18 : __?__ = 9 : 12

8 __?__ : 24 = 21 : 14

Express each percent as a fraction in simplest form. (Lesson 6.1)

9 58%

10 $24\frac{1}{3}\%$

11 9.4%

Express each percent as a decimal. (Lesson 6.1)

12 37%

13 67%

14 8.9%

Express each fraction as a percent. (Lesson 6.2)

15 $\frac{19}{20}$

16 $\frac{23}{25}$

17 $\frac{360}{400}$

Express each decimal as a percent. (Lesson 6.2)

18 0.07

19 0.62

20 0.8

Find the quantity represented by each percent. (Lesson 6.3)

21 55% of 600 liters

22 73% of $3,900

Write an algebraic expression for each of the following. (Lesson 7.1)

23 A number that is 7 more than 3 times x

24 The total cost, in cents, of 8 apples and 9 oranges if each apple costs $2y$ cents and each orange costs $3y$ cents

25 The perimeter of a rectangle whose sides are of lengths $(4z + 3)$ units and $(3z + 5)$ units

Evaluate each expression for the given value of the variable. (Lesson 7.2)

26 $4(x + 5) - \dfrac{2x}{3}$ when $x = 6$

27 $\dfrac{6y + 7}{3} + \dfrac{3y + 4}{4}$ when $y = 8$

Simplify each expression. (Lesson 7.3)

28 $36a + 12 - 6a - 7$

29 $21 + 34b - 8 - 5b + 8 + 23b$

Expand each expression. (Lesson 7.4)

30 $6(m + 4) + 3(m + 9)$

31 $8(n + 4) + 5(6 + n)$

Factor each expression. (Lesson 7.4)

32 $6a - 42$

33 $56 - 8b$

34 $23c + 37 - 5c + 8$

35 $58 + 40d - 9 - 19d$

Problem Solving

Solve. Show your work.

36 A factory produces 550 bottles of water in 25 minutes. How many bottles can it produce in 3 minutes? (Chapter 5)

37 A machine can stamp 75 caps per minute. At this rate, how long will it take to stamp 3,000 caps? (Chapter 5)

38 There were 65 students in the hall. 80% of them were girls. How many girls were in the hall? (Chapter 6)

39 Kenneth had $1,800. He spent 34% of it on a watch. How much did he pay for the watch? (Chapter 6)

40 28% of a number is 168. Find the number. (Chapter 6)

41 140% of a number is 364. Find the number. (Chapter 6)

42 Of the 90 students who sat for a test, 24 students passed. Find the ratio of the number of students who passed the test to the number of students who did not. Give your answer in simplest form. (Chapter 4)

43 On Saturday, Aaron spent $108. On Sunday, he spent $54 more than what he spent on Saturday. Find the ratio of Aaron's spending on Saturday to his spending on both Saturday and Sunday. Give your answer in simplest form. (Chapter 4)

44 A dalmatian weighs 72 pounds. A bullmastiff is 24 pounds heavier than the dalmatian. A bulldog is 12 pounds lighter than the bullmastiff. Find the ratio of the bulldog's weight to the dalmatian's weight. Give your answer in simplest form. (Chapter 4)

45 The ratio of the number of left-handers to the number of right-handers in a middle school is 6 : 15. If there are 120 left-handers, how many right-handers are there? (Chapter 4)

46 Mrs. Jackson gave a sum of money to her son and daughter in the ratio 8 : 9. Her daughter received $3,060. How much did Mrs. Jackson give to her two children in all? (Chapter 4)

47 The ratio of the number of boys to the number of girls in a school is 7 : 9. If there are 1,248 students in the school, how many girls are there? (Chapter 4)

48 A sum of money was shared among Daniel, Elliot, and Frank in the ratio 5 : 7 : 8. If Frank's share was $2,781 more than Daniel's share, what was the original sum of money shared among the three men? (Chapter 4)

49 A tank is filled with water at a rate of 2.4 liters per minute. At this rate, how long will it take to fill the tank with 84 liters of water? (Chapter 5)

50 A farmer uses 920 grams of grains to feed 8 chickens. (Chapter 5)

    a) At this rate, how many grams of grains does he use to feed 100 chickens?

    b) At this rate, how many chickens can he feed using 48.3 kilograms of grains?

51 The distance between School A and School B is 360 kilometers. (Chapter 5)

    a) If a bus leaves School A at 9:30 A.M. and reaches School B at 2:30 P.M., what is its speed in kilometers per hour?

    b) If a car travels at a speed of 80 kilometers per hour, how long will it take to travel from School A to School B?

52 A truck traveled from Town A to Town B, and then to Town C. The truck took 3 hours to travel from Town A to Town B at an average speed of 42 kilometers per hour. It then traveled from Town B to Town C at an average speed of 68 kilometers per hour. The truck took a total of 5 hours to travel from Town A to Town C. (Chapter 5)

    a) What is the distance between Town A and Town B?

    b) What was average speed of the truck for the whole journey?

53 Russell bought a CD player that cost $120 before it went on sale for a 15% discount. If he paid 5% sales tax on the sale price, how much did Russell pay for the CD player? (Chapter 6)

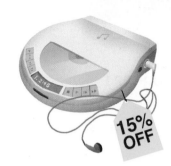

54 Last year, Jane had $2,800 in her bank account. This year, her savings increased by 4.5%. She plans to increase her savings by 5% next year. How much will Jane have in her account after the two-year period? (Chapter 6)

55 Two jackets were on sale. The first jacket cost $239 and was marked down 40%. The second jacket cost $159 and was given a 20% discount. Which of the two jackets cost less during the sale? Justify your reasoning. (Chapter 6)

56 One year, the price of a motorcycle was $3,000. It increased to $3,550 another year. What is the percent increase in its price? Round your answer to 2 decimal places. (Chapter 6)

57 Leonard has 5 times as many stamps as Alison. Melissa has 7 more stamps than Leonard. If Alison has q stamps, how many stamps does Melissa have? (Chapter 7)

58 Tim is k years old and Jennifer is 4 years younger than Tim. Find their average age in $3k$ years' time, in terms of k. (Chapter 7)

59 The length of a rectangular garden is 7 meters longer than its width. If its perimeter is $(12x + 14)$ meters, find its length in terms of x. (Chapter 7)

60 A cupboard weighs $(5y + 6)$ pounds more than a table. 3 cupboards and 4 tables weigh $(29y + 18)$ pounds in all. (Chapter 7)

a) Find the weight of the table in terms of y.

b) If $y = 15$, find the total weight of 2 cupboards and 3 tables.

61 A factory can produce 45 containers of yogurt in t minutes. 950 grams of fruit are used for every 25 containers of yogurt. (Chapters 5, 7)

a) Find, in terms of t, the number of containers of yogurt that the factory can produce in 5 minutes.

b) Find, in terms of t, the time taken by the factory to produce 100 containers of yogurt.

c) If $t = 6$, find the amount of fruit used in producing containers of yogurt in 8 minutes.

Selected Answers

CHAPTER 1

Lesson 1.1, Guided Practice (pp. 7–13)

1.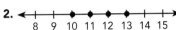

2.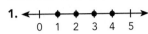

3.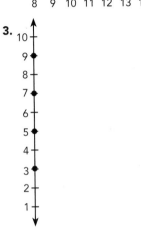

4.

5.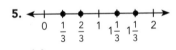

<; >

6.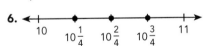

7.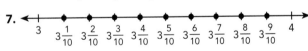

8.

9.

10.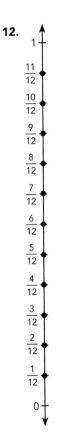

>; <

11.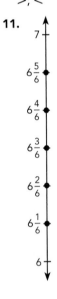

12.

13.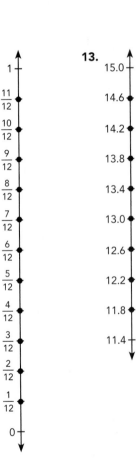

14.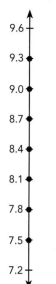

15.

11.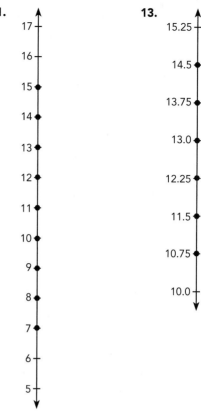

13.

16. >   **17.** <   **18.** >   **19.** >   **20.** 0.5; 0.5; left; >

21. <   **22.** >   **23.** >   **24.** >   **25.** >   **26.** <

Lesson 1.1, Practice (pp. 14–15)

1.
23 24 25   27   30   33

3.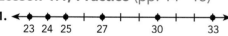
5.1   5.12 5.13   5.15   5.17   5.2

5.
0 1 2 3 4 5 6 7 8 9 10

7.
0   $\frac{1}{3}$ $\frac{2}{3}$ 1 $1\frac{1}{3}$ $1\frac{2}{3}$ 2

9.

15. <   **17.** <   **19.** >

21.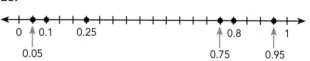
2   2.125   2.375 2.5   2.875   3

23.

0 ↑ 0.1   0.25   ↑ 0.8 ↑ 1
  0.05   0.75 0.95

25. <   **27.** <   **29.** <   **31.** >

33. Jina's model; 0.1 centimeter taller

Lesson 1.2, Guided Practice (p. 17)

1. Method 1:

$$
\begin{array}{c|c}
2 & 48 \\\hline
2 & 24 \\\hline
2 & 12 \\\hline
2 & 6 \\\hline
 & 3
\end{array}
$$

2; 2; 3

Method 2:

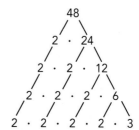

Lesson 1.2, Practice (p. 18)

1.

1	②	③	4	⑤	6
⑦	8	9	10	⑪	12
⑬	14	15	16	⑰	18
⑲	20	21	22	㉓	24
25	26	27	28	㉙	30

3. 3×5 **5.** $2 \times 3 \times 13$ **7.** $2 \times 2 \times 2 \times 3 \times 3 \times 5$

9. 7×7 **11.** $2 \times 2 \times 2 \times 2 \times 3 \times 3$

13. $2 \times 3 \times 5 \times 17$ **15.** $3 \times 3 \times 11 \times 11$

17. $2 \times 2 \times 3 \times 3 \times 5 \times 5$ **19.** Step 1: Find the factors of 42. They are 1, 2, 3, 6, 7, 14, 21, and 42. Step 2: Identify the factors that are also prime numbers. They are 2, 3, and 7. Step 3: The prime factors of 42 are 2, 3, and 7.

21. $2 \times 2 \times 2 \times 2 \times 2 \times 2 \times 2 \times 5 \times 5$

23a. $2 \times 2 \times 2 \times 2 \times 3 \times 5 \times 5$

23b. $2 \times 2 \times 2 \times 3 \times 5$

Lesson 1.3, Guided Practice (pp. 19–26)

1. 1; 2; 5; 10; 1; 2; 4; 7; 14; 28; 1; 2   **2.** 1, 2, 4, and 8

3. 1   **4.** 1 and 2   **5.** 1 and 2   **6.** Method 1: 1; 2; 4; 5; 10; 20; 1; 2; 4; 8; 16; 32; 1; 2; 4; 4; Method 2: 2; 5; 2; 2; 2; 2; 2; 4; 4;

Method 3:

```
2 | 20, 32
2 | 10, 16
      5, 8
```

2; 4; 4

7. 3   **8.** 18   **9.** 24   **10.** 20   **11.** 3; 3; 3; 5; 3; 3; 9; 9; 2; 9; 5; 9; 2; 5   **12.** 7(5 + 13)   **13.** 5(12 + 17)

14. 8(3 + 8)   **15.** 3; 6; 9; 12; 15; 18; 21; 24; 27; 30; 33; 36; 39; 42; 45; 5; 10; 15; 20; 25; 30; 35; 40; 45; 50; 15; 30; 45

16. First 10 multiples of 6: 6, 12, 18, 24, 30, 36, 42, 48, 54, 60; First 10 multiples of 12: 12, 24, 36, 48, 60, 72, 84, 96, 108, 120; Common multiples: 12, 24, 36, 48, 60   **17.** First 10 multiples of 7: 7, 14, 21, 28, 35, 42, 49, 56, 63, 70; First 10 multiples of 11: 11, 22, 33, 44, 55, 66, 77, 88, 99, 110; Common multiples: None   **18.** Method 1: 8; 16; 24; 32; 40; 48; 56; 64; 72; 80; 10; 20; 30; 40; 50; 60; 70; 80; 90; 100; 40; 80; 40; Method 2: 2; 2; 5; 2; 2; 5; 40; 40

Method 3:

```
2 | 8, 10
      4, 5
```

4; 5; 40; 40

19. 21   **20.** 60   **21.** 36   **22.** 66

Lesson 1.3, Practice (pp. 27–28)

1. 1, 3, and 9   **3.** 1, 2, 5, and 10   **5.** 1, 2, 13, and 26

7. 12   **9.** 14   **11.** 13   **13.** 30, 60, 90, 120, 150

15. 90, 180, 270, 360, 450   **17.** 75, 150, 225, 300, 375

19. 30   **21.** 40   **23.** 70   **25.** 2   **27.** 12   **29.** 3

31. 504   **33.** 210   **35.** 18,975   **37.** 5; 100

39. 27; 810   **41a.** 4 inches

41b. $84 + 116 = 4 \cdot 21 + 4 \cdot 29$

$\qquad\qquad = 4(21 + 29)$

The number inside the parentheses represents the number of pieces of rope that can be cut from each type of rope.

43. 10:48 a.m.

Lesson 1.4, Guided Practice (pp. 30–31)

1. 4   **2.** 36   **3.** 81   **4.** 121   **5.** 5   **6.** 8   **7.** 12   **8.** 14

Lesson 1.4, Practice (p. 32)

1. 9   **3.** 144   **5.** 6   **7.** 11   **9.** 36, 49, 64, 81   **11.** 3,136

13. 17   **15.** 22   **17.** 510   **19.** 152,100   **21.** $296

Lesson 1.5, Guided Practice (pp. 34–36)

1. 125   **2.** 216   **3.** 729   **4.** 6   **5.** 7   **6.** 10

7. 5; 5; 25; 5; 5; 5; 125; 25; 125; 150; 3,125   **8.** 232

9. 279   **10.** 1,206   **11.** 7   **12.** 76   **13.** 297

Lesson 1.5, Practice (pp. 37–38)

1. 512   **3.** 1,000   **5.** 8   **7.** 125, 216, 343, 512

9. 8 and 9   **11.** 964   **13.** $38\frac{1}{9}$ **15.** 740   **17.** 250

19. 2,331   **21.** 4,096   **23.** 12   **25.** 15   **27.** 140

29. 7,845   **31.** 8, 9, and 10

Lesson 1.5, Brain@Work (p. 38)

12 square tiles

Chapter Review/Test (pp. 40–41)

1.

3.

| 4 | $4\frac{1}{4}$ | $4\frac{2}{4}$ | $4\frac{3}{4}$ | 5 | $5\frac{1}{4}$ | $5\frac{2}{4}$ | $5\frac{3}{4}$ | 6 |

5. $2 \times 3 \times 7$ **7.** 1, 3, 7, and 21   **9.** 4   **11.** 20, 40, 60

13. 30   **15.** 196   **17.** 13   **19.** 64   **21.** 11   **23.** 100

25. 7,831   **27.** 396,900   **29.** 160   **31.** 12 and 13

33. After 630 minutes or 10 hours 30 minutes   **35.** 216 plastic cubes

CHAPTER 2

Lesson 2.1, Guided Practice (pp. 46–51)

1. −36°F **2.** −$10,540 **3.** −29,035 feet **4.** 45 yards
5. below **6.** 928 **7.** Death Valley, CA **8.** Pilot
Mountain, NC **9.** New Orleans, LA

10.
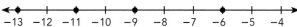

11.
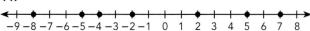

12.
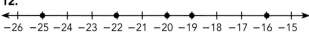

13. 14 **14.** 9 **15.** 17 **16.** −27 **17.** 23 **18.** −46
19. < **20.** > **21.** < **22.** < **23.** > **24.** <
25. 0°C > −5°C **26.** −131 feet < −92 feet
27. Answers vary. Sample: −61°F is less than −47°F.
28. Answers vary. Sample: An elevation of −520 feet is
greater than an elevation of −893 feet.

Lesson 2.1, Practice (pp. 52–53)

1. 438°C **3.** −8,327 feet **5.** −20 yards

7.
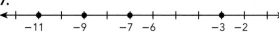

9. −8 **11.** −21 **13.** −24

15.

17.

```
  −90
  −91
  −92
● −93
  −94
● −95
  −96
● −97
  −98
● −99
  −100
● −101
  −102
  −103
  −104
```

19. < **21.** < **23.** > **25.** < **27.** > **29.** >
31. −9, −5, −2, 0, 3, 7 **33.** 43, 31, 19, −14, −20, −57
35. −5 and −9. Opposite of −5: 5, opposite of −9: 9
37. −22°C < −4°C **39.** −36,200 feet < −24,442
feet; Pacific Ocean **41.** Answers vary. Sample: An
elevation of −45 feet is closer to sea level than an
elevation of −80 feet.

Lesson 2.2, Guided Practice (pp. 55–56)

1. 10 **2.** 3 **3.** 8 **4.** 1 **5.** 7 **6.** 0 **7.** 23
8. 41 **9.** 38 **10.** 114 **11.** 132 **12.** 506
13a. Amount owed to Kelly: −18, amount owed by
David: 20 **13b.** Joe **14a.** Lowest part of garage:
−40, highest part of garage: 20, limousine parking
area: −23 **14b.** The highest part of the garage

Lesson 2.2, Practice (pp. 57–58)

1. 11 **3.** 6 **5.** 46 **7.** < **9.** > **11.** 16
13a. March, April, and July **13b.** $450 **13c.** March
13d. April **13e.** $870 **15a.** Earth **15b.** Uranus
15c. Earth **15d.** −218°C, −108°C, −53°C, 14°C

Lesson 2.2, Brain@Work (p. 58)

1a. −3 **1b.** 3 **2.** 23°C

Chapter Review/Test (pp. 60−61)

1. 47 **3.** 78

5.

−134 −132 −130 −128 −126 −124 −122 −120 −118
−133 −131 −129 −127 −125 −123 −121 −119

7.

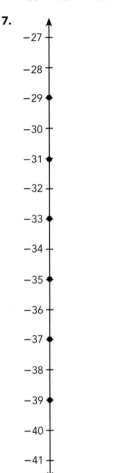

−27
−28
−29
−30
−31
−32
−33
−34
−35
−36
−37
−38
−39
−40
−41

9. −181°F **11.** −11 meters **13.** > **15.** <

17. 15, 7, 2, −5, −6, −9, −14 **19.** −112°C > −143°C

21. 79 **23.** 102 **25.** < **27.** < **29a.** 12:30 a.m.

29b. Between 4:30 a.m. and 8:30 a.m.

CHAPTER 3

Lesson 3.1, Guided Practice (pp. 66−75)

1. 3; $\frac{1}{6}$; 6; 3; 6; 3; 6; 18; 18; Speech bubble: 6

2. 3; 5; 15 **3.** 7; 4; 28 **4.** 8 **5.** 15 **6.** 30 **7.** 64

8. $\frac{4}{3}$; 7; $\frac{4}{3}$; 7; $\frac{4}{3}$; $\frac{28}{3}$; 9 $\frac{1}{3}$; Speech bubble 1: 9 $\frac{1}{3}$;

Speech bubble 2: $\frac{4}{3}$

9.

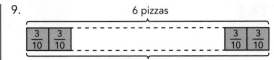

6 pizzas

3/10 3/10 ... 3/10 3/10

20 students

$\frac{3}{10}$; 6; $\frac{10}{3}$; 20; 20 **10.** 7 **11.** 21 **12.** 24 **13.** 6 $\frac{1}{2}$

14. 28 **15.** 13 $\frac{1}{3}$ **16.** $\frac{5}{7}$; $\frac{2}{7}$; $\frac{5}{7}$; $\frac{7}{2}$; $\frac{5}{2}$; 2 $\frac{1}{2}$; 2 $\frac{1}{2}$

17. $\frac{2}{3}$; $\frac{1}{9}$; $\frac{2}{3}$; 9; 6; 6 **18.** 4 **19.** 6 **20.** 1 $\frac{1}{2}$

21. $\frac{1}{4}$ **22.** $\frac{2}{3}$ **23.** 1 $\frac{1}{20}$ **24.** $\frac{13}{3}$; $\frac{3}{13}$; $\frac{1}{13}$; $\frac{5}{39}$

25. $\frac{13}{5}$; $\frac{17}{9}$; $\frac{13}{5}$; $\frac{9}{17}$; 1 $\frac{32}{85}$

Lesson 3.1, Practice (pp. 76−77)

1. 4 **3.** 6 **5.** 5

$\frac{1}{5}$

7. 1 $\frac{1}{3}$

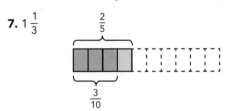

$\frac{2}{5}$

$\frac{3}{10}$

9. 28 **11.** 12 **13.** 4 **15.** $\frac{9}{11}$ **17.** 1 $\frac{3}{7}$ **19.** $\frac{4}{21}$

21. $\frac{1}{42}$ **23.** 1 $\frac{11}{17}$ **25.** $\frac{114}{131}$ **27.** 54 children

29. 18 servings **31.** $\frac{5}{6}$ mile **33.** 60 small cartons

Lesson 3.2, Guided Practice (pp. 80−84)

1. Method 1: 4; 0.9; 0.9; 9; 36; 3.6

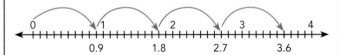

0   1   2   3   4
0.9 1.8 2.7 3.6

Method 2: 36; 3.6

2. Method 1: 3; 0.025; 25; 75; 0.075

0   0.025   0.050   0.075

Method 2: 75; 0.075

3. 0.63 **4.** 0.42 **5.** 0.315 **6.** 2.56 **7.** 2.16

8. 0.342 **9.** 10; $\frac{6}{10}$; $\frac{18}{100}$; 0.18 **10.** Step 1: 72;

Step 2:

```
    0.9    ←  1 decimal place
×   0.8    ←  + 1 decimal place
  ─────────
    0.7 2  ←  2 decimal places
```

0.72

11. Step 1: 192; 1.92;

Step 2:

$$\begin{array}{r} 3.2 \\ \times\ \ 0.6 \\ \hline 1.9\,2 \end{array}$$

3.2 ← 1 decimal place
× 0.6 ← + 1 decimal place
1.9 2 ← 2 decimal places

1.92

12. 24.51 **13.** Step 1: 356; 0.356

Step 2:

$$\begin{array}{r} 0.8\,9 \\ \times\ \ 0.4 \\ \hline 0.3\,5\,6 \end{array}$$

0.8 9 ← 2 decimal places
× 0.4 ← + 1 decimal place
0.3 5 6 ← 3 decimal places

0.356

14. 0.645

Lesson 3.2, Practice (p. 86)

1. 4; 0.3 **3.** 3 × 0.5 **5.** 10.8 **7.** 0.567 **9.** 0.02

11. 0.16 **13.** 0.63 **15.** 8.1 **17.** 0.28 **19.** 0.27

21. 0.45 **23.** 0.9 **25.** 0.75 **27.** 0.328 **29.** 0.72

31. 3.45 **33.** 30.87 **35.** 0.598 **37.** 0.12537

Lesson 3.3, Guided Practice (pp. 88–92)

1. Method 1: 2; Method 2: $\frac{5}{10}$ or $\frac{1}{2}$; $\frac{10}{5}$ or $\frac{2}{1}$; 2

2. $\frac{3}{10}$; $\frac{10}{3}$; 160

3.

98

0.14 0.14 … 0.14 0.14

4. 75; $\frac{15}{100}$; 75; $\frac{100}{15}$; 500 **5.** 156; $\frac{13}{100}$; 156; $\frac{100}{13}$; 1,200

6. 0.3; 0.9; 0.3; 3; 3; Speech bubble: three

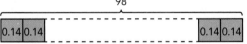

0   0.3   0.6   0.9

7. Method 1: 72; $\frac{3}{100}$; 72; $\frac{3}{100}$; $\frac{72}{100}$; $\frac{100}{3}$; $\frac{72}{3}$; 24;

Method 2: 0.03; $\frac{72}{3}$; 24 **8.** Method 1: $\frac{78}{100}$; $\frac{6}{10}$; $\frac{78}{100}$;

$\frac{6}{10}$; $\frac{78}{100}$; $\frac{10}{6}$; $\frac{78}{60}$; 1.3; Method 2: 0.6; $\frac{7.8}{6}$; 1.3; Thought

bubble: 7.8 **9.** Method 1: $\frac{675}{100}$; $\frac{3}{10}$; $\frac{675}{100}$; $\frac{3}{10}$; $\frac{675}{100}$;

$\frac{10}{3}$; $\frac{675}{30}$; 22.5; Method 2: $\frac{6.75}{0.3}$; $\frac{67.5}{3}$; 22.5

Lesson 3.3, Practice (p. 93)

1. 1 ÷ 0.2 **3.** 5 **5.** 25 **7.** 30 **9.** 40 **11.** 110

13. 172 **15.** 50 **17.** 40 **19.** 25

21.

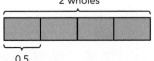

2 wholes

0.5

23. 100 **25.** 200 **27.** 150 **29.** 1,070 **31.** 600

33. 2 **35.** 13 **37.** 0.05 **39.** 22.5

Lesson 3.4, Guided Practice (pp. 94–104)

1. 8.60; 83.42; 83.42; Speech bubble: 8.60; 8.6

2.

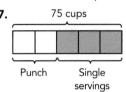

12 m

0.75 m 0.75 m … 0.75 m 0.75 m

16 pieces

÷; 0.75; 16; 16 **3.** 2.24; 0.16; 14; 14 **4.** 12.75; ÷;

0.85; 15; 15 **5.** 18; 6; 12; 12; 12; $\frac{1}{4}$; 12; 4; 48; 48;

Thought bubble: $\frac{1}{4}$ s **6.** 17; $\frac{1}{2}$; 17; 2; 34; 34

7.

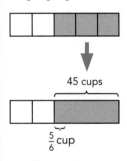

75 cups

Punch   Single
servings

Speech bubble: 5; 75; 75; 5; 15; 3; 3; 15; 45

1; $\frac{2}{5}$; $\frac{3}{5}$; $\frac{3}{5}$; 75; 45; 45

45 cups

$\frac{5}{6}$ cup

45; $\frac{5}{6}$; 45; $\frac{6}{5}$; 54; 54

8a. 5; $\frac{4}{3}$; $6\frac{2}{3}$; 6 **8b.** 6; $4\frac{1}{2}$; $4\frac{1}{2}$; $\frac{1}{2}$; $\frac{1}{2}$

8c. 6; $\frac{5}{6}$; $\frac{5}{6}$ **9.** 7; $\frac{5}{2}$; $17\frac{1}{2}$; 18 **10a.** Method 1:

$\frac{5}{12}$; Method 2: $\frac{2}{3}$; $\frac{2}{3}$; $\frac{1}{4}$; $\frac{2}{3}$; $\frac{1}{4}$; $\frac{5}{12}$; $\frac{5}{12}$

10b. Method 1: 12; 540; 12; 45; 5; 5; 45; 225; 225;

Method 2: $\frac{5}{12}$ 225; 225 **11a.** $\frac{2}{3}$; $\frac{1}{9}$; $\frac{2}{3}$; 9; 6; 6

11b. $\frac{2}{3}$; 30; 30; 6; 5; 5 **12a.** $\frac{3}{5}$; $\frac{1}{10}$; $\frac{3}{5}$; 10; 6; $\frac{2}{5}$;

$\frac{1}{5}$; $\frac{2}{5}$; 5; 2; 6; 2 **12b.** 8; 24; 24; 4; 4

Lesson 3.4, Practice (pp. 105–107)

1. $3.50 **3.** 640 packets **5a.** 7 pieces

5b. $\frac{2}{5}$ foot **7a.** 6 pieces **7b.** 0.2 meter

9a. 6 sashes **9b.** $\frac{3}{16}$ yard **11a.** 23 copies

11b. $3.95 is close to $4 and $6.95 is close to $7.
$100 − $7 = $93. $93 ÷ $4 is close to $92 ÷ $4 = 23. So,
the answer to part a) is reasonable.

13a. 26 rows   **13b.** $\frac{1}{2}$ yard   **15.** 240 marbles

17. $300

Lesson 3.4, Brain@Work (p. 107)

$3,388

Chapter Review/Test (pp. 109−110)

1. 45   **3.** $\frac{1}{2}$ **5.** 2.4   **7.** 1.68   **9.** 0.18   **11.** 2.28

13. 10   **15.** 50   **17.** 20   **19.** 600   **21.** 29

23. 15 times   **25.** 50 days   **27.** 96 pies

29. 880 students   **31a.** $3,600   **31b.** $800

Cumulative Review Chapters 1−3
(pp. 111−113)

1.

3. 2 × 2 × 3 × 7   **5.** 4   **7.** 36   **9.** 16   **11.** 12

13. 347   **15.** 12,544

17.

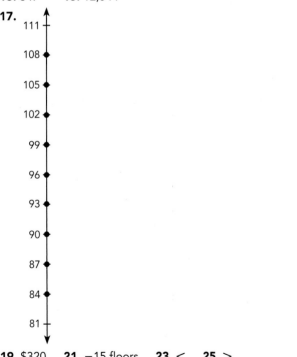

19. $320   **21.** −15 floors   **23.** <   **25.** >

27. 84 kilometers > 76 kilometers   **29.** <   **31.** <

33. 63   **35.** $\frac{3}{4}$

37. 29.61   **39.** 74.95061   **41.** 27   **43.** 6,400

45. 7 and 8   **47.** 21 pieces   **49.** 375 loaves of bread

51a. 65 boxes   **51b.** 3 bags of rice, 5 blankets, and 7
bottles of water

CHAPTER 4

Lesson 4.1, Guided Practice (pp. 119−124)

1. 3; 5   **2.** 4; 7   **3a.** 12; 13   **3b.** 13; 12   **4.** Yes

5. Yes   **6.** No   **7.** 200; 13; 200; Think: 200   **8.** 5,000;
13; 5,000; 13; Think: 5,000   **9.** 9; 7,000; 9; 7,000;
Think: 7,000

10a.

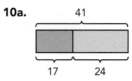

17; 24

10b. 17; 24; 41; 24; 41

11.

72 cm

31 cm   41 cm

31; 41; 41; 41; 72; 41; 72; 41; 72

12a. $32   **12b.** 45 : 32   **13.** 7; 8; 15; 8; 15; $\frac{8}{15}$

14a. $\frac{9}{14}$ **14b.** $\frac{5}{14}$ **15a.** $\frac{4}{1}$; 4   **15b.** $\frac{1}{4}$; $\frac{1}{4}$

Lesson 4.1, Practice (pp. 125−126)

1. 9 : 5 and 5 : 9   **3.** 8 : 7 and 7 : 8   **5.** No   **7.** Yes

9a. 37 : 150   **9b.** 150 : 187   **11.** $\frac{2}{3}$ **13a.** $\frac{3}{5}$

13b. $\frac{1}{7}$ **15.** Answers vary. Sample: There are 98 cars
and 3 buses in a parking lot.

Lesson 4.2, Guided Practice (pp. 128−137)

1. 10; 20   **2.** 5; 10; 5; 10   **3.** 1; 2; 1; 2   **4.** 5; 10; 1; 2;
10; 20; 5; 10; 1; 2   **5.** 4; 4; 3; 16   **6.** 7,000; 7,000; 21;
7,000; 7; 21; 7; 1,000; 3   **7.** No   **8.** Yes   **9.** No
10. Yes   **11.** Ratio 1: 14; 16; Ratio 2: Answers vary.
Sample: 3; 3; 21; 24; Ratio 3: Answers vary. Sample: 4; 4;
28; 32; 14; 16; 21; 24; 28; 32; $\frac{14}{16}$; $\frac{21}{24}$; $\frac{28}{32}$ **12.** 1 : 4; 2 : 8;
3 : 12; 4 : 16; 6 : 24; 8 : 32; 12 : 48; Speech bubble: 2, 3, 4,
6, 8, 12, and 24   **13.** 5; 5; 35   **14.** 7; 7; 4   **15.** 6

16. 81   **17a.** 31 : 33   **17b.** 124; 930   **17c.** 132; 990

18a. 7,000 gallons   **18b.** 19 : 350   **18c.** 760 gallons

18d. 21,000 gallons   **18e.** Oil: 1,520 gallons; Water:
28,000 gallons; Speech bubble: 19; 350; 7,000; 19; 350;
760; 19; 350; 21,000; 19; 350; 1,520; 28,000; 19; 350

Lesson 4.2, Practice (pp. 138−139)

1. 1 : 3   **3.** 5 : 3   **5.** 5 : 9   **7.** 13 : 200   **9.** 7 : 24

11. Yes   **13.** No   **15.** Yes   **17.** 60   **19.** 143   **21.** 5

23. 11   **25.** 3 : 1; 6 : 2; 12 : 4; 21 : 7; 24 : 8; 42 : 14; 84 : 28

27. 21   **29.** 20   **31.** 25   **33.** 42   **35a.** 9 : 5

35b. 20 ounces   **35c.** 81 ounces

37.

Number of Baskets	Weight of Fruits (lb)		
	Bananas	Apples	Pears
1	4	6	5
2	8	12	10
3	12	18	15

Lesson 4.3, Guided Practice (pp. 141–147)

1a.

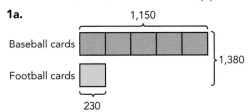

5; 1; 6; 6; $\frac{1,380}{6}$; 230; 230; 5; 230; 1,150; 1,150

1b.

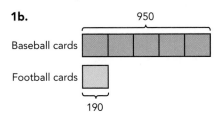

5; 950; $\frac{950}{5}$; 190; 190   **2.** 1; 2; 3; 6; 6; 18,000; $\frac{18,000}{6}$;

3,000; 3,000; 2; 3,000; 6,000; 6,000; 3; 3,000; 9,000; 9,000

3a.

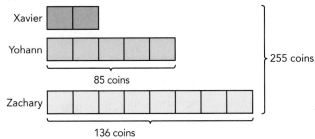

85; $\frac{85}{5}$; 17; 8; 8; 17; 136; 136

3b. 2; 5; 8; 15; 15; 15; 17; 255; 255

4a.

Ride bike : Walk = 3 : 4   Walk : Take bus = 12 : 7

$\times 3$ ( ) $\times 3$

= 9 : 12

9; 12; 7; 9; 12; 7; 28; 28; $\frac{560}{28}$; 20; 9; 20; 180; 180

4b. 12; 12; 20; 240; 240   **4c.** 7; 7; 20; 140; 140

5. Before: 2; 1; After: 4; 5; green; green; 4; 5; 18

5a. 18; $\frac{18}{3}$; 6; 4; 4; 6; 24; 24   **5b.** 5; 5; 6; 30; 30

Lesson 4.3, Practice (pp. 148–149)

1. P: 81 inches; Q: 135 inches; R: 189 inches

3a. 85,800 points   **3b.** 257,400 points   **5a.** 40 liters

5b. 18 liters   **7.** 18 clarinets   **9a.** 16 men

9b. 20 women   **11.** 40 liters   **13.** Altogether they have

7 + 3 =10 units. For both of them to have equal number

of beads, they should have $\frac{10}{2}$ = 5 units each. So, Jane

needs to end with 7 − 5 = 2 units and Jill needs to end

with 3 + 2 = 5 units. It is possible if Jane gives Jill 2 units

of beads.   **15.** $210

Lesson 4.3, Brain@Work (p. 150)

1a. 2 : 7   **1b.** 42 square centimeters   **2.** 8 chickens,

7 sheep

Chapter Review/Test (pp.152–153)

1. 1 : 3   **3.** 3 : 10   **5.** 2 : 7   **7.** 3 : 8   **9.** 18

11. 5   **13.** 5   **15.** 42   **17.** 7 : 9   **19.** 2 : 5

21a. 72 right-handed batters   **21b.** 5 : 13

23. 350 girls   **25.** $3,304   **27.** 56 bottles

CHAPTER 5

Lesson 5.1, Guided Practice (pp. 160–165)

1. Yes   **2.** Yes   **3.** No   **4.** Yes   **5.** 9; 45; 45; minute;

Thought bubble: 45; 9   **6.** 1.25; 1.25; $\frac{10,000,000}{125}$;

80,000; 80,000   **7.** 63; 22.5; 2.80; 2.80

8. 4.00; 5; 0.80; 0.80; 3.00; 5; 0.60; 0.60; 2.50; 2; 1.25;

1.25; onions; carrots; potatoes; onions; 0.60; 0.80; 1.25;

onions   **9.** Method 1: 280; $\frac{280}{4}$; 70; 70;

Method 2: $\frac{280}{4}$; 70; 70   **10.** $\frac{1}{2}$ kilometer per hour

Lesson 5.1, Practice (pp. 166–167)

1. 30 T-shirts   **3.** 0.2 liter   **5.** 90 meters per minute

7. $3.60 ÷ 60 = $0.06

The cost of the pipe per centimeter is $0.06.

1 m = 100 cm

1 cm ⟶ $0.06

1 m ⟶ $0.06 × 100 = $6

100 m ⟶ 100 × $6 = $600

100 meters of the same kind of pipe cost $600.

9. 2$\frac{1}{2}$ acres   **11.** Smith; Both Sebastian's speed and

Steve's speed are less than 10 meters per second. Smith's

speed is greater than 10 meters per second. So, Smith is

the fastest sprinter.

Lesson 5.2, Guided Practice (pp. 169–176)

1a.

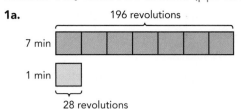

196; $\frac{196}{7}$; 28; 28; Speech bubble: 28

1b.

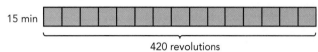

15; 15; 28; 420; 420

2a. 5; 60; 60; 5; 12; 12　**2b.** 14; 12; 168; 168　**3.** 4; 3.00; 2.50; 5.00; 3; 5.00; 15.00; 3.00; 15.00; 18.00; 18.00

4. Chloe: 87; 87; 17.4; 17.4; Fiona: 45; 45; 2; 22.5; 22.5; Fiona; Fiona　**5.** Method 1: 65; 2; 2; 65; 130; 130

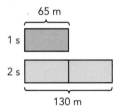

Method 2: 65; 2; 130; 130; Thought bubble: 65; 2

6. Method 1: 54; 1; 216; $\frac{216}{54}$; 4; 4; Method 2: 216; 54; 4; 4; Thought bubble: 216; 54

7.

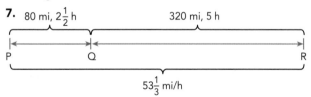

320; 400; 5; $7\frac{1}{2}$; $\frac{400}{7\frac{1}{2}}$; 400; $7\frac{1}{2}$; $53\frac{1}{3}$; $53\frac{1}{3}$; $53\frac{1}{3}$

8. 400; 800; 4; 6; 10; $\frac{800}{10}$; 80; 80

Lesson 5.2, Practice (pp. 177–178)

1. 600 tennis balls　**3.** 640 kilocalories　**5.** 162 kilometers

7. 1 kilometer　**9.** Car A: 58.5 miles per gallon, Car B: 58.2 miles per gallon; David should buy Car A.

11. 75.6 kilometers per hour

Lesson 5.2, Brain@Work (p. 178)

a. 200 seconds　**b.** 1,440 meters

Chapter Review/Test (pp.180–181)

1. 20 video game disks　**3.** 12 minutes　**5a.** 325 grams

5b. 34 square meters　**7a.** Plan A　**7b.** $4　**9a.** $\frac{3}{4}$ hour

9b. 1.1 kilometers per minute　**11.** To find average speed, Brian should not divide the sum of the speeds by 2. He should find the total distance and divide this value by the total time of the trip.; 48 miles per hour

CHAPTER 6

Lesson 6.1, Guided Practice (pp. 186–187)

1. $\frac{14}{25}$; 14; 25; 56; 56; 56　**2a.** $\frac{32}{400}$; 8; 8; 8　**2b.** 100; 8; 92; 92　**3.** 100; $\frac{12}{25}$　**4.** $\frac{11}{20}$　**5.** $1\frac{2}{25}$　**6.** $\frac{13}{100}$; 0.13　**7.** 0.08　**8.** 1.26

Lesson 6.1, Practice 6.1 (p. 188)

1. 13%　**3.** 18%　**5.** $\frac{13}{20}$　**7.** $\frac{23}{25}$　**9.** $2\frac{19}{25}$　**11.** 0.06

13. 0.8　**15.** 5.79　**17.** 95%

Lesson 6.2, Guided Practice (pp. 190–191)

1. 100; $\frac{400}{7}$; $57\frac{1}{7}$　**2.** 100; 14; 100; $155\frac{5}{9}$　**3.** $83\frac{1}{3}$%

4. $187\frac{1}{2}$%　**5.** Method 1: 82; 82%; Method 2: 0.82; 82%

6. 4%　**7.** 98%　**8.** 60%　**9.** $\frac{5}{6}$　**10.** $\frac{211}{250}$

Lesson 6.2, Practice (p. 192)

1. 60%　**3.** $33\frac{1}{3}$%　**5.** 775%　**7.** 46%　**9.** 6%

11. 603%　**13.** $\frac{23}{400}$　**15.** $\frac{341}{400}$　**17.** $\frac{339}{800}$　**19.** 61%

21. 29%　**23.** School A; Percent of students who plan to go to college in School A = $\frac{432}{450} \times 100\%$ = 96%; Percent of students who plan to go to college in School B = $\frac{361}{380} \times 100\%$ = 95%; 96% > 95%; So, a greater percent of students in School A plan to go to college.

Lesson 6.3, Guided Practice (pp. 194–195)

1. Method 1:

720 cm (100%)

288 cm (40%)

720; $\frac{720}{100}$; 7.2; 40; 7.2; 288; 288; Method 2: 40; 288; 288

2. Method 1:

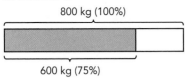

800 kg (100%)

600 kg (75%)

$800; \frac{800}{100}$; 8; 75; 8; 600; 600; Method 2: $\frac{75}{100}$; 600; 600

3. 135   **4.** $135   **5.** 176   **6.** $605

7.

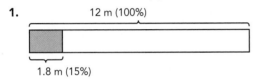

2,000 students (100%)

540 students (27%)

27; 540; $\frac{540}{27}$; 20; 20; 2,000; 2,000

8. 60; 720; $\frac{720}{60}$; 12; 100; 12; 1,200; 1,200   **9.** 815

10. 333 $\frac{1}{3}$

Lesson 6.3, Practice (pp. 196–197)

1.   12 m (100%)

1.8 m (15%)

3. $162   **5.** 975 girls   **7.** $1,000   **9.** 50 CDs

11. 1,040 ducks   **13.** 37.5   **15.** 11.25   **17.** 9,000

19. $262.50

Lesson 6.4, Guided Practice (pp. 199–202)

1a. Method 1: $\frac{52}{80}$; $\frac{52}{80}$; 100; 65; 65;

Method 2: 80; 80; 52; 52; 80; 65; 65

1b. 65; 35; 35   **2.** Method 1: 7; $\frac{7}{100}$; 50.40; 50.40;

770.40; 770.40; Method 2: 720; $\frac{720}{100}$; 7; 7; $\frac{720}{100}$; 50.40;

50.40; 770.40; 770.40   **3.** 100; 78.50; 100; $\frac{100}{78.50}$; 4.71;

4.71; $\frac{100}{78.50}$; 6; 6   **4.** 3; 2,880; $\frac{2,880}{3}$; 960; 960; 96,000;

96,000   **5.** 2; 30,000; $\frac{2}{100}$; 30,000; 600; 600

6. 4; 500,000; $\frac{1}{2}$; 10,000; 10,000

Lesson 6.4, Practice (p. 203)

1a. 28%   **1b.** 72%   **3.** $468   **5.** 64%

7. $180,000   **9.** $3,840

Lesson 6.5, Guided Practice (pp. 205–211)

1.

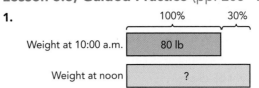

100%   30%

Weight at 10:00 a.m.   80 lb

Weight at noon   ?

Method 1: $\frac{30}{100}$; 80; 24; 24; 24; 104; 104; Method 2: 0.8;
30; 30; 0.8; 24; 24; 24; 104; 104

2.

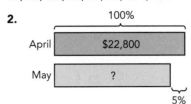

100%

April $22,800

May   ?

5%

95; 22,800; 22,800; 228; 95; 95; 228; 21,660; 21,660

3a.

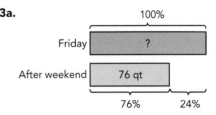

100%

Friday   ?

After weekend   76 qt

76%   24%

24; 76; 76; 76; 76; 76; 1; 1; 100; 100

3b.

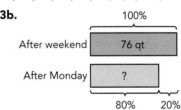

100%

After weekend   76 qt

After Monday   ?

80%   20%

20; 80; 80; $\frac{80}{100}$; 76; 60.8; 60.8

4.

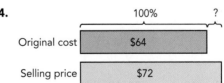

100%   ?

Original cost $64

Selling price $72

Speech bubble: 100

72; 64; 8; 8; 64; $\frac{100}{64}$; 8; $\frac{100}{64}$; 12.5; 12.5;

5.

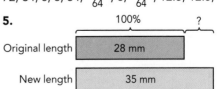

100%   ?

Original length   28 mm

New length   35 mm

35; 28; 7; 7; $\frac{7}{28}$; 25; 25   **6a.** 5; $\frac{5}{50}$; 10; 10

6b. 5; $\frac{5}{45}$; 11 $\frac{1}{9}$; 11 $\frac{1}{9}$ **7.** 150; 150; 150; 150; 45; 45

Lesson 6.5, Practice (pp. 212–213)

1. $720   **3.** $540   **5.** $87.50   **7a.** 1.6 meters
7b. 0.4 meter   **9.** 6.94%   **11.** Jason. Jason should take the height of the candle at 20 cm as 100% instead of its original height of 25 cm.

Lesson 6.5, Brain@Work (p. 214)

1a. $502   **1b.** $722.50   **2.** 15.38%

Chapter Review/Test (pp. 216–217)

1. $\frac{23}{50}$ **3.** $\frac{11}{125}$ **5.** 0.6   **7.** 85%   **9.** 90%   **11.** 63%
13. 175 kilograms   **15.** 27 women   **17.** 200
19a. 25%   **19b.** 75%   **21.** $2,996   **23.** $6.30
25. 6 months   **27.** 15.79%

CHAPTER 7

Lesson 7.1, Guided Practice (pp. 223–224)

1. $x + 10$ **2.** $y - 7$ **3a.** $(z + 4)$ years old
3b. $(z - 3)$ years old   **4.** $6z$ **5.** $\frac{w}{8}$ **6a.** $5p$ dollars
6b. $\frac{p}{4}$, or $\frac{1}{4}p$ dollars

Lesson 7.1, Practice (p. 225)

1. $4 + p$ **3.** $3r$ **5a.** $(x + 24)$ years old
5b. $(x - 2)$ years old   **5c.** $2x$ years old
5d. $\frac{x}{3}$ years old   **7.** $\frac{m}{7} - 4$ **9.** $\frac{1}{3}z + \frac{1}{5}z$
11. $(7x + 9)$ square centimeters

Lesson 7.2, Guided Practice (p. 227)

1. 7; 24; 5; 5; 12; 18; $\frac{2}{5}$

Lesson 7.2, Practice (p. 228)

1. 19   **3.** 7   **5.** 11   **7.** 14   **9.** 12   **11.** $5\frac{1}{3}$ **13.** $3\frac{1}{5}$
15. 61   **17.** 34   **19.** $1\frac{1}{2}$ **21.** 18   **23.** 48   **25.** 18
27. $2\frac{1}{3}$

Lesson 7.3, Guided Practice (pp. 231–236)

1. $5x$; 5   **2.** $2y + 6$; 2   **3.** $3m + 9$; 3   **4.** $6n + 4$; 6
5.

x; x; x; 4x; 4x

6.

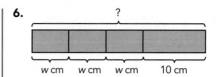

w; w; 10; $3w + 10$; $(3w + 10)$

7.

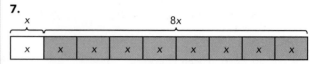

9x

8. $5r$ **9.** $11y$ **10.** Equivalent   **11.** Equivalent
12. Not equivalent   **13.** Not equivalent
14. Not equivalent   **15.** Equivalent

16.

3s

17. $5z$ **18.** 0   **19.** Not equivalent
20. Equivalent   **21.** $4j$; $6j$ **22.** $11j$ **23.** $2t$ **24.** 0
25. $5w$ **26.** $3w$ **27.** $8x$; 8; $(8x + 8)$ **28.** $7x - 3$
29. $3y + 4$ **30.** $4y - 7$ **31.** $5z + 7$ **32.** $17z + 1$
33. $5g + 17$ **34.** $2g + 7$ **35.** $18r + 18$

Lesson 7.3, Practice (pp. 237–238)

1. $4u$; 4   **3.** $6w + 8$; 6   **5.** $9p$ **7.** $6p$ **9.** Equivalent
11. Equivalent   **13.** Not equivalent   **15.** $7x + 11$
17. $3w + 5$ **19.** $(4b + 4)$ inches   **21.** Anne: $2h$ years old;
Bill: $3h$ years old; Charles: $(8 + h)$ years old; Sum: $(6h + 8)$ years
23. $(10y + 2)$ yards   **25a.** $(2m + 22)$ units
25b. $(4m + 2)$ units   **25c.** 60 units   **25d.** 8 units

Lesson 7.4, Guided Practice (pp. 240–243)

1. $3x + 12$ **2.** $12x + 18$ **3.** $14 + 12x$ **4.** $5y - 15$
5. $16y - 4$ **6.** $45x - 18$ **7.** Equivalent   **8.** Equivalent
9. Not equivalent   **10.** Not equivalent   **11.** $3(x + 1)$
12. $2(2x + 3)$ **13.** $2(4 + 3y)$ **14.** $5(y - 2)$
15. $2(2 - 5z)$ **16.** $4(3 - 2x)$ **17.** $2(4f + 3)$
18. $4(3t - 2)$ **19.** $5(3 + q)$ **20.** $8(4m - 5)$
21. Equivalent   **22.** Equivalent   **23.** Not equivalent
24. Not equivalent   **25.** Equivalent   **26.** Not equivalent

Lesson 7.4, Practice (pp. 244–245)

1. $5x + 10$ **3.** $4y - 12$ **5.** $3x + 33$ **7.** $6(p + 1)$
9. $3(4 + q)$ **11.** $2(7r - 4)$ **13.** Equivalent
15. Equivalent   **17.** $7m + 30$ **19.** $10k + 37$
21. $5(y + 6)$ **23.** $28x$ **25.** $(3w + 80)$ cents

27a. $(x + 2)$ centimeters; $(3x + 6)$ square centimeters

27b. Unshaded rectangle $= 3x$ square centimeters, shaded rectangle $= 6$ square centimeters   **27c.** Sum of area of the shaded and unshaded rectangles $=$ Area of rectangle $ABCD = 3(x + 2) = 3x + 6$. Thus, the expressions $3x + 6$ and $3(x + 2)$ are equivalent.

Lesson 7.5, Guided Practice (pp. 247−250)

1a. $(y + 6)$ **1b.** $(y − 4)$ **1c.** y; 4; 12; 4 ; 8; 12; 8; 20; 20

2a. 14; $3p$; 14; $42p$; $42p$ **2b.** 1; v; 14; $\frac{v}{14}$; $\frac{v}{14}$; $\frac{v}{14}$; $\frac{56}{14}$; 4

3a. First question: m points

Second question: $2m$ points

m; $2m$; $3m$; $3m$

3b.   25 points

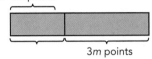

$3m$ points

$(25 − 3m)$

3c. 5; 10; 5; 15; 10; 5; 10; 10

Lesson 7.5, Practice (pp. 251−252)

1a. $(x − 5)$ years old   **1b.** $3x$ years old   **1c.** 24 years older   **3a.** $(2x + 3)$ fruit   **3b.** $(90x + 150)$ cents

3c. $\frac{15x + 25}{2}$ cents   **5a.** $(18y + 6)$ dollars   **5b.** $110

Lesson 7.5, Brain@Work (p. 252)

$(6x + 32)$ centimeters; 65 centimeters

Chapter Review/Test (pp. 254−255)

1. $2x + 5$ **3.** $\frac{r}{4}$ units   **5.** 17   **7.** $19k + 7$

9. $7m + 31$ **11.** $5(a − 5)$ **13.** $5(z + 5)$

15. Equivalent   **17.** Not equivalent   **19.** $(4p − 5)$ marbles   **21.** $(8y + 8)$ meters   **23a.** $(11p − 4)$ quarts

23b. 84 quarts

Cumulative Review Chapters 4−7
(pp. 256−259)

1. $3 : 7$ **3.** $4 : 9$ **5.** 7   **7.** 24   **9.** $\frac{29}{50}$ **11.** $\frac{47}{500}$

13. 0.67   **15.** 95%   **17.** 90%   **19.** 62%

21. 330 liters   **23.** $3x + 7$ **25.** $(14z + 16)$ units

27. $25\frac{1}{3}$ **29.** $52b + 21$ **31.** $13n + 62$ **33.** $8(7 − b)$

35. $7(7 + 3d)$ **37.** 40 minutes   **39.** $612   **41.** 260

43. $2 : 5$ **45.** 300 right-handers   **47.** 702 girls

49. 35 minutes   **51a.** 72 kilometers per hour

51b. $4\frac{1}{2}$ hours   **53.** $107.10   **55.** The second jacket

cost less during the sale.; $\frac{60}{100} × \$239 = \$143.40$.

The first jacket cost $143.40 after the markdown.

$\frac{80}{100} × \$159 = \$127.20$. The second jacket cost $127.20 after the discount. $143.40 > $127.20; So, the second jacket cost less during the sale.   **57.** $(5q + 7)$ stamps

59. $(3x + 7)$ meters   **61a.** $\frac{225}{t}$ containers

61b. $\frac{20t}{9}$ minutes   **61c.** 2,280 grams

Glossary

A

absolute value

The distance of a number from zero on a number line.

algebraic expression

An expression that contains at least one variable.

Examples : $3y - 2$ and $\frac{y}{4}$ are algebraic expressions.

average speed

The average distance traveled per unit time.

B

base (of an exponent)

In an expression of the form a^n, the base a is used as a factor n times: $a^n = \underbrace{a \cdot a \cdot a \ldots a}_{n \text{ times}}$

base (of a percent)

The whole quantity of which a percent is found.

Example: In 20% of 85, the base is 85.

C

coefficient

The numerical factor in a term of an algebraic expression.

Example: In the term $8z$, the coefficient is 8.

commission

A percent of the total sales earned by a salesperson.

common factor

A number that is a factor of two or more whole numbers.

common multiple

A number that is a multiple of two or more whole numbers.

composite number

A counting number that has more than two factors.

cube (of a number)

The value of the number raised to an exponent of 3.

Example: $2^3 = 2 \times 2 \times 2 = 8$.

cube root

A number which, when cubed, is equal to a given number.

Example: The cube root of 27 (written as $\sqrt[3]{27}$) is 3 since $3 \times 3 \times 3 = 27$.

D

discount

The amount by which an original price of something is reduced.

E

equivalent expressions

Expressions that are equal for all values of the variables.

Example: $5x + 7x$ and $12x$ are equivalent expressions because they are equal for all values of x.

equivalent ratios

Ratios that are of different forms, but have the same value when simplified.

Example: 8 : 12 and 2 : 3 are equivalent ratios.

evaluate

To find the value.

expand

To write an expression that uses parentheses as an equivalent expression without parentheses.

Example : $4(y + 1) = 4y + 4$

exponent

The number to which the base is raised.

Example: In 4^5, the exponent is 5.

F

factor

To write an expression that does not use parentheses as an equivalent expression with parentheses.

Example : $4x + 4 = 4(x + 1)$

factor (of a number)

A whole number that divides evenly into a whole number.

Example: The factors of 10 are 1, 2, 5, and 10.

G

greatest common factor

The common factor of two or more numbers that has the greatest value.

I

improper fraction

A fraction in which the numerator is greater than or equal to the denominator.

Example: $\frac{10}{3}$ and $\frac{4}{4}$ are improper fractions.

inequality

A number sentence which states that two values are unequal.

Examples: $6 > 3$, $8 < x$.

interest

The amount charged for borrowing money, or the amount of money earned from savings or investments.

interest rate

The rate at which money earns interest.

L

least common multiple

The common multiple of two or more numbers that has the least value.

like terms

Terms that have the same variables with the same corresponding exponents.

Example: In the expression $2x + 4 + x + 1$, the terms $2x$ and x are like terms, as are 4 and 1.

M

markup

The rate at which a seller raises the price of goods over their cost.

mixed number

A number with a whole number part and a fraction part.

Example: $3\frac{2}{5}$

multiple

The product of a whole number and any whole number.

Example: 16 is a multiple of 4.

N

negative number

A number that is less than zero.

number line

A horizontal or vertical line representing whole numbers, fractions, and decimals.

Examples:

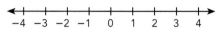

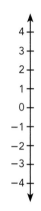

numerical expression

A collection of numbers and operations symbols that represent a single value.

Example: 3 × 2 + 7

O

opposite

Having the same numeral but different signs.
Example: −6 is the opposite of 6.

P

percent

A ratio that compares a number to 100.

Example: 28% is equivalent to the ratio 28 : 100.

perfect cube

The cube of a whole number.

Example: 343 is a perfect cube, since
343 = 7 × 7 × 7.

perfect square

The square of a whole number.

Example: 64 is a perfect square, since 64 = 8 × 8.

positive number

A number that is greater than zero.

prime factor

A factor of a number that is also a prime number.

prime number

A counting number that has exactly two different factors, 1 and itself.

Example: 5 is a prime number, because its only factors are 1 and 5.

R

rate

A ratio that compares two quantities with different units.

ratio

A comparison of two or more numbers or quantities. It describes the relative sizes of the numbers or quantities.

Example: In the ratio 2 : 1, the first term, 2, is twice the second term, 1.

reciprocals

Two numbers whose product is 1.

Examples: $\frac{1}{4}$ and 4 are reciprocals because
$\frac{1}{4} \times 4 = 1$.

$3\frac{1}{3}$ and $\frac{3}{10}$ are also reciprocals, because

$3\frac{1}{3} \times \frac{3}{10} = \frac{10}{3} \times \frac{3}{10} = 1$.

S

sales tax

A tax that is imposed on purchased goods. It is usually expressed as a percent of the selling price.

simplest form (of a ratio)

A ratio whose terms are whole numbers and have no common factor other than 1.

simplify

To write an equivalent expression by combining like terms.

speed

A special rate that expresses distance per unit time.

square (of a number)

The value of the number raised to an exponent of 2.

Example: $5^2 = 5 \times 5 = 25$.

square root

A number which, when squared, is equal to a given number.

Example: $\sqrt{100} = 10$ since $10 \times 10 = 100$.

substitute

To replace the variable by a number.

T

term (of a ratio)

The numbers or quantities that are being compared in a ratio.

Example: In the ratio 7 : 4, the first term is 7, and the second term is 4.

terms (of an expression)

Part of an algebraic expression that can be a number, a variable, or a product of both.
Example: In the expression $2x + 14$, the terms of the expression are $2x$ and 14.

U

unit rate

A ratio that compares a quantity to one unit of a different quantity.

V

variable

A quantity represented by a letter that can take different values.

Example: In the expression $2x + 1$, x is the variable.

W

whole number

Any of the numbers 0, 1, 2, 3, 4 and so on.

Table of Measures, Formulas, and Symbols

METRIC	CUSTOMARY
Length	
1 kilometer (km) = 1,000 meters (m)	1 mile (mi) = 1,760 yards (yd)
1 meter = 10 decimeters (dm)	1 mile = 5,280 feet (ft)
1 meter = 100 centimeters (cm)	1 yard = 3 feet
1 meter = 1,000 millimeters (mm)	1 yard = 36 inches (in.)
1 centimeter = 10 millimeters	1 foot = 12 inches
Capacity	
1 liter (L) = 1,000 milliliters (mL)	1 gallon (gal) = 4 quarts (qt)
	1 gallon = 16 cups (c)
	1 gallon = 128 fluid ounces (fl oz)
	1 quart = 2 pints (pt)
	1 quart = 4 cups
	1 pint = 2 cups
	1 cup = 8 fluid ounces
Mass and Weight	
1 kilogram (kg) = 1,000 grams (g)	1 ton (T) = 2,000 pounds (lb)
1 gram = 1,000 milligrams (mg)	1 pound = 16 ounces (oz)

TIME

1 year (yr) = 365 days	1 week = 7 days
1 year = 12 months (mo)	1 day = 24 hours (h)
1 year = 52 weeks (wk)	1 hour = 60 minutes (min)
leap year = 366 days	1 minute = 60 seconds (s)

CONVERTING MEASUREMENTS

You can use the information below to convert measurements from one unit to another.

To convert from a smaller unit to a larger unit, divide.	To convert from a larger unit to a smaller unit, multiply.
Example: 48 in. = __?__ ft	Example: 0.3 m = __?__ cm

Recall: 12 in. = 1 ft
48 ÷ 12 = 4
48 in. = 4 ft

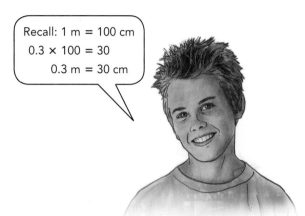

Recall: 1 m = 100 cm
0.3 × 100 = 30
0.3 m = 30 cm

PERIMETER, CIRCUMFERENCE, AND AREA

Square

length (ℓ)

length (ℓ)

Perimeter = 4ℓ
Area = ℓ^2

Rectangle

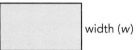

width (w)

length (ℓ)

Perimeter = $2\ell + 2w$
= $2(\ell + w)$
Area = ℓw

Circle

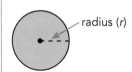

radius (r)

Circumference = πd
= $2\pi r$
Area = πr^2

Triangle

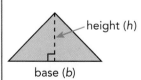

height (h)

base (b)

Area = $\frac{1}{2} bh$

Parallelogram

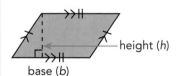

height (h)

base (b)

Area = bh

Trapezoid

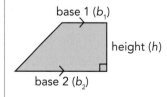

base 1 (b_1)

height (h)

base 2 (b_2)

Area = $\frac{1}{2} h(b_1 + b_2)$

Centimeters
0 1 2 3 4 5 6 7 8 9 10 11 12 13 14 15 16 17 18 19 20

SURFACE AREA AND VOLUME

Cube

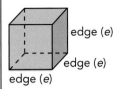

edge (e)
edge (e)
edge (e)

Surface Area = $6e^2$
Volume = e^3

Rectangular Prism

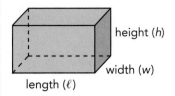

height (h)
width (w)
length (ℓ)

Surface Area = $2(\ell w + wh + \ell h)$
Volume = $\ell wh = Bh$*

Prism

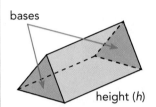

bases
height (h)

Surface Area
= Sum of the areas of the faces
= Perimeter of base × height + Area of two bases
Volume = Bh*

Pyramid

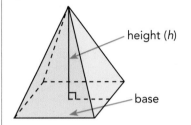

height (h)
base

Surface Area = Sum of the areas of the faces
Volume = $\dfrac{1}{3} Bh$*

Cylinder

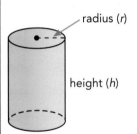

radius (r)
height (h)

Surface Area = $2\pi r^2 + 2\pi rh$
Volume = $\pi r^2 h$

Cone

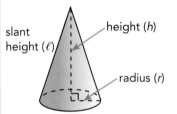

slant
height (ℓ)
height (h)
radius (r)

Surface Area = $\pi r(\ell + r)$,
where ℓ is the slant height
Volume = $\dfrac{1}{3} \pi r^2 h$

Sphere

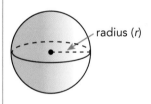

radius (r)

Surface Area = $4\pi r^2$
Volume = $\dfrac{4}{3} \pi r^3$

*B represents the area of the base of a solid figure.

PYTHAGOREAN THEOREM

Right Triangle

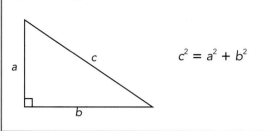

$$c^2 = a^2 + b^2$$

PROBABILITY

Probability of an event, A happening

$$P(A) = \frac{\text{Number of favorable outcomes}}{\text{Number of equally likely outcomes}}$$

Probability of an event not happening
$= 1 - P(A)$

LINEAR GRAPHS

The slope, m, of a line segment joining points $P(x_1, y_1)$ and $Q(x_2, y_2)$ is given by

$m = \dfrac{y_2 - y_1}{x_2 - x_1}$ or $m = \dfrac{y_1 - y_2}{x_1 - x_2}$.

Given the slope, m, the equation of a line intercepting the y-axis at b is given by $y = mx + b$.

The distance, d, between two points $P(x_1, y_1)$ and $Q(x_2, y_2)$ is given by

$d = \sqrt{(x_2 - x_1)^2 + (y_2 - y_1)^2}$ or $d = \sqrt{(x_1 - x_2)^2 + (y_1 - y_2)^2}$.

RATE

Distance = Speed × Time	
Average speed = $\dfrac{\text{Total distance traveled}}{\text{Total time}}$	
Interest = Principal × Rate × Time	

TEMPERATURE

Celsius (°C)	$C = \dfrac{5}{9} \times (F - 32)$
Fahrenheit (°F)	$F = \left(\dfrac{5}{9} \times C\right) + 32$

SYMBOLS

$<$	is less than	$\lvert a \rvert$	absolute value of the number a
$>$	is greater than	(x, y)	ordered pair
$\leq$	is less than or equal to	$1 : 2$	ratio of 1 to 2
$\geq$	is greater than or equal to	$/$	per
$\neq$	is not equal to	$\%$	percent
$\approx$	is approximately equal to	$\perp$	is perpendicular to
$\cong$	is congruent to	$\parallel$	is parallel to
$\sim$	is similar to	$\overleftrightarrow{AB}$	line AB
10^2	ten squared	$\overrightarrow{AB}$	ray AB
10^3	ten cubed	$\overline{AB}$	line segment AB
2^6	two to the sixth power	$\angle ABC$	angle ABC
$2.\overline{6}$	repeating decimal 2.66666...	$m\angle A$	measure of angle A
7	positive 7	$\triangle ABC$	triangle ABC
-7	negative 7	$^\circ$	degree
$\sqrt{a}$	positive square root of the number a	π	pi; $\pi \approx 3.14$ or $\pi \approx \dfrac{22}{7}$
$\sqrt[3]{a}$	positive cube root of the number a	$P(A)$	the probability of the event A happening

Credits

Cover: © Henri Faure/Dreamstime.com   Chapter 1: 3, © Comstock Images/Getty Images; 5, © Tetra Images/Getty Images; 6 (t), © Annworthy/Dreamstime.com; 6 (c), © Ron Chapple/Dreamstime.com; 7 (t), © Plush Studios/Bill Reitzel/Getty Images; 7 (b), © Comstock Images/Getty Images; 8, © Barbara Penoyar/Getty Images; 9, © Image Source; 10, © Flying Colours Ltd/Getty Images; 12, © Plush Studios/Bill Reitzel/Getty Images; 13, © Ron Chapple/Dreamstime.com; 17, © Flying Colours Ltd/Getty Images; 19, © Image Source; 20, © Image Source; 23, © Tetra Images/Getty Images; 24, © Plush Studios/Bill Reitzel/Getty Images; 25, © Barbara Penoyar/Getty Images; 29 (t), © Image Source; 29 (b), © Tetra Images/Getty Images; 30, © Annworthy/Dreamstime.com; 31, © Kris Timken/Getty Images; 33 (t), © Comstock Images/Getty Images; 33 (b), © Barbara Penoyar/Getty Images; 34, © Plush Studios/Bill Reitzel/Getty Images; 35, © Ron Chapple/Dreamstime.com   Chapter 2: 45, © Plush Studios/Bill Reitzel/Getty Images; 46, © Ron Chapple/Dreamstime.com; 47, © Comstock Images/Getty Images; 48 (t), © Barbara Penoyar/Getty Images; 48 (c), © Jose Luis Pelaez, Inc/Getty Images; 51, © Image Source; 55, © Annworthy/Dreamstime.com   Chapter 3: 65 (t), © Plush Studios/Bill Reitzel/Getty Images; 65 (b), © Kris Timken/Getty Images; 66 (t), © Jose Luis Pelaez, Inc/Getty Images; 66 (c), © Ron Chapple/Dreamstime.com; 66 (b), © Annworthy/Dreamstime.com; 68 (t), © Barbara Penoyar/Getty Images; 68 (c), © Comstock Images/Getty Images; 69 (t), © Jose Luis Pelaez, Inc/Getty Images; 69 (c), © Tetra Images/Getty Images; 71, © Image Source; 72, © Flying Colours Ltd/Getty Images; 74 (t), © Ron Chapple/Dreamstime.com; 74 (c), © Annworthy/Dreamstime.com; 75, © Image Source; 78 (t), © Tetra Images/Getty Images; 78 (b), © Jose Luis Pelaez, Inc/Getty Images; 79, © Image Source; 81 (t), © Plush Studios/Bill Reitzel/Getty Images; 81 (c), © Flying Colours Ltd/Getty Images; 82, © Comstock Images/Getty Images; 84, © Jose Luis Pelaez, Inc/Getty Images; 87, © Tetra Images/Getty Images; 88, © Jose Luis Pelaez, Inc/Getty Images; 89 (c), © Image Source; 89 (b), © Plush Studios/Bill Reitzel/Getty Images; 90, © Flying Colours Ltd/Getty Images; 91 (c), © Image Source; 91 (b), © Ron Chapple/Dreamstime.com; 92, © Comstock Images/Getty Images; 94 (t), © Kris Timken/Getty Images; 94 (b), © Annworthy/Dreamstime.com; 95, © Barbara Penoyar/Getty Images; 96 (t), © Tetra Images/Getty Images; 96 (c), © Jose Luis Pelaez, Inc/Getty Images; 97, © Image Source; 98, © Jose Luis Pelaez, Inc/Getty Images; 99, © Flying Colours Ltd/Getty Images; 100 (t), © Ron Chapple/Dreamstime.com; 100 (b), © Plush Studios/Bill Reitzel/Getty Images; 103, © Barbara Penoyar/Getty Images   Chapter 4: 118 (tl), © MCE; 118 (b), © Plush Studios/Bill Reitzel/Getty Images; 119 (c), © Barbara Penoyar/Getty Images; 119 (bl), © MCE; 119 (br), © MCE; 121 (t), © Comstock Images/Getty Images; 121 (c), © Kris Timken/Getty Images; 122, © Comstock Images/Getty Images; 123 (t), © Ron Chapple/Dreamstime.com; 123 (c), © Plush Studios/Bill Reitzel/Getty Images; 125 (t), © MCE; 125 (c), © loskutnikov/iStock; 127, © MCE; 128 (l), © MCE; 128 (r), © russellart/iStock; 132 (c), © Tetra Images/Getty Images; 132 (b), © Comstock Images/Getty Images; 133 (tl), © Image Source; 133 (tr), © Annworthy/Dreamstime.com; 133 (bl), © Flying Colours Ltd/Getty Images; 133 (br), © Image Source; 136, © Barbara Penoyar/Getty Images; 137, © Comstock Images/Getty Images; 142, © Ron Chapple/Dreamstime.com; 143, © Plush Studios/Bill Reitzel/Getty Images; 144, © Annworthy/Dreamstime.com; 146, © Flying Colours Ltd/Getty Images; 147, © Image Source; 150 (l), © MCE; 150 (r), © globalP/iStock   Chapter 5: 159, © Tetra Images/Getty Images; 160 (c), © Image Source; 160 (b), © Ron Chapple/Dreamstime.com; 164 (t), © Annworthy/Dreamstime.com; 164 (b), © Barbara Penoyar/Getty Images; 165, © Comstock Images/Getty Images; 168 (t), © Tetra Images/Getty Images; 168 (b), © Jose Luis Pelaez, Inc/Getty Images; 169, © Image Source; 172, © Flying Colours Ltd/Getty Images; 173 (t), © Image Source; 173 (b), © Ron Chapple/Dreamstime.com; 174 (t), © Annworthy/Dreamstime.com; 174 (b), © Plush Studios/Bill Reitzel/Getty Images; 175 (l), © Comstock Images/Getty Images; 175 (r), © Kris Timken/Getty Images   Chapter 6: 185, © Image Source; 188, © alexnika/iStock; 189, © Kris Timken/Getty Images; 190 (t), © Comstock Images/Getty Images; 190 (b), © Barbara Penoyar/Getty Images; 191, © Jose Luis Pelaez, Inc/Getty Images; 193, © Tetra Images/Getty Images; 200, © Plush Studios/Bill Reitzel/Getty Images; 201, © Ron Chapple/Dreamstime.com; 204, © Jose Luis Pelaez, Inc/Getty Images; 206, © Comstock Images/Getty Images; 208, © Flying Colours Ltd/Getty Images; 210, © Image Source; 211, © Ron Chapple/Dreamstime.com; 213 (l), © Jose Luis Pelaez, Inc/Getty Images; 213 (r), © Plush Studios/Bill Reitzel/Getty Images   Chapter 7: 221, © Comstock Images/Getty Images; 222 (t), © Ron Chapple/Dreamstime.com; 222 (b), © Jose Luis Pelaez, Inc/Getty Images; 223, © Tetra Images/Getty Images; 224, © Plush Studios/Bill Reitzel/Getty Images; 225, © MCE; 227, © Barbara Penoyar/Getty Images; 229, © Comstock Images/Getty Images; 230 (t), © Kris Timken/Getty Images; 230 (b), © Annworthy/Dreamstime.com; 233, © Tetra Images/Getty Images; 234, © Jose Luis Pelaez, Inc/Getty Images; 236, © Barbara Penoyar/Getty Images; 237, © MCE; 237, © Krys Bailey/Alamy; 237, © Tom Uhlman/Alamy; 239 (t), © Jose Luis Pelaez, Inc/Getty Images; 239 (b), © Flying Colours Ltd/Getty Images; 240 (cr), © Annworthy/Dreamstime.com; 240 (cl), © Tetra Images/Getty Images; 242 (t), © Image Source; 242 (c), © Image Source; 242 (b), © Jose Luis Pelaez, Inc/Getty Images; 246, © Barbara Penoyar/Getty Images

Index